D1737224

Populism,
Progressivism,
and the
Transformation
of Nebraska
Politics,
1885–1915

Populism, Progressivism, and the Transformation of Nebraska Politics, 1885-1915

Robert W. Cherny

Published by the
UNIVERSITY OF NEBRASKA PRESS
Lincoln and London
for the
Center for Great Plains Studies
University of Nebraska–Lincoln

Library of Congress Cataloging in Publication Data

Cherny, Robert W
  Populism, progressivism, and the transformation of Nebraska politics,
1885–1915.

  Bibliography: p.
  Includes index.
  1. Nebraska—Politics and government.   2. Populism—Nebraska.
3. Progressivism (United States politics).   4. Voting — Nebraska.
5. Political parties — Nebraska.   I. University of Nebraska–Lincoln.
Center for Great Plains Studies.   II. Title.
F666.C49   320.9782   80–11151
ISBN 0–8032–1407–3

To my grandmothers and
to the memory of my grandfathers,

Mollie Bartosovsky Cherny and
Joseph Cherny,

Rixte Saathoff Hobbs and
John Hobbs

Contents

List of Maps, Tables, and Figures   ix

Preface   xiii

ONE: Nebraska Politics in the 1880s   1

TWO: Voting Behavior and Political Leadership in the 1880s   13

THREE: Nebraska's Populist Revolt: Campaigns, Issues, and
    Personalities, 1890–95   32

FOUR: Voting Behavior, Leadership, and the Nature of the Political
    System, 1890–95   53

FIVE: Fusion Victory and Republican Redemption, 1896–1904   74

SIX: Voting Behavior and Political Leadership, 1896–1904   89

SEVEN: Nebraska Progressivism, 1905–15: Campaigns, Issues,
    and Personalities   109

EIGHT: Voting Behavior and Political Leadership in the Progressive
    Era, 1906–14   123

NINE: Populists, Progressives, and the Transformation of
    Nebraska Politics   149

APPENDIX A: Methodology and Data Sources   167

APPENDIX B: Correlation and Regression Coefficients, All General
    Election Dependent Variables and Major Independent Variables 181

Notes   189

Selected Bibliography   211

Index   223

Maps, Tables,
and Figures

MAPS

1. Study Area   xvii
2. Population Density, 1890   4
3. Railroad Lines, ca. 1890   5

TABLES

1. Pearson Coefficients of Correlation, Representative Population Variables with Indexes of Party Strength, 1886 and 1888   16
2. Party Strength Indexes, for Counties, 1886 and 1888, Broken down by Population Characteristics by Quartiles   17
3. Distribution of Counties by Attitude on Prohibition and by Farm Income   18
4. Indexes of Party Strength by Counties, 1888, Counties Distributed by Attitude on Prohibition and by Farm Income   18
5. Stepwise Multiple Regression Summary Table Republican Vote for Governor, 1886   19
6. Stepwise Multiple Regression Summary Table, Democratic Party Index, 1888   20
7. Percentage Distribution of Nebraska Poltical Leaders by Occupation and Place of Birth, 1880–90   27
8. Percentage Distribution of Nebraska Political Leaders by Various Biographical Characteristics, 1880–90   28
9. Percentage Distribution of Support for Major Parties, 1892   42

10. Percentage Distribution of Total Vote Cast, 1894, by Party and Office 47
11. Populist Party Strength Indexes, for Counties, 1890–93, with Counties Grouped by Socioeconomic Quartiles 54
12. Index of Populist Strength and Difference from Overall Mean by Counties, 1890, with Counties Distributed by Attitude on Prohibition and Farm by Income 55
13. Stepwise Multiple Regression Summary Table, Index of Populist Party Strength, 1892 56
14. Index of Democratic Party Strength and Difference from Overall Mean by Counties, 1890, with Counties Distributed by Attitude on Prohibition and by Farm 58
15. Stepwise Multiple Regression Summary Table, Index of Democratic Party Strength, 1892 59
16. Percentage Distribution of Nebraska Political Leaders by Occupation and Place of Birth, 1890–95 68
17. Percentage Distribution of Nebraska Political Leaders by Various Biographical Characteristics, 1890–95 69
18. Party Legislative Strengths, 1897–1903 75
19. Appropriations, Number of Patronage Appointees, and Party Distribution of Fusion Nominees for Statehouse Offices, 1896–1904 76
20. Party Strength Indexes, for Counties, 1898, with Counties Grouped by Socioeconomic Quartiles 91
21. Stepwise Multiple Regression Summary Table, Democratic Vote for President, 1904 96
22. Stepwise Multiple Regression Summary Table, Populist Vote for President, 1904 97
23. Ticket-splitting in Presidential and Gubernatorial Elections, 1886–1904 98
24. Significance Measures, Three Independent Variables, 1896–1904 101
25. Percentage Distribution of Nebraska Political Leaders by Occupation and Place of Origin, 1896–1904 105
26. Percentage Distribution of Nebraska Political Leaders by Various Biographical Characteristics, 1896–1904 106
27. Pearson Coefficients of Correlation between Indexes of Party Voting Strength and Independent Variables, 1906–14 125

28. Mean Indexes of Party Strength, for Counties, 1906–14, with Counties Grouped by Socioeconomic Quartiles — 126
29. Ethnic Characteristics of Twelve Counties — 128
30. Vote for Candidates in Party Primaries, for Counties, 1908, 1910, and 1912, with Counties grouped into Homogeneous Socio-economic Clusters — 138
31. Percentage Distribution of Nebraska Political Leaders by Occupation and Place of Origin, 1906–12 — 144
32. Percentage Distribution of Nebraska Political Leaders by Various Biographical Characteristics, 1906–12 — 145
33. Comparison of Support for Populism and La Follette — 153

FIGURES

1. Voting Behavior, 1898, Counties Distributed by Ethnicity and Farm Income · — 92
2. Voting Behavior, 1898, Counties Distributed by Ethnicity and Degree of Urbanization — 93
3. Changes in Voting Behavior, 1898–1902, Counties Distributed by Ethnicity and Degree of Urbanization — 102
4. Voting Behavior, 1906–14, Counties Distributed by Ethnicity and Degree of Urbanization — 127
5. Coefficients of Correlation between Voting Support for Clark, Metcalfe, and Shallenberger in Democratic Primaries, 1908–12 — 134
6. Coefficients of Correlation between Voting Support for Dahlman, Harmon, Hitchcock, and Morehead in Democratic Primaries, 1908–12 — 134
7. Coefficients of Correlation between Voting Support for Brown, Burkett, Cady, and Taft in Republican Primaries, 1910 and 1912 — 135
8. Coefficients of Correlation between Voting Support for Aldrich, La Follette, Norris, and Whedon in Republican Primaries, 1910 and 1912 — 135
9. The Democratic Party in Nebraska—Core and Periphery — 140
10. The Republican Party in Nebraska—Core and Periphery — 141
11. Groups within the Republican and Democratic Parties — 143

Preface

My country, 'is [*sic*] of thee,
Once land of liberty,
Of thee I sing.
Land of the Millionaire;
Farmers with pockets bare;
Caused by the cursed snare—
The Money Ring.
The Alliance Songster[1]

So sang the angry farmers of Kansas and Nebraska during the summer of 1890. Politics that summer raged like the hot sun that glared down day after day, parching the corn crop. Agrarian discontent, smoldering for more than a decade, erupted as thousands of farm families drove their wagons down the dusty Main Streets of a hundred towns, parading both their unity and their defiance of the small-town bankers, lawyers, and merchants who dominated the social, economic, and political life of their communities. The parades culminated in picnics and rallies. There the embittered farmers put new words to old songs and sang of their frustrations:

Worm or beetle, drouth or tempest,
On a farmer's land may fall,
But for first-class ruination
Trust a mortgage 'gainst them all.

And they sang their condemnation of political parties that seemed oblivious to their distress:

> I was a party man one time
> The party would not mind me,
> So now I'm working for myself,
> The party's left behind me.

The rallies concluded with arm-waving speeches attacking Wall Street, international bankers, monopolies, and the railroads. Thousands of farmers did leave their parties behind them in November. Two years later they formed a new national party, the People's party. They were quickly dubbed Populists.[2]

The People's party was the most successful of the agrarian third parties that swept the plains and prairies of the Middle West and the piney woods of the South during the two generations following the Civil War. It was also one of the most successful of America's so-called populist movements. As such, it has held the attention of American historians for three-quarters of a century, and they have found in it everything from the darkest protofascism to a blueprint for a socialist America. The historians of the 1920s and 1930s, writing in the progressive tradition, saw Populism both as a response to immediate grievances and as an episode in the continuing battle between "the people" and "the interests"—the forces of democracy and the forces of privilege. They traced a direct line from the Locofocos through the Populists to the progressivism of Robert La Follette, William Jennings Bryan, and George W. Norris. In the late 1940s and 1950s, historians influenced by pluralist political analysis described Populism as irrational, provincial, aberrant, nativist, anti-Semitic, even protofascist. Progressive reformers, by contrast, were "more informed, more moderate, more complex . . . less rancorous," seeking to restore political power to "the responsible middle class," to curb the power of "the plutocracy," and to mitigate the "poverty and restlessness of the masses." Recently various historians have differed with the pluralist view and have variously reinterpreted Populism as simple interest-group politics, or as a humanitarian and collectivist movement oriented to restructuring American society, or as a power-oriented protest movement. Others have intensified the differentiation between Populism and progressivism until progressivism has emerged, in one view, as the political expression of corporate industrial capitalism, aimed at centralizing public decision-making, reducing popular participation in it, and using government "to attain conditions of stability, predictability, and security in the economy."[3]

During the last decade, some of the most rewarding insights into the nature of Populism and progressivism have come from works focused on a single state or locality, often employing quantitative analysis in addition to the more traditional historical sources.[4] Aware of the difficulties of attempting to determine whether Ignatius Donnelly or James B. Weaver, William V. Allen or Sarah E. V. Emery better voiced the sentiments of Populism, historians have sought other means of measuring the sentiments of the wider movement. One such method is to compile a collective biography of political leadership, compare Populist and progressive leaders with their opposition counterparts, and draw conclusions regarding the social and economic origins of the movements' leadership. The historian cannot conduct surveys of voter opinion, but the decennial censuses include a great deal of information on the economic, ethnic, and religious characteristics of counties; by employing quantitative analysis, the historian can measure the extent of the statistical relationship beween these population characteristics and voting behavior. This study employs several statistical techniques in combination with more traditional methods of historical inquiry to explore the political system of Nebraska during and immediately before the Populist and progressive period.[5]

Nebraska is an excellent setting for such a study. From 1885 to 1915, Nebraska politics saw the tumultuous birth and lingering death of the Populist party, the capture of the Republican party by the forces of progressivism, and a running battle between prohibitionists and their opponents. William Jennings Bryan and George W. Norris were only the best known of a number of Nebraskans prominent in national politics, including J. Sterling Morton, secretary of agriculture in Cleveland's second administration, George D. Meiklejohn, McKinley's assistant secretary of war, and William V. Allen, chairman of the 1896 Populist national convention. A number of equally striking figures, less known nationally, moved through the warp and woof of the state's political fabric, ranging from the long-bearded Bible-reading Populist John H. Powers to the Irish Catholic Democratic boss Arthur F. Mullen, and from the radical scion of New York society Charles H. Van Wyck to the former Texas cowboy and mayor of Omaha James C. Dahlman. In addition to the stress of the prohibition controversy and the strain of Populist radicalism, Nebraska's political system was wracked by intense intraparty struggles deriving from issues and ambition, from idealism and opportunism.

Within a short period, the state's political system was forced to grapple with the most significant political conflicts that raged through the Middle West between the Civil War and World War I—prohibition, Populism, and progressivism. The state contained within its boundaries a wide ethnocultural and economic range, varying from camp-meeting revivalists to High Church Episcopalians, from corn-farming to cattle-raising, from almost totally immigrant communities to those almost totally native-born, from isolated farm homesteads to the hustle of Omaha. In 1900 about half the people of the state were either foreign-born or of foreign-born parentage. Somewhat over a third of these foreign-stock Nebraskans were from Germany, about a tenth each from Great Britain, Ireland, Sweden, and Bohemia. Catholics made up about a quarter of the state's church members in 1906, old-stock American Protestant groups about half. In 1900 population densities ranged from 425 persons per square mile in Douglas County to fewer than one in western Nebraska. Countywide average values of farm land in 1900 varied from nearly $55.00 an acre to less than $1.50. Some eastern counties produced more than forty bushels of corn an acre in 1900, but corn productivity in western parts of the state fell as low as six and a half bushels an acre.[6] This heterogeneity of the people and the economy forms the canvas upon which the following chapters will portray developments within the political system.

Statistical analysis was limited to the sixty-one geographically contiguous counties that contained more than five persons to the square mile at the time of the censuses of 1890, 1900, and 1910. These counties are shown on map 1. Excluding from the analysis any county without such a population density had the effect of limiting analysis to relatively populated and relatively stable counties. The excluded area consisted of the cattle-raising counties of the sandhills and those of the panhandle, many of which experienced boundary changes during 1885–1915, as well as considerable fluctuation in population. Current county boundaries did not become fixed until 1913. The sixty-one counties analyzed included most of the population of the state, 90.4 percent as of 1890, 91.8 percent in 1900, and 87.6 percent in 1910, though they included only 51.1 percent of the land area.

This study began nearly ten years ago as a doctoral dissertation at Columbia University. It has since been extended, and the statistics have been extensively reworked. My debts and gratitude, as a result, span nearly a decade as well as a continent.

Among the various libraries and archives where I did research, the Nebraska State Historical Society stands out for the warmth and helpfulness of the staff, as well as for the amount of time I spent there. Director Marvin F. Kivett was most generous in making his facilities available. Archivists Duane Reed and James Potter and their staff were always willing to consult when problems arose. Research Associate Paul Riley was most generous with his own research. They deserve more thanks than I can adequately

STUDY AREA

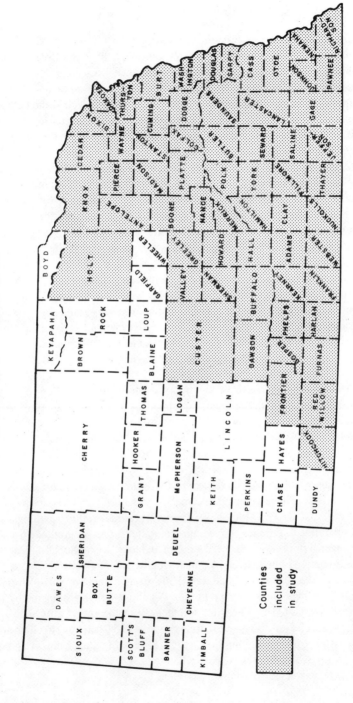

Counties
included
in study

MAP 1. Study area

xviii / POPULISM, PROGRESSIVISM, AND NEBRASKA POLITICS

express. Thanks are also due to the staffs of the Library of Congress, the National Archives, Butler Library of Columbia University, Love Memorial Library of the University of Nebraska, Spencer Research Library of the University of Kansas, Leonard Library of San Francisco State University, Bancroft Library of the University of California at Berkeley, the Pettigrew Museum of Sioux Falls, South Dakota, and the South Dakota Department of History. Thanks are also due for the assistance received from the office of the Nebraska secretary of state and the county clerks of Boone, Butler, Clay, Greeley, Harlan, Hitchcock, Jefferson, and Pawnee counties, Nebraska.

Special thanks must go to Professor John A. Garraty of Columbia University, my dissertation adviser, who was unsparing of his time for the discussion of concept and method and who insisted that my dissertation—the basis for this present study—have some literary style rather than being simply a written thread among masses of statistics. Professor Walter Metzger of Columbia University first aroused my interest in the uses of statistical analysis and provided thoughtful comments and suggestions on my dissertation in his role as second reader. Others who have read versions of this manuscript and provided thoughtful and helpful suggestions have included Allan G. Bogue, Phil B. Johnson, Stanley B. Parsons, Ronald Rogowski, and Dennis Van Essendelft. Special thanks must go to Frederick C. Luebke of the University of Nebraska–Lincoln for his many suggestions and his assistance throughout the project.

The Woodrow Wilson Foundation provided the dissertation fellowship that was important to the financial support of my research in 1969. Assistance in compiling and analyzing data was rendered by the staffs of the Columbia University Computer Center, Columbia's Bureau for Applied Social Research, the Inter-University Consortium for Political and Social Research at the University of Michigan, and the Computer Center at San Francisco State University. The SFSU Computer Center staff earned my admiration for their expertise in somehow shoehorning an operating version of SPSS onto a CDC 3150; they earned my gratitude for their willingness to take the time to familiarize me with that system. Special gratitude is due to the manuscript service of the School of Behavioral and Social Sciences of San Francisco State University and especially to Lorraine Whittemore, who prepared the manuscript and saved me from numerous small errors by careful editing. Maps 1–3 and figures 1–4 and 9–11 were prepared by Jean Ann Carroll of The Thematic Mappers, Burlingame, California. And, finally, special thanks are due to Rebecca Marshall Cherny for her long hours of assistance during the summer of 1969, for her tolerating Nebraska politics for so long, and for her encouragement.

All mistakes are, of course, my own.

CHAPTER ONE

Nebraska Politics
in the 1880s

[As] we approached Beaver City . . . the road ran diagonally
through a field of corn that I thought was the finest I had ever
seen. . . . On that September day of 1885, . . . the skies were
clear and blue; the sun was brilliant and pleasantly warm. . . .
Here was the place of all places where it seemed to me everything was designed for the happiness and prosperity of the
farmer.

George W. Norris, *Fighting Liberal*

The skies were clear and blue for many who, like the
young lawyer George W. Norris came to Nebraska in the 1880s. It was a
decade of rosy optimism, and the only things that grew faster than the state
were the dreams and aspirations of Nebraskans. The most optimistic hope
was undoubtedly that of the Kearney city fathers who hoped to lure the
national capital from the eastern seaboard to a more central location—
Kearney, Nebraska. Everything seemed possible.[1]

From 1880 to 1890 Nebraska's population grew by about 118 percent, and
the state's two urban centers, Omaha and Lincoln, grew even more rapidly,
Omaha gaining about 236 percent and Lincoln about 165 percent. But this
rapid growth did not bring significant changes in the ethnic composition of
the population. Most Nebraskans had been born either in the Middle West or
in the Middle Atlantic states; more than 40 percent had either one or both
parents foreign-born. In 1880, 59 percent of the Nebraska labor force was
engaged in agriculture; by 1890 this had fallen to 46 percent.[2]

Early historical treatments of Nebraska politics in the 1880s, notably
those of Albert Watkins and Addison E. Sheldon, took the basic attitude of
the progressives—that politics was a struggle between corporations and
honest men, fought out at the state level. Both men's histories focused on
state-level events such as elections, party conventions, and state legislative

1

sessions, and both were harshly critical of corporate influence in state politics, especially the influence of the state's two leading railroads, the Union Pacific and the Burlington.[3] An important new perspective came in 1964, when Stanley B. Parsons directed his attention not to state-level politics but to the grass roots, where he found that the county-seat "village" dominated politics at all levels. The "town fathers" not only were preeminent in the economic and political life of their own counties, they also dominated government at the state level, to the proportionate disadvantage of both farmers and city dwellers. Such village businessmen and professionals often opposed "reform" politicians who seemed to threaten the villagers' ambitious plans to attract railroads and manufacturing.[4]

One of the guiding concepts of this study is that state-level politics was an end product of grass-roots politics. Although grass-roots politics may be studied at the level of such primary political units as the school district and the township, for the purposes of this synthesis the county will be considered the basic community. The typical Nebraska farming county was composed of sixteen townships, each six miles square. The county seat, typically the largest town in the county and usually centrally located, was therefore often not only the political center of the county but the commercial center as well. Here were the county offices (including those for the payment of taxes), the county fairground, the GAR post (sometimes the only one in the county), and the lodge halls of several fraternal organizations. The population of these political commercial centers averaged one to five thousand; thus most men probably knew most others at least by name and reputation.[5]

The lowest level of relevant, describable political activity was the county, although the actual lowest level of political activity was the township of thirty-six square miles, the unit of organization of the primary caucus preceding county conventions. County conventions were held frequently, before the many state or district conventions: the state nominating conventions for executive officers; the state conventions that selected delegates to national nominating conventions; the state nominating conventions for off-year offices, supreme court judge, and university regents; the congressional district nominating conventions; and in some cases separate conventions for the nomination of district court officials (judge, attorney, clerk), state senator, and member of the lower legislative house. In short, it was a rare year that did not see at least two political conventions above the county level, and some years there might be as many as four. County-level conventions preceded most of these conventions, typically meeting at the county seat, often in a room of the courthouse. The county chairman was the key figure.

He communicated with the state committee and candidates above, and with the township or precinct chairmen below.[6]

The county-seat town was the location of the "county ring," accused by agrarian radicals in the 1880s and later of monopolizing the access to political power. According to Parsons, such "rings" were largely figments of the agrarian imagination. A relatively tightly knit group might well exist, composed of county officials, county-seat lawyers, leading merchants, bankers, and town-oriented successful farmers, but the implications of "ring" are misleading. The prominent figures of the county were naturally thrown into numerous face-to-face contacts and seemed inevitably to dominate the school boards, churches, fraternal lodges, GAR posts, local commercial organizations, booster activities, and the Republican party. To outsiders they may have seemed like "rings," and the political structure may have appeared fraught with implications of "machine control"; to the members they were performing the natural functions of the "better sort." While some controversies existed within local elites, most members agreed on certain essentials—essentials that generally included a belief in the Republican party as necessary to good government. This belief, shared with a majority of the county's residents, meant that members of the local elite of a county-seat town were allowed to exercise the functions of party leadership so long as they fulfilled certain minimal expectations for that role: making July Fourth orations, mounting campaign rallies and extravaganzas, delivering GOP majorities on election day, and rewarding campaign workers. In addition, possessing power allowed them to build support groups through rewards for campaign work and through access to railroad passes, which were generally made available to railroad lawyers and surgeons, elected officials, and often county chairmen. These were generally not considered bribes by either giver or recipient, but rather were seen as the prerogatives of the local elite. The county-seat elite was able to dominate the county's politics through dominating the Republican party and to operate with some impunity not through corruption, but through the general apathy of the party rank and file.[7]

Despite the isolation inherent in the concept of "island community," the community *elites* were far from isolated. In northeastern, southeastern, and southcentral Nebraska, the railroads, especially the Burlington, bound together the many county seats and other commercial centers and provided an easy route for the local elites to travel. Maps 2 and 3 indicate population density and the extent of railroad development as of about 1890. The lines connected county centers with Lincoln and Omaha, and also with other

1890 POPULATION

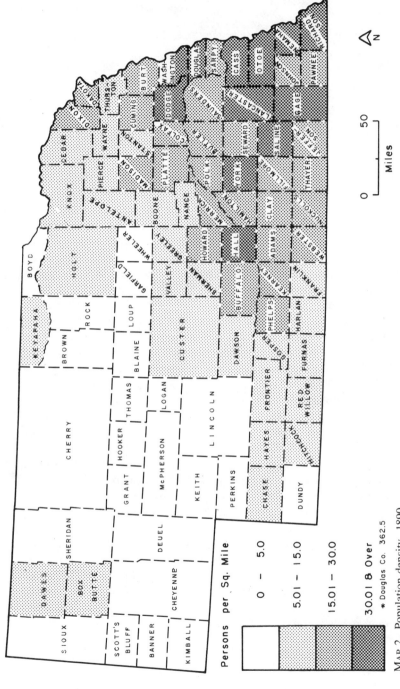

Persons per Sq. Mile

	0 – 5.0
	5.01 – 15.0
	15.01 – 30.0
	30.01 & Over

* Douglas Co. 362.5

MAP 2. Population density, 1890.

1890   RAILROADS

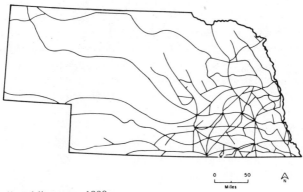

MAP 3. Railroad lines, ca. 1890.

county centers. Local elites frequently met their counterparts, both at non-political activities such as church conferences, lodge conventions, and GAR encampments and at the frequent political conventions. They traveled to state conventions on the same railroads and frequently on the same trains. Railroads provided special rates, and sometimes passes, for those attending state party conventions and some nonpolitical statewide events as well. Webs of relationships among local elites often developed along rail lines. Persons living in the Burlington area would often act together at state conventions—and not solely because of pressures from railroad representatives, as charged by the reformers, although such pressures undoubtedly existed. When a county community elite chose to promote one of its members for a state or district nomination, contacts with other community elites were eased by the rail network. The promotion of a local leader for nomination to a higher political sphere often tended to unite a local community and its neighbors in a species of boosterism.[8]

The state convention, focus of these promotional efforts, had other functions in addition to creating a slate composed of villagers from various parts of the state. Three distinct elements emerge from accounts of Republican state conventions. The first is convention as ritual: flaying the Democrats and praising the Republicans as the saviors and only legitimate servants of the Union. This invocation of the past and of tradition promoted unity and solidarity among the ritual's participants, but this unity was sorely tried by the second function of the convention: the nomination of state candidates. With only two exceptions in the 1880s, a two-term rule was adhered to in nominating state executive officers. When an office was occupied by an incumbent in his second term (or when the occupant of an office had become controversial in some way) the state convention was rarely united in choosing a successor. James W. Dawes, state chairman for several years, was nominated for governor in 1882 on the third ballot; the first ballot had given him 121 votes to 108 for his nearest competitor with 190 scattered among six other candidates. The selection of delegates to national nominating conventions was also closely contested. In 1880 three factions sought control of the state delegation, with the winning anti-Grant faction averaging 238 votes, compared with about 129 for the Grant supporters. Despite the clear-cut victory of the anti-Grant forces, the state convention could not muster a majority to instruct for any candidate. In 1884 a motion to instruct the state delegation for Blaine was tabled by a vote of 220 to 207. Election of state convention chairman was often equally hard-fought. Off-year conventions and congressional conventions exhibited similar intraparty divisions.[9]

The third function of the Republican conventions, writing the state party platform, was often a means of reuniting a party that had split while making nominations. Most platforms attacked the Democrats as the party of treason, lauded the GOP as the party of the Union, and included virtually every noncontroversial demand, grievance, or complaint voiced by any party member. Democratic leaders were characterized as "inherently dishonest." Nebraska Republicans took fearless stands against the excesses of Tweed in New York and against the imposition of white supremacy in Mississippi, and they were equally staunch in support of Irish home rule, the regulation of interstate commerce, and a national Labor Day. When some specific controversial topic arose, however, the Republicans invariably straddled. In 1882, for example, when railroad rate regulation was a prominent issue, the party platform opposed "unjust discrimination and extortion by railroad companies" but also recognized "the importance of fostering and protecting them as necessary factors in our progress and prosperity." No Republican platform spoke more clearly on prohibition than to favor a popular vote on the issue, but the 1888 platform did announce in favor of "virtue," "sobriety," and "purity" and sympathized with "all wise and well-directed efforts for the protection of temperance and morality."[10] After the convention came the campaign, and the focus of activity shifted to the county and to the local trading centers, where state-level candidates and the state committees traded charges of personal and party incompetence and malfeasance. The state was saturated with orators: the state committees, the state executive nominees, and party notables.[11]

State government reflected the primacy of the local community. For most state officeholders government service was anything but a lifetime occupation. Upon completing their terms, most returned to their home towns and took up their businesses or professions, perhaps with their reputations enhanced. Silas Garber, governor from 1875 to 1879, returned to Red Cloud and engaged in merchandising, banking, and cattle-raising. James W. Dawes, state party chairman from 1876 to 1882 and governor from 1883 to 1887, thereafter resumed his law practice in Crete and entered the real estate business. John Milton Thayer, elected governor in 1886 and reelected in 1888, retired in 1892 to follow "literary pursuits." None of the three took an active part in politics after leaving office. Similar patterns characterized most state executive officers in the 1880s. Like some county officials, a few state officials used state office as a stepping-stone to personal advancement. When Albinus Nance completed his second term as governor in 1883, he left Nebraska to become a Chicago stock and bond broker. Heman A. Babcock of Ord, in central Nebraska, served two terms as state auditor in the 1880s, then remained in Lincoln as a banker.[12]

A very few men continued a high level of political activity over a long period. Edward Rosewater, editor and publisher of the *Omaha Bee*, was an influential, but seldom regular, Republican spokesman from 1870 to his death in 1906. Charles Gere was editor and publisher of the state's semiofficial Republican organ, the *Nebraska State Journal*, from its founding in 1867 to his death in 1904. Charles Van Wyck, leader of the radical-reform wing of the GOP, had represented a New York district in Congress, was elected to the United States Senate from Nebraska in 1881 and defeated for reelection in 1887, became a Populist in 1890, and was the Populist candidate for governor in 1892. Charles Manderson was the only Nebraskan to serve two full consecutive terms in the United States Senate before 1916; he was senator from 1883 to 1895. Algernon Sidney Paddock was territorial secretary from 1861 to 1867, senator from 1874 to 1881, member of the Utah Commission from 1882 to 1886, and senator again from 1887 to 1893. Church Howe served six terms in the state legislature before 1890, was Republican national committeeman from 1884 to 1888, and unsuccessfully sought election to the House of Representatives in 1886. These six men were exceptions to the general trend, and of the six Manderson and Paddock were largely preoccupied at a national level during the 1880s, and Rosewater and Gere were neither officeholders nor officeseekers.[13]

This high level of turnover in the personnel of the political system was coupled with a low level of activity by most officeholders. Most state officials were conscientious and honest, but nearly all were political amateurs, filling office on a short-term basis. The state political system, like the national system, defined executives as administrators rather than innovators. Governor Nance described the duties of governor as "to secure the effective enforcement of the law, and to guard the interests of the state so as to avoid useless expenditures, and encourage frugality in the management of the state institutions.'' Governors' reports to the state legislature were typically catalogs of the activity of each state institution during the preceding two years; they occasionally suggested areas for legislative activity, but only in the most general terms. These amateur administrators sometimes proved susceptible to influence from various sources, including party leaders and corporate agents who had done favors during the campaign. Some favors, such as obtaining railroad passes, were not generally considered corrupt. Opportunities for corruption were, in fact, limited. When opposition orators spoke of corruption, they usually referred to patronage matters and to governmental inaction vis-à-vis corporate regulation. Such inaction did not necessarily suggest official corruption, for corporate growth was usually equated with community growth, and regulating the former was thought to limit the latter. One Republican, upon being urged to run for governor, described his views as follows: ''I have no love for monopolies but do not feel . . . that they should be ground to powder. R.R. interests, individual interests and State interests should be mutual.''[14]

If most executive officers were amateurs with little to do, members of the state legislature were no more experienced or busy. The state legislature met for two or three months once every two years. Most legislative nominating conventions rigidly adhered to a two-term rule, but many incumbents apparently did not even seek a second term. Few legislators had prior experience, and not one served more than a few consecutive terms. The court system was the only branch of state government where officials developed long periods of consecutive service. The three state supreme court judges served six-year terms and were generally renominated so long as they did not become centers of controversy. Opposition to the renomination of judges most often took the form of simple competition for office. A correspondent wrote to Supreme Court Judge Samuel Maxwell after the 1881 nominating convention that ''there was no opposition to you personally; the votes given for others being chiefly from a desire to put others *in* office, not to put you out.''[15] The same was true of the district courts, although these offices sometimes served as stepping-stones to higher office, usually congressman.

The Republican-dominated political system, in sum, was built upon party loyalty, a loyalty deriving from tradition and renewed by the rituals of rhetoric, convention, and campaign. The system of minimal government, where innovation and activism were divisive and thus discouraged, had little ability to respond to crisis. Throughout the 1880s, the party was faced with two potential sources of discord: criticism by reformers of supposed corporate influence in party councils and state government, and rare instances of dishonest or unethical practices by elected officials. The party's response to both was identical—it refused to renominate the offending official, whether his offense was embezzlement or criticism of his party.[16]

The Democrats, a perpetual minority, had little to do with the structure of state government. Since statehood was achieved in 1867, Democrats had held only two significant offices, state treasurer and congressman, each for only one term and each as a result of divisions within the Republican ranks. Yet many of the generalizations about Republicans also apply to Democrats. Fewer members of the county-seat elites were Democrats, but Democrats did exist there. Party differences little affected relationships among members of the town elites. Willa Cather, describing two small-town aristocrats in a short story, noted that they "sometimes discussed politics, and joked each other about the politics and pretensions of their respective parties. . . . Each man seemed to enjoy hearing his party ridiculed, took it as a compliment." Democratic county organizations tended to include more farmers proportionally than did their Republican counterparts, partly because there were fewer Democrats in the professions and commerce, and partly because the Democrats tended to attract some dissatisfied agrarians and seemed more receptive to agrarian issues than were the more secure Republicans.[17]

At a state level, Democratic gatherings were more personality-oriented than were the Republicans. J. Sterling Morton, later secretary of agriculture in Cleveland's second administration, occupied a position of prominence throughout the 1880s, as he had since the earliest days of the territory. Morton had served in the territorial government and had unsuccessfully sought election to Congress and the governorship. Dr. George L. Miller, editor and publisher of the *Omaha Herald* from 1865 to 1887, was Morton's chief rival in the Nebraska Democracy. Miller had also served in the territorial legislature, had run for Congress in 1864, and had been a prominent member of the Tilden wing of the national party. Other Omahans, with Miller, made up the leadership of the urban "packing-house" faction in contradistinction to Morton's rural "slaughter-house" faction. Many of the other leading Omaha Democrats were Irish entrepreneurs. Typical of this group were James Boyd, who had investments in railroads, banking, meat-packing, and Omaha's most prominent theater; John McShane, president of the Union Stock Yards; and John A. Creighton, whose fortune came from construction and was invested in banks, stockyards, railroads, and land.[18]

Democratic state platforms usually praised national party leaders, called for tariff reform if not free trade, attacked Republican extravagance and malfeasance, opposed sumptuary legislation (especially prohibition), and favored Irish home rule. They frequently attacked corporations, especially railroads, and urged their regulation. Democrats in 1882 demanded the abolition of railroad passes and, in 1888, condemned "the republican creature known as the trust." Subsidies to corporations, specifically further land grants to railroads and the state sugar-beet bounty, were denounced. The Democrats courted labor, "the producer of the wealth of the nation," by opposing Chinese immigration, promising to remove all of "the Mongolian race" from American territory, and backing laws to protect "the interests and welfare of the industrial masses" and to outlaw prison labor contracts. The Republicans were pictured as rapacious plunderers of the public trust, "under the dominion of false doctrine and animated by enormous pecuniary interest in the perpetuation of existing abuses." Two platforms called for either a sound currency (1880) or for no further coinage of silver dollars (1885). Democratic statements about the nature of government somewhat contradicted some of their specific demands for governmental action: "The prosperous commonwealth is that one which legislates the least as to the relations between labor and capital, which enacts the fewest laws of a regulatory character, most unfrequently invades the domain of political economy with statutes, and draws the least amount of annual taxes from its citizens."[19]

At the state level, Democrats were appealing to three overlapping groups—opponents of prohibition, antimonopolists, and labor. Prohibition had strong and vocal support in Nebraska throughout the 1880s; pro-hibitionists finally succeeded in getting a referendum on constitutional prohibition in 1890. Where Republicans avoided taking a position on the issue, Democrats specifically opposed prohibition in their 1882 platform as "contrary to the fundamental rights of the individual, and to the fundamental principle of social and moral conduct." Similar sentiments were to be found in the platforms of 1883, 1884, 1886, 1887, 1888, and 1889.[20]

The greatest opposition to prohibition in Nebraska was in the communities of Germans, Czechs, Irish, Poles, and some other immigrant groups. These groups moved to the Democratic party as prohibition and nativist sentiment grew, and Democratic leaders did all they could to estrange such groups from the Republicans. J. Sterling Morton, candidate for governor in 1882 and 1884, made special efforts to link advocacy of prohibition to support for the GOP: "Show me a radical pulpit-hanger of any denomination or sect—one who preaches politics every Sunday mixed with the Puritan doctrine of prohibition and I will show you always, without exception an individual who is voting for Dawes and the Republican ticket throughout." Such strong statements, according to Morton, were necessary "to direct the German mind to an observation of a peculiar type of mental and moral man who has carried prohibition into effect in Iowa and Kansas." In Irish communities he concluded his addresses by stressing Democratic commitment to Irish home rule and condemning "English tyranny."[21]

Democrats also tried to attract antimonopolists and labor, but the most radical of the antimonopolists formed the various third parties that contested state elections through the 1880s—Greenback Labor in 1880, Anti-Monopoly in 1882, Anti-Monopoly and Greenback in 1884, National Union in 1886, and Union Labor in 1887, 1888, and 1889. The antimonopoly or reform wing of the Republican party, led by Edward Rosewater of the *Omaha Bee* and Senator Charles H. Van Wyck, occasionally bolted regular Republican candidates it found objectionable. The state Farmers' Alliance, maintaining a precarious grip on life throughout the decade, formed another center of antimonopoly sentiment, as did the Knights of Labor. Labor, represented not only by the Knights but also by craft unions in the larger cities, was active in the 1880s, most notably in a smelting strike and riot in Omaha in 1880, a railroad laborers' strike in Omaha in 1882, strikes by Burlington employees in Omaha and Lincoln in 1886, the national railway strike of 1888, and an 1888 Burlington strike at Plattsmouth, which culminated in a riot between Pinkertons and strikers. In 1888 correspondents in parts of the state as geographically separate as Fairbury and North Platte wrote to Governor John Thayer that the Knights of Labor state lecturer was campaigning for John McShane, the Democratic candidate for governor.[22]

Of these various disaffected groups, the Democrats were most successful in attracting the antiprohibition immigrants and much less so in attracting the antimonopolists, despite repeated efforts by some leaders in both camps to promote fusion. Fusion between Democrats and antimonopolists in 1882 elected Phelps D. Sturdevant state treasurer, with the assistance of repeated attacks by Rosewater's *Bee* upon the Republican nominee. Complete state-level fusion of Democrats with antimonopoly and Greenback forces in 1884 failed to secure the election of any of its nominees, even the reelection of Sturdevant. Similar coalitions between Democrats and antimonopoly forces occasionally occurred in congressional districts and on county tickets, and the latter were sometimes successful.[23]

This impressionistic survey of Nebraska's political system has concentrated on the dominant Republicans. Republicanism mirrored the attitudes of the community leaders who dominated party conventions and state committees. Preoccupied with promoting the growth of their communities and of the state and clearly in the majority on election day, Republican leaders shunned controversy and related to politics as no more a full-time occupation than the fraternal lodge, the church, the GAR post, or the school board. Government and the Republican party were largely synonymous. Most Republican state officials saw themselves as short-term administrators; few maintained a long-term involvement in the process of government.

The minority Democrats sought to better their status through vociferous opposition to sumptuary legislation, attacks on corporate power, and cooperation with radical third parties. Republicanism expressed the bland optimism of community leaders; the Democracy spoke to the dissatisfied or the threatened. To be a Republican was to be "normal" as defined by most communities' delineators of social values. To be a Democrat was to admit deviation from those values in some way.

CHAPTER TWO

Voting Behavior
and Political Leadership
in the 1880s

I am not afraid of defeat. If I had been I would have left this
crowd a good many years ago. . . .I will undertake to lead this
forlorn hope. . . .There is certainly not the remotest danger of
[winning the] election.

J. Sterling Morton,
Democratic candidate for
governor, 1882

Morton knew whereof he spoke. Nebraska's growth
seemed to have been paralleled by the growth of Republican supremacy. In
Nebraska's first gubernatorial election in 1866, only a few percentage points
separated the two major candidates; by 1880 Republican voters outnum-
bered Democrats two to one. Although this wide margin began to narrow
somewhat by the late 1880s, Republican dominance remained secure until
the end of that decade.[1]

Historians have advanced two quite different explanations for the appeal
of the GOP to Nebraska voters, one looking to economic factors, the other to
ethnocultural conflict. Robert Manley summarizes the economic explanation as follows: "the continuing strength of the Republican party in Nebraska in the 1870's and 1880's derived in large measure from the willingness
of that party to ask for governmental assistance to agriculture." Republican
officials did much to encourage the settlement of the state's unimproved, and
even marginally productive areas. A list of such actions is long indeed,
beginning with the Homestead Act and encouragement of railroad construction and including numerous state actions and pledges. Nebraska's dominant
Republicans also promoted growth through such devices as establishing
state institutions, offering cash awards for the discovery of minerals, and
giving a direct subsidy for the manufacture of beet sugar. Democrats, by

13

contrast, tended to oppose such measures, condemning subsidies to railroads and to the beet-sugar industry, opposing the construction of state buildings "not absolutely and imperatively demanded in behalf of the welfare of the whole people," and asking "vigorous frugality" in all government. They specifically opposed appropriations to irrigate "desert lands" on the basis that the nation had "already enough arable land to glut a home market."[2] In light of these party attitudes, it would not be surprising for the speculative farmer—that is, the farmer on unimproved or even marginally productive land, paying high mortgage interest rates and hoping for a large increase in land value—to support the expansive generosity of the Republicans.

A very different interpretation of the basis of Republican success is found in the writings of Samuel P. Hays, Paul Kleppner, and Frederick C. Luebke, who have looked to ethnocultural differences as the major determinants of voting behavior in the Middle West in the late nineteenth century. For these historians, party affiliations are to be understood as only one aspect of larger social patterns. Ethnicity and religion are crucial elements in understanding these social patterns, for late nineteenth century social attitudes tended to coincide with a spectrum of ethnoreligious values.[3]

Groups at one end of the ethnoreligious spectrum, termed "pietistic" or "evangelical," emphasized the intensely personal nature of the religious conversion experience and the need to be "born again" in order to become a full participant in the life of the church. Such groups often defined acceptable social behavior with both narrowness and precision. *The Doctrines and Discipline of the Methodist Episcopal Church* for 1896 provides a list of "imprudent and unchristian conduct" for which a church member might be expelled:

indulging sinful tempers or words, the buying, selling, or using intoxicating liquors as a beverage, signing petitions in favor of granting license for the sale of intoxicating liquors, becoming bondsmen for persons engaged in such traffic, renting property as a place in or on which to manufacture or sell intoxicating liquors, dancing, playing at games of chance, attending theaters, horse races, circuses, dancing parties, or patronizing dancing schools, or taking such other amusements as are obviously of misleading or questionable moral tendency.

The same source defines "complete legal prohibition of the traffic in alcoholic drinks" as "the duty of civil government." While the Methodists were essentially Arminian in their emphasis on the need for each person methodically to perfect his or her own life, and in their belief that such perfection was attainable, other old-stock Protestant groups often came to similar conclusions regarding proper social behavior while still retaining Calvinist concepts of predestination and the impossibility of attaining a sinless state. Whether Calvinist or Arminian in theology, groups at the pietist end of the spectrum of ethnoreligious values placed a strong emphasis on the conversion experience and on the need "to evidence their desire of salvation" by their daily behavior. Also important was the need to "bring the world to Christ" by eliminating sin from it and by converting others so that they too might perfect their own lives and thus be saved. Old-stock groups closest to the pietist end of this spectrum included Methodists, Baptists, and Disciples of Christ. Many Congregationalists and Quakers also are to be placed very near the extreme pietist end of the spectrum. While some Presbyterians also belong there, most were somewhat closer to center. Episcopalians belong at the center or perhaps somewhat toward the opposite end. A number of immigrant groups also typify the pietist perspective, notably Norwegian and Swedish Lutherans, British Methodists, and Ulster Presbyterians.[4]

At the opposite end of the spectrum of ethnoreligious values stood the "ritualist" or "liturgical" perspective. The differences in theology, social values, and church practices are numerous. Where pietist groups required that a person be "born again" to become a full communicant but seldom required anything more than such a personal declaration of faith, ritualistic groups typically required lengthy catechism classes so that the communicant would have detailed knowledge of the faith. Ritualistic groups generally defined acceptable social behavior—and sin—much differently than did the pietists. The ritualists did not see alcohol as sinful in itself, though overindulgence might be. Unlike the extreme abhorrence toward alcohol of the extreme pietist, the ritualist groups usually considered it a normal part of life, to be taken with meals or with friends and to be served to celebrate such sacred occasions as weddings. Where pietist groups defined gambling as sinful, ritualist groups might conduct a lottery (gambling, by the definition of the pietists) to raise money for the church. The extreme ritualistic perspective is best typified by the Catholics, with such traditionalist German Lutheran groups as the Missouri Synod very close to the same point of view. Other German Lutherans, German Calvinists, and some Danish Lutherans would be placed somewhere between the extreme ritualist end of the spectrum and the center.[5]

These ethnoreligious perspectives provided not just a standard of behavior for Sunday mornings, but also a way of organizing the many social patterns that profoundly affected political behavior. According to Hays, party divisions in the late nineteenth century are to be understood almost entirely in terms of "the impact of evangelical Protestantism on the political world of the late 1840's and early 1850's." Kleppner, basing his conclusions on study of several Middle Western states, argues that "the more ritualistic the religious orientation of the group, the more likely it was to support the Democracy; conversely, the more pietistic the group's outlook the more intensely Republican its partisan affiliation." While conflict between the two perspectives ranged over a wide range of issues, including the public schools, Sunday closing laws, and woman suffrage, it came to focus especially on the issue of prohibition, which in turn came to symbolize much of the larger ethnocultural conflict.[6]

To explore the nature of Nebraska's voting behavior in the 1880s, this analysis began with some forty indicators of population characteristics, derived from the federal censuses of 1880 and 1890 and from popular referenda in 1882 and 1890. These variables included such things as place of birth of the foreign-born, sentiment on prohibition, place of residence (urban or rural), occupation, type of agriculture, and agricultural prosperity. The derivation of a matrix of Pearson (product-moment) coefficients of correlation indicated three major clusters of population characteristics, the first focusing upon ethnicity, the second upon place of residence, and the third upon agricultural development and prosperity.[7]

The next step in measuring relationships between these population attributes and voting behavior was to derive coefficients of correlation between representative population variables and party support in the elections of 1886 and 1888. Table 1 summarizes these coefficients. It appears from this table that the vote for prohibition, reflecting the ethnocultural antagonisms described by Kleppner, Hays, Luebke, and others, is the most reliable predictor of the party vote. The strong relationship between prohibition and party preference can be seen quite clearly by dividing the sixty counties into quartiles based on their prohibition vote, then calculating the mean party

TABLE 1. PEARSON COEFFICIENTS OF CORRELATION, REPRESENTATIVE POPULATION VARIABLES WITH INDEXES OF PARTY STRENGTH, 1886 AND 1888

Dependent Variables	Percentage of the Vote in Favor of Prohibition, 1890	Percentage of the Population Living in Incorporated Areas, 1890	Mean Income per Farm, 1889
Republican party index, 1886	+0.5687	−0.2265	−0.3546
Republican party index, 1888	+0.7387	−0.1939	−0.2791
Democratic party index, 1886	−0.7828	+0.1890	+0.2378
Democratic party index, 1888	−0.8484	+0.2028	+0.2609

TABLE 2. PARTY STRENGTH INDEXES, FOR COUNTIES, 1886 AND 1888,
BROKEN DOWN BY POPULATION CHARACTERISTICS BY QUARTILES

Independent Variables	Democratic Party Index		Republican Party Index	
	1886	1888	1886	1888
Vote for prohibition, 1890				
Quartile most opposed	49.68%	50.55%	47.04%	45.28%
Second quartile	39.23	40.10	54.61	52.66
Third quartile	32.65	35.42	59.02	56.27
Quartile most in favor	29.95	31.33	59.43	58.13
Mean income per farm, 1889				
Most prosperous quartile	41.37%	43.29%	53.67%	51.22%
Second quartile	38.18	39.16	51.79	51.88
Third quartile	36.52	37.86	54.64	53.96
Poorest quartile	35.14	36.88	60.26	55.46
Percentage of the population living in incorporated areas, 1890				
Most urban quartile	39.44%	41.05%	52.86%	51.35%
Second quartile	37.54	37.21	56.17	55.46
Third quartile	39.05	41.79	52.05	50.19
Most rural quartile	34.68	36.73	59.57	55.72

vote for each quartile. This form of cluster analysis is presented in table 2, which also includes quartile breakdowns for the percentage of the population living in incorporated areas and for the mean farm income. This table clearly points up the central importance of ethnicity in the determination of party vote. Democrats were in the majority *only* in those counties most opposed to prohibition. When the counties are broken down by nonethnic criteria, Republicans held majorities in every quartile.

The coefficients of correlation and the quartile breakdowns alone do not indicate a totally monocausal relationship between ethnicity and political behavior. The coefficients of correlation between farm income and the index of party strength, and the quartile breakdowns for the same variables, both allow for the possibility of a secondary relationship between party preference and the viability of agriculture. A problem arises, however, in sorting out the effects of ethnicity and agricultural prosperity, for they were not related to each other in a random fashion. The coefficient of correlation between the vote for prohibition and the farm income variable is a rather low

TABLE 3. DISTRIBUTION OF COUNTIES BY ATTITUDE ON PROHIBITION AND BY FARM INCOME

	Farm Income above the Median	Farm Income below the Median
Prohibition Vote below the Median		
	11 counties	18 counties
Prohibition Vote above the Median		
	20 counties	11 counties

-0.2545. However, if we divide the counties into two groups on the basis of their vote for prohibition, then split each of these groups on the basis of farm income, the counties most opposed to prohibition are disproportionately prosperous, and the counties most in favor of prohibition are similarly overrepresented among the less prosperous counties. Table 3 summarizes these data. One way of examining the possibility that agricultural viability may have had a secondary influence on voting behavior, once the effects of ethnicity are held constant, is to calculate the mean party vote for *each cell* in table 3; this is done in table 4, using the party index for 1888. Table 4 suggests that agricultural prosperity had little influence on party preference, once the effect of ethnicity is held constant. There is virtually no difference in the Democratic vote in the more prosperous and less prosperous counties,

TABLE 4. INDEXES OF PARTY STRENGTH BY COUNTY, 1888, COUNTIES DISTRIBUTED BY ATTITUDE ON PROHIBITION AND BY FARM INCOME

Party Index	Farm Income above the Median	Farm Income below the Median
Prohibition Vote below the Median		
Democratic	45.68%	45.40%
Republican	48.94	48.78
Prohibition Vote above the Median		
Democratic	32.82%	34.20%
Republican	57.84	56.11

holding constant the effect of prohibition sentiment. The Republican vote does tend to be somewhat higher among the less prosperous counties, but the tendency is very slight indeed. Both minor parties, the Prohibitionists and the Union Laborites, showed their greatest strength in the lower right quadrant of table 4, the cell where the Republican vote was most different from expectations. If table 4 were to be recalculated using only the vote for the two major parties, some of this variation would be eliminated; doing so suggests that among the counties most opposed to prohibition, three persons out of five hundred may have voted Republican out of economic motives, and that, among the counties most in favor of prohibition, three voters out of two hundred may have done so. In point of fact, table 4 suggests that the impact of economic situation on voting behavior in 1888, once ethnicity is held constant, is so slight as to be almost unmeasurable.

Another method of evaluating the influence of a second independent variable on voting behavior, once the explanatory powers of a first are explored, is stepwise multiple regression. Stepwise multiple regressions were calculated for the party vote in 1886 and 1888, the vote for governor in 1886 and 1888, and the vote for president in 1888. In only two instances did adding a second variable to the regression equation increase the square of the multiple coefficient by more than 0.04. Table 5 presents the instance where adding a second variable produced the largest increase in explanatory power. Table 6 presents a more typical example. The conclusion is obvious: adding a second and third independent variable does not significantly improve the explanatory power of ethnicity. Similarly, a comparison of actual precincts

TABLE 5. STEPWISE MULTIPLE REGRESSION SUMMARY TABLE, REPUBLICAN VOTE FOR GOVERNOR, 1886

Independent Variables	Multiple R	Multiple R^2	Change in R^2	Simple r
Vote in favor of prohibition, 1890	0.55435	0.30731		+0.55435
Mean income per farm, 1889	0.59979	0.35975	0.05244	−0.36256
Percentage of the population living in incorporated areas, 1890	0.62168	0.38648	0.02673	−0.16350

TABLE 6. STEPWISE MULTIPLE REGRESSION SUMMARY TABLE,
DEMOCRATIC PARTY INDEX, 1888

Independent Variables	Multiple R	Multiple R^2	Change in R^2	Simple r
Vote in favor of prohibition, 1890	0.84836	0.71971		−0.84836
Percentage of the population living in incorporated areas, 1890	0.86106	0.74142	0.02171	+0.20284
Mean income per farm, 1889	0.86831	0.75397	0.01255	+0.26094

and counties indicate that ritualistic antiprohibitionists held strong Democratic preferences in marginally productive areas, and highly productive areas peopled by old-stock American Protestants were typically Republican.

The preceding analysis clearly suggests that the Democratic party in Nebraska in the 1880s was largely a single-interest party, with Democratic voting determined almost solely by the voter's ethnocultural outlook. Any relationship between agricultural prosperity and voting for the two major parties was more apparent than real, deriving from the tendency of certain ethnic groups to settle disproportionately in more prosperous areas. This tendency is clearly seen in table 3 and can also be discerned in some of the coefficients of correlation among various population attributes. The mean farm income for example, correlates at +0.28 with the percentage of the population born in Germany, Bohemia, Ireland, or Poland. Obviously there is no strict linear relationship between ethnicity and prosperity. But the majority of the ritualistic groups were concentrated in the more prosperous areas of eastern Nebraska, and the less productive central and western areas of the state were peopled disproportionately by old-stock American pietists. Contemporary observers and historians alike have commented on the different attitudes toward the land among immigrants and old-stock Americans.[8] Immigrants, it appears, were more likely to view the land as almost an extension of themselves, to work the land more intensively, and to seek to establish their offspring on farms near themselves. Old-stock Americans, by contrast, were more prone to sell out when offered a good price, and to move farther west where land values were lower and—at least in central Nebraska—the risk of failure was greater. This suggests that a propensity to view agriculture speculatively—a willingness to take risks in the expectation of future gains—may have sprung from the same old-stock attitudes that predisposed these marginal farmers to Republican voting.

The importance of immigrant culture to this view of party identification dictates a closer examination of immigrant voting patterns. Germans were the largest foreign-born group in the state. Swedes and Czechs were in close contention for second place. Smaller groups included Danes, Irish, other British, Russian-Germans (the Wolgadeutsch), Poles, and Norwegians. Frederick C. Luebke found strong Democratic partisan preferences among German immigrants. In 1884, eight voting precincts in which more than three-quarters of the voters were German averaged 73 percent Democratic for governor, and in 1890 the same eight precincts averaged 92 percent opposed to prohibition. During the 1880s, Luebke concludes, "the identification of the German voters with the Democratic Party was strengthened under the pressure of continued agitation for woman suffrage, prohibition, and Sabbatarianism." Furthermore, Luebke found that Catholic Germans were most strongly Democratic, Missouri Synod Lutherans "only slightly less Democratic though there were some significant exceptions," and that Nebraska Synod Lutherans or non-Lutheran Protestants showed greater Republican proclivities. He concluded that "church affiliation is the best guide to variation in political behavior among the Germans of Nebraska."[9]

John R. Kleinschmidt applied Luebke's social analysis and methods to Nebraska's Swedish and Czech groups. His findings further reinforce the argument that ethnocultural factors are the most significant predictors of partisan preference. Five precincts in which more than 75 percent of the voters were Czech averaged 92 percent against prohibition in 1890; three precincts in which more than 75 percent of the voters were Swedish averaged 88 percent in favor of prohibition. Just as the ethnocultural conflicts of the 1880s had pushed Catholic and Lutheran Germans ("ritualistic" groups) into a closer alignment with the Democratic party, so did these conflicts push the Czechs in the same direction—most strongly for Catholics, less so for the considerable number of freethinkers. Similarly, Swedish immigrants, whose Lutheranism was highly "pietistic," became more committed to the GOP.[10]

Four other relatively large immigrant groups have not been studied intensively. Of these four, the non-Irish British were too dispersed to permit the location of voting precincts where they were numerically dominant. The remaining three—the Irish, Danish, and Russian-German groups—can be isolated into relatively homogeneous precincts and examined, although the scope of this study does not permit depth comparable to that of Luebke's. The analyses that follow combine quantifiable material with impressionistic evidence to indicate the general trends among each of these groups.

Irish fondness for the Democracy was as strong on the prairies of Ne-

braska as on the streets of Boston or the sidewalks of New York. O'Connor
Precinct, Greeley County, named for Bishop James O'Connor of Omaha,
was part of a farming settlement promoted by the Irish Catholic Colonization
Association. The proportion of Irish was extremely high—well over half and
perhaps 80 percent—but an exact measurement is not possible because
O'Connor Precinct did not exist at the time of the 1885 state census. The
1900 census shows O'Connor Precinct 76 percent Irish. O'Connor voted 82
percent Democratic for governor in 1888 and 99 percent against prohibition
in 1890. A physician and Democratic politician in neighboring Boone
County described the Greeley County Irish as "unanimously democrats and
Catholics"—for him, the two characteristics obviously went together. Arthur F. Mullen, who grew up in O'Neill, an Irish colony sixty miles north of
Greeley, noted a similar Irish affinity for the Democracy, especially among
the some two score former Molly Maguires in and around O'Neill. Summit
Precinct, Dakota County, in the extreme northeast corner of Nebraska, was
about 80 percent Irish in 1885. No election returns were located for Summit
before 1890, but in that year the precinct was unanimously opposed to
prohibition and 99 percent Democratic for governor.[11]

Three predominantly Danish precincts were studied, one in Kearney
County, two in Howard County. Cosmo Precinct, Kearney County, about 80
percent Danish in 1885, voted 76 percent against prohibition in 1890 but
split its 1888 gubernatorial votes, giving 41 percent to the Democrats, 47
percent to the Republicans, and 11 percent to the Union Labor party.
Dannebrog and Dannevirke precincts, Howard County, were at least 50
percent Danish, but Dannevirke also contained a significant proportion of
Polish immigrants.[12] The two precincts were quite similar in their voting
behavior, casting about 70 percent of their votes for the Democratic candidate for governor in 1888. Both opposed prohibition in 1890, Dannebrog by
62 percent and Dannevirke by 89 percent. The differing behavior of the
Howard County and Kearney County Danes suggests there existed no bloc
Danish vote, even in areas where Danes were concentrated geographically.
Although the other Scandinavian groups in Nebraska, the Swedes and the
Norwegians, were both strongly Republican,[13] the Kearney County Danes
were split between the two major parties and the Howard County Danes
showed a tendency to vote Democratic. An explanation may well lie in the
nature of Danish Lutheranism. Swedish Lutheranism and Norwegian
Lutheranism, in Nebraska, were strongly influenced by pietistic movements, but Danish pietism was a rather late develpment and was counterbal-
anced by the development of a folk-culture movement led by the Danish
bishop N. F. S. Grundtvig. All the churches in or near the three precincts

sampled were aligned with the pietistic branch of Danish Lutheranism; yet the most significant cultural center in Dannebrog was the folk high school, a Grundtvigian institution frowned upon by Danish pietist leaders. The division within Danish Lutheranism over pietism, and even within Danish communities with only one church, suggests that there was no well-defined social basis for bloc voting.[14]

Russian-born immigrants, most of them German in language and culture, can be isolated into several voting precincts that allow a comparison of their voting behavior. Cub Creek Precinct, Jefferson County, was the center of a large Mennonite settlement; the precinct voted 53 percent Democratic for governor in 1888 and opposed prohibition by 80 percent of its vote in 1890. Sutton and School Creek townships, Clay County, were evangelical in their religious attitudes and were less Democratic in their voting than Cub Creek. The Clay County precincts voted 37 percent and 27 percent Democratic, respectively, in the 1888 gubernatorial election and also split their votes on prohibition in 1890, voting 51 percent and 41 percent in favor.[15] As with the Danes, the absence of a single immigrant church seems to indicate a division within the group itself which worked against significant levels of bloc voting.

Polish immigrants were few in number in Nebraska but were concentrated in a few locations. The largest settlement was in Howard County, but the exact proportions cannot be determined because precinct boundaries were changed soon after the 1885 state census. Kelso Precinct, Howard County, was probably at least 30 percent Polish in 1888 and likely considerably higher; Dannevirke Precinct may have been as much as 30 percent Polish in 1888 but also included a significant number of Danes.[16] Burrows Township, Platte County, was about 25 percent Polish in 1885; Poles were the largest group there, followed by Germans and Irish. The electoral behavior of these three precincts is consequently only suggestive of Polish voting behavior. Kelso voted 92 percent Democratic for governor in 1888 and 92 percent against prohibition in 1890. Dannevirke, as already noted, voted 70 percent Democratic in 1888 and 89 percent against prohibition in 1890. Burrows registered 72 percent Democratic in 1888 and 83 percent against prohibition in 1890. Such evidence suggests that Polish immigrants were quite similar in their political preferences to their fellow Slavs, the Czechs, and to their fellow Catholics.

The ethnocultural conflict that centered on temperance measures and included woman suffrage, Sabbatarian legislation, and disputes over the proper role of the public schools had a dramatic effect on party affiliations. The movement of ritualistic groups into Democratic ranks during the decade of the 1880s helped Democratic gubernatorial candidates increase their share of the vote from 26 percent in 1878 to 42 percent in 1888. The most striking Democratic gains came in 1880 when saloon licensing was a major issue and in 1888 when the Democratic candidate for governor was a "sopping wet" Irish Catholic. These developments not only greatly improved Democratic standings at the polls, but also gave the party a new complexion, made it almost totally a single-interest party composed of immigrants, ritualistic church members, and opponents of moral reforms. By the late 1880s, Democratic voting was most strongly associated with an ethnocultural perspective common to German, Czech, Irish, and Polish immigrants, to Catholics and many Lutherans—a perspective that found sumptuary legislation, especially prohibition, highly distasteful. Republican voting tended to be related to an opposing ethnocultural perspective, more Arminian, that took a proselytizing approach to the world, advocating not only temperance but other perfectionist moral reforms as well. In Nebraska, old-stock American Protestants were also likely to be disproportionately represented in marginally productive areas, seeking government assistance in the form of subsidies or land grants.

There were, throughout the 1880s, two minor parties who routinely contested state elections—the Prohibitionists and a series of agrarian radical parties variously labeled Greenbackers, Anti-Monopolists, and Union Labor. The Prohibitionists received between 2 percent and 6.4 percent of the statewide vote from 1884 to 1888; agrarian radical parties got 18 percent in 1878 and 19 percent in 1882, but less than 1 percent in 1884 (when one group of Anti-Monopolists fused with the Democrats) and in 1886. The Union Labor party of 1888 got just over 2 percent. Of course, both minor parties had local strongholds. In 1886 fifteen counties voted more than 10 percent Prohibitionist, and one—Polk County—exceeded 20 percent; the following major election, 1888, saw only two counties exceed 10 percent. Similarly, the National party of 1886 received more than 20 percent in one county (also Polk) but failed to receive a single vote in more than half the counties in the state. In 1888 some votes were cast in most counties, but the Union Labor ticket got more than 10 percent in only three counties. Attempts to determine some statistical relationship between Union Labor or Prohibition party voting and population characteristics are not particularly fruitful. Pearson coefficients of correlation are weak; of the three independent variables used in stepwise multiple regression and cluster analyses, the most significant is the vote in favor of prohibition. For the Prohibition party votes, the coefficients vary from +0.41 to +0.53; for the agrarian parties (National in 1886 and Union Labor in 1888), from +0.23 to +0.31. Other variables stepped into the regression equations do not significantly increase the value of the multiple coefficient. Although we might anticipate some relationship between agrarian radical voting behavior and the farm income level, the coefficients of correlation are weak; the strongest is for the 1888 vote for governor, +0.2. Although the historical literature suggests the likelihood of a relationship betweeen wheat farming and agrarian radicalism,[17] such is not indicated by the coefficient of correlation (+0.1). Some weak relationship appears, however, if we divide counties into groups according to degree of dependence on wheat farming. The fifteen counties most dependent upon wheat averaged just over 4 percent for the Union Labor party in 1888, ranging from 0 to 14 percent, and the twenty-eight counties with the lowest ratios (those least dependent on wheat) averaged just over 2 percent, ranging from 0 to 21 percent.[18]

Quantitative analysis seems to be of little help in evaluating the appeal of agrarian radicalism in the late 1880s. Certain nonquantifiable factors undoubtedly influenced the Union Labor vote—most obviously the method of ballot distribution. In the late 1880s ballots were still printed and distributed by political party organizations. County chairmen presented bundles of ballots to precinct chairmen who then carried the party tickets to the voters.[19] Such a system placed a premium on complete party organization. In some counties there was no Union Labor organization, hence no ballots, and therefore not a single vote was cast for Union Labor candidates. This situation apparently was most likely to occur in the newly organized counties of central and western Nebraska—the regions where agricultural distress might have made voters receptive to the appeals of the agrarian radicals. In the longer-settled, more politically organized, and more prosperous sections of eastern Nebraska, the Union Labor Party did best in those counties where prohibition sentiment was strongest, probably as the result of two factors: (1) ritualistic voters, by the late 1880s, were firmly wedded to the Democratic party, as the protector of their ethnocultural value patterns; and (2) the crusading, proselytizing style of the agrarian radicals may have had its greatest appeal to voters of pietistic background and have been a negative influence on ritualistic voters who associated such style with the "cold water" warriors of temperance. Indeed, many of the most prominent agrarian spokesmen were of old-stock Protestant background, committed in varying degrees to temperance.

Voting patterns in Nebraska in the 1880s are best characterized as ethnically linked deviations from a Republican norm. The stereotype of the Republican voter—native-born of old American stock, pietistic Protestant, Civil War veteran, GAR member, prosperous farmer or small-town businessman—has some validity but conceals the presence in Republican ranks of immigrants from Sweden, Norway, and other lands, of some Lutherans, Jews, and Free Thinkers, of struggling homesteaders and urban laborers, of debtors and bank presidents, of prohibitionists and saloon-keepers. The stereotype of the Democratic voter—immigrant and ritualistic—also has its shortcomings, concealing Texas-born cattlemen and Vermont-born Jacksonians, Indiana-born Copperheads and New York–born free traders. Despite such variations, the preceding analysis has established the Democratic party as being largely based on the single issue of opposition to sumptuary legislation and as composed largely of immigrants and ritualistic religious groups. In 1890, 45 percent of Nebraska males twenty-one years of age or older were either foreign-born or of foreign parentage. If we accept males of voting age as roughly approximating the electorate (foreign-born males who had filed their first citizenship papers were allowed to vote), and if we assign half of the foreign-stock voters to the Democrats, then 56 percent of Democratic voters and 42 percent of Republican voters were of foreign stock. If two-thirds of the foreign-stock voters are assigned to the Democrats (i.e., virtually all the ritualistic groups), then 75 percent of Democratic voters and 28 percent of Republican voters were of foreign stock. The convergence of these projections with other forms of analysis[20] suggests that it would not be far afield to project that by the late 1880s *probably* at least two-thirds of Democratic voters and *probably* no more than a third of Republican voters were of foreign birth or foreign parentage.

Political Leadership

The Nebraska Democratic leadership during the 1880s centered on J. Sterling Morton of Nebraska City and on a group of Omaha businessmen, notably Dr. George Miller, James E. Boyd, and John McShane. During the eighties, an animosity developed between these factions. Morton favored free trade unreservedly and supported Senator Thomas F. Bayard at the 1884 national convention: Miller leaned toward the modified free-trade views of the Ohio-Pennsylvania Democrats and adhered to the Tilden-Cleveland-Manning wing of the national party. Both groups ardently opposed prohibition. Conflict had appeared during the 1883 senatorial contest and again in 1884 when Morton had accepted the Anti-Monopoly nomination for governor in addition to that of the Democrats. The distribution of patronage made possible by the national victory of 1884 ripped the state party apart, Morton favoring distribution through the state committee, of which he was chair-

TABLE 7. PERCENTAGE DISTRIBUTION OF NEBRASKA POLITICAL LEADERS BY OCCUPATION AND PLACE OF BIRTH, 1880–90

Characteristics	Republicans	Democrats
Occupation	N=253	N=79
Agriculture	30.4%	21.5%
The professions		
Law	21.7	20.3
Journalism	3.7	3.8
Total, professions	31.2	35.4
Business		
Merchandising	16.6	12.7
Finance	11.1	11.4
Total, business	35.6	36.7
All other occupations	2.8	6.3
Place of birth	N=356	N=106
Born in U.S.		
New England	7.0%	4.7%
Middle Atlantic	27.2	25.5
Middle West	42.7	31.1
Border	4.2	5.7
Confederate South	2.0	8.5
Total born in U.S.	83.1	75.5
Foreign-born		
Britain (exc. Ireland)	6.2	8.5
Germany	3.9	7.6
Ireland	2.8	4.7
Total foreign-born	16.3	22.6
Unspecified	0.6	1.9

Note: Columns may not add to 100 owing to rounding.

man, and Miller looking for rewards from his wing of the national party. After 1886 the Miller-Boyd Omaha group established control over the state party.[21] There were some able Democratic leaders in the rest of the state, but they were few in number and their voices were not loud.

Personalities played a different role in the GOP than in the Democracy: with a few exceptions, mostly in the reform wing of the party, Republican leaders tended to a bland facelessness. Governors Nance and Dawes took no further part in state politics after they retired from executive office. United States senators were in faraway Washington much of the time, concentrating their energies on patronage and on procuring federal largesse for the state. Although congressional districts did not follow a two-term tradition (as state

28 / POPULISM, PROGRESSIVISM, AND NEBRASKA POLITICS

TABLE 8. PERCENTAGE DISTRIBUTION OF NEBRASKA POLITICAL LEADERS
BY VARIOUS BIOGRAPHICAL CHARACTERISTICS, 1880–90

Biographical Characteristics	Republicans	Democrats
Date of birth	N=291	N=89
Born before 1831	9.6%	14.6%
Born 1831–40	19.9	27.0
Born 1841–50	52.9	33.7
Born 1851–60	15.8	20.2
Born after 1860	0.3	1.1
Unspecified	1.4	3.4
Union Army service among		
leaders born 1836–45	63.3%	18.5%
Attendance at or graduation from	N=253	N=79
college or normal school	31.2%	30.3%
Date of arrival in Nebraska	N=253	N=79
Before 1865	11.5%	30.4%
1865–75	62.5	39.2
After 1875	24.9	26.6
Unspecified	1.2	3.8
Associational memberships	N=59	N=23
Grand Army of the Republic	37.3%	13.0%
Mason	52.5	56.5
Other fraternal lodges	45.8	52.2
Professional and commercial		
organizations	10.2	21.7

Note: Data for date of birth and date of arrival in state may not add to 100 owing to rounding. Percentages for associational memberships are based on the number indicating memberships rather than on total number of subjects and columns do not add to 100 because of multiple memberships.

offices did), death and retirements combined to produce enough turnover in the three-man House delegation to preclude the development of powerful personal followings during the 1880s.[22]

A profile of party leadership may be deduced from a collective biography. Compiling data on a large number of men might well be expected to yield certain insights into the nature of partisan differences. Biographical data were tabulated for more than three hundred political officeholders, nominees, and party notables.[23] The following aspects were examined: place of birth, date of birth, Union Army service during the Civil War, education, occupation, religion, and organizational affiliations. Tables 7 and 8 summarize the most interesting of these data. The same measures were derived for thirty-one Republicans who occupied the highest party and state positions. The data reveal that Republicans were more likely than Democrats to have been born in New England, the Middle West, or Scandinavia; Democrats were more likely to have been born in the Confederate South, Germany, or Ireland. More than half of the Republican leaders were born in the decade 1841–50. This is the generation that came to political awareness fifteen to twenty years later, in the period 1855–70—that is, the generation for whom the struggle to preserve and rebuild the Union was the central focus of political identity. Only about a third of the Democratic leadership was born in that decade. This relationship between Republican leaders and the Civil War experience may also be observed in the Union Army service of party leaders. Among the most significant Republican leaders, four out of five were Union veterans. The equivalent figure for the state as a whole, as of 1890, was 31 percent. The Democratic leadership group included two Confederate veterans; no Confederate veterans appeared in the Republican leadership. Denominational information, unfortunately, is available for only 15 percent of the Republicans and 10 percent of the Democrats, but these very limited data indicate that Republicans were nearly four times more likely to be old-stock pietistic Protestants than were Democrats, and that Democrats were more than two and a half times more likely to be ritualistic than were Republicans.

These several elements—place of birth, Civil War experience, and religion—tap the major vein of Republican party distinctiveness. Republican leadership appears to have been profoundly affected by the Civil War experience—or, perhaps, to have come from a sociocultural milieu that was susceptible to being profoundly affected by the war. The typical Republican leader was from a strongly Unionist area of the nation, was—so far as the data allow generalization—an old-stock pietistic Protestant, and had participated in the Civil War either as a combatant or as a person of impressionable age who likely had brothers or cousins who were combatants. After the war he came West, often to take advantage of the cheap or free land provided though Republican generosity. Data for the most significant Republican leaders intensify the direction of these relationships. These leaders were more likely than the larger group to have been born in New England or the Middle Atlantic states and much less likely to have been foreign-born. They had more education in general and were much more oriented to the law in particular than the entire Republican group. The major difference between these top leaders and the larger Republican leadership group was in occupation: the top leadership contained only one-third as many agriculturists but had twice as many in finance and in law. Organizational affiliations, education, and occupation show little significant difference between the two party leadership groups.

The Political System, 1880–90

From statehood to the election of 1890, Republican dominance of Nebraska politics was almost total and the level of interparty competitiveness was low, although less so at the beginning and end of the time span. The majority Republicans avoided controversy in their platforms and denied renomination to controversial Republican officeholders. Democrats and antimonopolists were more issue oriented, the Democrats with regard to sumptuary legislation and, among a few leaders, free trade, and the antimonopolists with regard to economic issues relating to corporate control. Even together, Democrats and antimonopolists were a minority.

Throughout the period there was a high rate of turnover among elected officials—typically, 80 to 90 percent of the state legislators had *no* previous legislative experience[24]—and this in turn suggests a relatively open political system, within certain limits. Occupation seems to have been a major limiting factor, with the unskilled totally unrepresented among the political leadership, artisans greatly underrepresented, and farmers somewhat underrepresented. Place of residence was similarly limiting, with small trading centers and county-seat towns disproportionately represented vis-à-vis both farms and urban areas. The foreign-born were underrepresented, and those of New England or New York background were overrepresented. But these limiting factors should not obscure the essential openness of the system. The two-term tradition for most offices operated to keep tenure to a minimum in state government. The Democrats, who had extreme difficulty in getting elected to even one term, were wracked by factional feuds that prevented long-term dominance by one faction or one man. State-level figures with long-term involvement were few—no more than ten in each major party.

The high level of leadership turnover and low level of party competitiveness combined to produce what may be termed an amateur system. The securely dominant Republicans refused to orient their campaigns to current economic issues, and party affiliations tended to be tied either to the events of 1855–70 or to prohibition. In such a context, few demands were placed on the state political system. With the high rate of turnover among elected leaders, positions of power were dominated by political amateurs, and controversial actions in office were not tolerated. The low level of demands placed on the system, the desire to avoid controversy, the Whiggish view of the executive, and the virtual absence of long-term political experience all combined to produce very little output from the system itself. Such a system carried within it the seeds of its own destruction. Should demands increase, the party leaders, locked into the system, would be too inexperienced to deal with them or too opposed to controversy to wish to do so, with the result of a continued agitation of the demands and also popular frustration with the system itself.

By the closing months of 1889 it had become apparent to seasoned political observers that 1890 was to be a year of heavy demand on the political system. Throughout the 1880s, ever more insistent pressures for regulation of railroad rates had brought no response from the Republican-dominated state government. A bumper corn crop in 1889 raised many farmers' hopes for a good financial return, but prices plummeted and railroad rates remained so high that some farmers found it cheaper to burn their corn for fuel than to sell it and buy coal. The Republican party showed no ability to respond to the fast-approaching crisis. Indeed, the state convention in 1889 refused to renominate Supreme Court Judge Manoah B. Reese, who had become controversial through his antirailroad sentiments, and nominated in his stead an alleged "railroad tool." A congressional district convention, meeting to nominate for a seat vacated by a death, spurned Republican antimonopolists and nominated another alleged railroad man. Membership in the Farmers' Alliance boomed, and the orators of the Alliance and the Union Labor party, long-practiced but unable to attract crowds for the past seven years, began to draw throngs of hard-pressed farmers with their tirades against the moneylenders, railroads, and grain dealers. During the winter of 1889–90, politicians began to anticipate 1890—regular Republicans with dread, antimonopolists with hope.[25] The weather took a hand, and events moved beyond the capacity of the old system, for 1890 was a drought year. Hot winds seared the corn. Farmers, with no corn, raised hell.

CHAPTER THREE

Nebraska's Populist Revolt: Campaigns, Issues, and Personalities, 1890–95

I cannot sing the old songs,
My heart is full of woe;
But I can howl calamity
From Hell to Broken Bow.
—J. L. Bixby

The emergence of Populism in 1890 provoked the fiercest political battle so far known in Nebraska. Radicals saw the issue as between "the insatiable greed of organized wealth and the rights of the great plain people." Republicans saw it as between "the best intelligence of the section that was loyal to the union" and "bloody anarchists" and "calamity howlers." Farmers, thousands strong, defiantly paraded down Main Street, then gathered to sing Populist versions of old songs and hear orators indict moneylenders, the railroads, the political system, and sometimes the entire economic system. An opponent of the Populists described their 1890 campaign as "a composite of Hugo's pictures of the French Revolution and a western religious revival. The popular emotion more nearly approached obsession than . . . had theretofore seemed possible for the American temperament." Contemporaries and later historians alike have described the fiery zeal that crumbled the old party alignments as a "revolution."[1]

In Nebraska during the 1880s, the Democrats' consistent opposition to prohibition brought them a loyal following among the antiprohibition portion of the electorate. Republicans, eschewing controversy, maintained a hold on the loyalties of a different part of the electorate by appealing to memories of the Civil War and to old-stock American and pietist values. Such ethnoculturally derived party preferences might be susceptible to disruption in two possible ways: a widespread change in ethnocultural attitudes, an unlikely occurrence; or the emergence of strong political determinants not of an ethnocultural nature. At least half of Nebraska's voters, and probably somewhat more, changed their traditional voting behavior at some time during 1890–95. Many who did not change parties probably analyzed the issues and candidates as intensely as did the voters who did switch.[2] A survey of political events, especially campaigns, is essential for understanding the context in which these voters reevaluated their political affiliations. What follows is not a comprehensive narrative of all political events but is limited to the public means whereby parties defined their appeal to voters.

The 1889 election had given Nebraska antimonopolists cause for both despair and hope. The 1889 Republican conventions seemed to be more railroad-dominated than ever, but county-level independent tickets based on the Farmers' Alliance captured several courthouses, sometimes with the backing of local Democrats. Men who kept a close count on the pulse of politics began, as early as December 1889, to voice the opinion that 1890 was to be the year of political upheaval. Prominent Republicans, including Attorney General William Leese, former Supreme Court Judge Manoah B. Reese, and Edward Rosewater of the *Omaha Bee*, attempted to counteract growing third-party agitation by holding an antimonopoly Republican convention in mid-May. The conference produced a platform that highly praised the Republican party, demanded an end to the political activities of railroads, the abolition of railroad passes, and a railroad freight rate law; opposed the McKinley tariff; and favored ballot reform. The conference also appealed to antimonopoly Republicans throughout the state to "rally and rescue our state from corporate domination by actively participating in the primary elections [i.e., the party caucuses] and nominating conventions."[3]

Agitated farmers, however, did not follow the advice of these established political leaders. Farmers' Alliance membership rolls burgeoned with the expectation that the Alliance would soon enter the political arena. Alliance officers initially resisted, but by mid-May they agreed to call a political convention if Alliance members should request one through petitions. Within five weeks, fifteen thousand signatures had been collected, and the Alliance and Knights of Labor issued a convention call. Rosewater's *Bee*, long sympathetic to the Republican antimonopoly sentiment, condemned Alliance leaders as "ambitious visionaries and wildcat cranks" and repeated the appeal to Republican farmers to stay in the GOP and force the selection of antimonopoly Republican candidates.[4]

The Republican state committee, under these pressures, called their state convention early, to precede the Alliance convention by six days. Republican antimonopolists won early victories in the selection of the chairman and the writing of the platform, which included all the demands of the May antimonopoly convention and others as well. The convention balked when asked actually to criticize the actions of office-holding Republicans, however, and tabled, 486 to 330, an attack on the state board of transportation.[5]

The selection of nominees for state office pointed up the same unwillingness to depart from the practices of the past. No prominent reformer or antimonopolist was nominated for any statewide office. The nomination for governor went to Lucius D. Richards of Fremont, a forty-three-year-old Vermont-born Civil War veteran, prominent GAR member, and self-made man who had worked his way up through a railroad construction crew to construction supervisor and roadmaster, then entered the business of selling real estate and insurance and making loans. Antimonopoly Republicans left the convention dissatisfied but not bolting.[6]

The Alliance-sponsored convention, meeting a few days later, took the name Independent party and drafted a platform that demanded silver coinage and paper issue sufficient to increase the money supply in circulation to fifty dollars per capita, declared that land monopolization must be abolished, and demanded government ownership of the railroad system. John H. Powers, state Alliance president, was nominated for governor on the first ballot. If Lucius Richards was in many ways a typical Republican leader, long-bearded John Powers was the stereotype Populist. He had worked in Illinois as a schoolteacher, carpenter's assistant, and farmer before the Civil War. He enlisted but was discharged because of illness. Resuming farming in Illinois, he joined the Grange and was elected lecturer of the local organization. He moved to Nebraska in 1874, won election to the local offices of township supervisor and justice of the peace, joined the Alliance in 1884, and held the office of state organizer and state president. A deeply religious Presbyterian licensed as a lay evangelist, Powers held local church offices in both Illinois and Nebraska. Modest and unassuming, he was well-read and quietly eloquent. Six of the remaining seven nominees for statewide office had longtime third-party, Alliance, or Labor experience. Of the eight statewide candidates, only the nominee for attorney general was not a farmer, and he had been counsel to labor organizations in Omaha.[7]

The Democrats convened some two weeks later, the convention securely controlled by the Omaha faction. The Democratic platform, like the Republican, sought to preempt the radicals' issues and, in addition, to disparage Republican dedication to reform. It closed with a denunciation of prohibition and an indictment of Republican hypocrisy on that issue. Just as the Republicans and Independents had selected men typical of their parties, the Democrats gave the head of the ticket to James E. Boyd. Born in Ireland, Boyd had come to Nebraska in 1856. Unquestionably the wealthiest of the three major candidates for governor, Boyd had risen from humble beginnings to acquire a wide range of financial interests by 1890; he had served as president of the Omaha Board of Trade in 1880–81. A "sopping wet," his long experience in the state's Democratic politics began the year he arrived and included two terms as mayor of Omaha in the 1880s. None of the eight Democratic statewide candidates was a farmer. Four of them were foreign-born, one was a Union veteran, and one was a Confederate veteran.[8]

Just as 1890 saw the culmination of more than a decade of agrarian and radical agitation, so it also saw the culmination of an equally long term effort to bring prohibition to the Nebraska plains. The 1888 session of the legislature had directed that a constitutional amendment proposing prohibition go on the 1890 ballot. Of the three major parties, only the Democrats took a position on this issue.

Republican campaigners, claiming that "in no other state of the Union are the people, as a whole, more prosperous, contented and happy than the people of Nebraska," attributed this condition to uninterrupted Republican rule and maintained that "every consideration affecting the future welfare of Nebraska demands republican success." Democrats, they said, were motivated solely by a desire for office and would "reverse the principles and politics which have contributed to the progress and prosperity of the state." Rosewater's *Bee* described Independent leaders only as "wild and visionary," but the *Nebraska State Journal* saw them as "demagogues and shysters," "arrant hypocrites," "shiftless lazy and improvident," and "a herd of hogs . . . in the parlor of a careful housekeeper." Richards embodied typical Republican traits: "the soldier boy, the patriot, the honest man who came west after the war to grow up with the country," "an honorable, moral and able champion of the people," and a "dignified, upright, able successful business man." Boyd was Richards's opposite in every particular: "the speculator and old time bourbon . . . whose record as a private citizen cannot with propriety be fully discussed in the newspapers." Republicans waved the bloody shirt vigorously, admonishing that votes for either Democrats or Independents might mean the control of Congress by "the rebel brigadiers" or the election of "the ex-confederate surgeon" as lieutenant governor. Republicans also constantly claimed that the Independent movement was promoted and exploited by the Democrats in their greed for office.[9]

Huge gatherings of farm families characterized the campaign of the Independents, often preceded by a parade of hundreds of farm wagons and floats through the town and climaxed by the singing of Independent versions of popular songs and speeches by prominent Alliancemen, Knights of Labor, and Independent party nominees. Independent rhetoric typically repeated the demands of their platform and the economic analysis of the Alliance, of the Knights of Labor, and of the third-party radicals of the 1880s. The songs were in a lighter vein but were thoroughly imbued with the same view of society. When Independent orators spoke of the desperate financial conditions of the farmer, the problems of the urban laborer, and the responsibility of the corporations and the old parties for these conditions, Republicans decried them as "calamity howlers."[10]

Democrats generally refrained from attacking the Independents, reserving their fire for accusations of prohibition-leanings on the part of Richards, although Powers was well known as a temperance advocate. In late April, Gilbert Hitchcock's *Omaha World-Herald,* the state's leading Democratic daily, had proposed that the Democrats endorse an Alliance state ticket in return for Alliance support of Democratic congressional candidates. Although no coalition was arranged, in the second congressional district Democrats endorsed the Independent nominee, William McKeighan. In the third congressional district, a move to give the Democratic nomination to Omer M. Kem, the Independent candidate, failed by a close vote in the district Democratic convention. In the first district, former Senator Charles Van Wyck declined the Independent nomination for Congress, a move apparently designed to benefit William Jennings Bryan, the Democratic candidate. Although Democrats sought the Independent nomination for Bryan, they were unsuccessful. In some counties, however, local arrangements were made whereby Democratic county conventions made the Independent candidates for county office their own in return for pledges to support Bryan on election day. Bryan and his supporters assiduously courted the Independent vote throughout the campaign.[11]

The campaign of 1890 saw the three parties campaigning on three issues, not necessarily in direct conflict. Democrats campaigned against prohibition. Independents campaigned against deflation, high interest rates, railroad rate discrimination, corporate abuses, and political corruption. Republicans appealed to tradition and pointed to their successful promotion of the state's growth and prosperity. When the campaign had burned to its close and the votes were counted, Independents secured majorities in both houses of the state legislature. The second and third congressional districts went to Independents, the first to Bryan. Boyd became the first Democrat to win the governorship, albeit with only 33.3 percent of the vote. Powers, the Independent, ran second with 32.8 percent. Richards, the Republican, was a close third with 32.2 percent. The average vote for the other seven statewide offices, a reliable indicator of party preferences, suggests that the GOP remained the largest party in the state with 34.7 percent. The new Independent party was second with 33.1 percent and the Democrats were third with 30.0 percent. Boyd's victory and the Democratic party vote were both closely tied to the defeat of the prohibition amendment. In the first congressional district, some Independents apparently supported Bryan, but others broke agreements to do so and supported their own party candidate instead.[12] The Independents cut a broad swathe across central Nebraska but were weak in the east and in the panhandle.

Independents had majorities in both houses of the 1890 legislature. The House elected Samuel M. Elder as speaker. A jovial one-armed Union veteran, Elder's highest previous political office had been county coroner. Independents charged fraud in the 1890 state elections and hoped to seat their own candidates, but in the official canvass of the returns before the house, Speaker Elder did not assert—indeed, may not have known—the prerogatives of the Speaker. When the returns were accepted on their face in the house, the Independents lost their first chance for a challenge.[13] They lost their final chance for a challenge when the senate rejected hearing the contest by a vote of 14 to 11, with three Independents joining Republicans and Democrats to make up the majority. The Independents' other major embarrassment of the 1891 session came with their attempt to pass a railroad rate bill. Known as the Newberry bill after its sponsor, it became a symbol of the independent movement. The bill passed the house 78 to 17, but a senate vote was delayed when an Independent senator disappeared from the state. Senate rules required that all members be present or excused, and the missing Independent was neither; all Senate business was held up until he could be found or until all those present could agree to suspend that rule. Ultimately the rules were suspended and the bill passed the senate by a vote of 23 to 7, but Democratic Governor Boyd then vetoed it. The house voted to override, but the senate failed, 18 to 13, to muster the two-thirds majority necessary to override. The legislature did enact a number of other reforms long discussed by antimonopolists and reformers.[14] Shortly after the legislature adjourned, the state supreme court ousted Boyd from the governorship on the basis that he was technically not a citizen.[15]

The campaign of 1891, to elect a supreme court judge and two university regents, began with the Independent convention in mid-August. Their platform stressed demands for currency inflation by paper issue and silver coinage, the prohibition of alien land ownership, a graduated income tax, government ownership of all means of public communication and transportation, and the direct election of the president, vice-president, and senators. The Independent nominee for judge was Joseph Edgerton, the 1890 nominee for attorney general.[16]

Nebraska Democrats continued to court the Independents. Their platform condemned "grasping corporations and usurious money lenders," repeated their opposition to "paternalism and favoritism in government," and attacked the growing power of the anti-Catholic American Protective Association (APA) as "un-American and treasonable." After the convention adjourned, Jefferson H. Broady, the Democratic nominee for judge, declined the nomination, forcing the Democratic state committee to act on the vacancy. Dr. George Miller and other conservative Democrats demanded that a candidate be named, but Governor Boyd broke with his Omaha ally to join Congressman Bryan and Gilbert Hitchcock of the *World-Herald* in convincing the committee that no Democratic candidates should appear on the ballot for any state office. Assuming that Democratic voters would give the Independent candidates their margin of victory, the *World-Herald* confidently predicted that Edgerton would win election as judge with 75 percent of the vote.[17]

Republicans convened in late September. Their platform spoke glowingly of Nebraska's "marvelous prosperity," opposed free silver, supported the McKinley tariff, and accused the Democrats of deception. Incumbent Judge Amasa Cobb, accused of favoritism toward the railroads, was denied renomination when antimonopoly Republicans waged a strong campaign for Manoah B. Reese, the former supreme court judge denied renomination in 1889. Reese led on an informal ballot, with Cobb a close second, but on the fourth official ballot the nomination went to a compromise candidate, Alfred M. Post, a state district judge.[18] Expectations that Democratic voters would support the Independent ticket proved unfounded. Republicans won all three races, polling 49 percent for judge and 48 percent for regent.

Nebraska's high state of political excitement continued through 1892. The Populist national convention met in Omaha in midsummer.[19] State nominating conventions were complete by early September, and the fall campaign was further intensified both by the presidential contest and by a series of debates between the Republican and Independent gubernatorial candidates.

The Republican platform, distinctly less of an attempt to preempt the radicals' issues than in 1890, proclaimed the GOP the friend of labor "in the factory, mill, mine, and on the farm" but deplored conflict between labor and capital. The convention favored measures to protect workers and farmers, to regulate express company rates, to establish an elective railroad commission with power to fix rates, and to establish a postal telegraph, postal savings banks, and rural free delivery. Democrats, more verbose in their praise of party candidates and traditions and in their pronouncement of friendship for ''the toiling interest,'' also favored an elected state railroad commission. They repeated their support for the direct election of senators and their opposition to government bounties and subsidies. Prohibition, they declared, was ''contrary to the fundamental principles of social and moral conduct'' and the APA was ''undemocratic and un-American.'' Independents, now widely known as Populists, endorsed their national platform, demanded state railroad rate legislation, and repeated their support for the direct election of president, vice-president, and senators. The convention favored equal pay for equal work for men and women and demanded prompt delivery of Populist campaign mailings.[20] Each party seems to have elected its most capable and representative campaigners for state office.

The Populist convention made its nominations first. Powers refused to contest the gubernatorial nomination, and the convention with near unanimity gave the honor to Charles H. Van Wyck, Powers's strongest competitor in the 1890 convention. Scion of the New York Van Wyck family, he had helped to organize the New York Republican party, had been elected to Congress in 1858 and 1860 by a New York district, had recruited a regiment in the summer of 1861, and had compiled an impressive military record. Temporary chairman of the 1866 New York Republican state convention, he was again elected to Congress in 1866 and 1868. Upon completion of his fourth term, he moved to Nebraska and was elected to the state constitutional convention in 1875, to the state senate in 1878 and 1880, and to the United States Senate in 1881. A vocal proponent of tariff reform, retrenchment, and corporate regulation, Van Wyck became anathema to regular Republicans and railroad supporters and was not reelected in 1887. His defeat embittered him toward the GOP, and he spent the years until 1890 trying to organize an effective force to defeat the railroad supporters and regular Republicans who, he felt, dominated state politics.[21]

The Republican state nominating convention met under the firm control of the new national committeeman, Edward Rosewater, antimonopoly editor of the *Omaha Bee*. Rosewater drew upon his quarter-century of experience in Nebraska politics to select a candidate who best combined respectability, reform sympathy, and, above all, electability. Lorenzo Crounse, fifty-six years old, born in upper New York State, was an able lawyer and Civil War veteran who had been wounded in action. He had moved to Nebraska in 1864, was elected to the territorial legislature that year, helped to draft the state constitution, was elected to the state supreme court in 1866 and to the house of representatives in 1872 and 1874, and sought election to the senate in 1877. Unsuccessful, he retired from active electoral politics, serving as state convention delegate, internal revenue collector, and assistant secretary of the treasury. His political activities made him well known, but he had not been recently active and had few personal enemies. Perhaps most fortuitously, he was father-in-law of Gilbert Hitchcock, thus neutralizing the *World-Herald*, the state's leading Democratic daily.[22]

The Democrats could not have selected a nominee more closely identified with the entire span of the party's history in Nebraska than J. Sterling Morton. Morton, like Crounse and Van Wyck, was born in New York State. He came to Nebraska in 1854, was elected to the territorial legislatures of 1855 and 1857, served as assistant territorial secretary from 1858 to 1861, and unsuccessfully sought election as territorial delegate in 1860 and as governor in 1866. After a ten-year absence from politics, he again plunged into activity as a free trade advocate, a railroad lobbyist in Washington, state party chairman, and candidate for governor in 1882 and 1884. Control of the state party passed out of his hands in 1884, but he ran for Congress in 1888 and remained a power to be reckoned with at all Democratic gatherings. While Morton and his supporters may have thought he had a chance of winning in 1892, his nomination for governor served at least two equally important functions—it eliminated any chance of fusion with the Populists, and it strengthened Morton's position vis-à-vis the federal patronage expected from a Cleveland victory.[23]

Republican reformers and antimonopolists were pleased with the nomination of Crounse. Populists, with few exceptions, were united behind Van Wyck. The Democrats, by contrast, were divided. Morton and his supporters opposed silver coinage, but Bryan based much of his reelection campaign on the silver issue, and only four Democratic editors in the entire state opposed silver. Morton leveled a constant attack on Van Wyck; Bryan's supporters reportedly offered to trade support for Van Wyck for Populist support of Bryan.[24] Hitchcock's *World-Herald* was largely silent.

Republican campaigners based their appeal upon their party's responsibility for "progress, prosperity and sound government," "honest money and industrial progress." The "calamity lamentation" of the Populists, they claimed, was responsible for "curtailing investments, driving out capital, and checking the inflow of population" and was therefore "the most serious form of disloyalty next to open treason." Every "loyal citizen" was urged to "stand up for Nebraska." Rosewater's *Bee* saw two classes of Populist leaders:

Class I. Visionaries and rattle-brained reformers who sincerely believe in the doctrines set forth in the crazy-quilt platform adopted in Omaha on the Fourth of July. Class II. Demagogues, mountebanks and imposters, whose sole aim and purpose is to ride into power and place on the tidal wave of popular discontent.

Van Wyck, a man of wealth, could not rationally accept Populist doctrine, the Republican campaigners reasoned, and therefore must be actuated by some ulterior motives. The Democrats, as usual, were motivated solely "by an inordinate desire to capture the spoils," and the entire Populist movement was only a Democratic device to fool unsuspecting Republicans.[25]

The *Alliance-Independent,* the Populist state organ, claimed the state faced two paramount issues:

I. Shall the corporations which have so long dominated and corrupted our politics, and robbed our people through extortionate charges, be retired from power, and the people given freight rates no higher than those now in force in Iowa? II. Shall our state offices be administered by selfish men who ignore the law, and violate their official oaths that they may enrich themselves at the expense of the taxpayers, and under whose past administration the most monstrous and shameful corruption has prevailed, or shall these offices be administered by honest men in the interest of the people?

The paper featured frequent exposés of Republican corruption in the state, estimating the total loss at seventy thousand dollars. State leaders told local campaign workers that "it is [especially] important that the exposures of corruption at the state capital should be kept before the people. . . . This reaches directly to the pocket of every taxpayer."[26]

Crounse and Van Wyck held a series of debates across the state. Van Wyck generally concentrated on the issues of the Populist national platform—trusts, the tariff, silver, railroad rates. Crounse sympathized with Alliance aims but criticized the Populist party, reviewed Republican accomplishments, sometimes complimented Morton, and slashingly attacked Van Wyck's public record. Van Wyck became defensive and angry and spent most of his remaining time defending his own past. Crounse's tactic of angering the former senator was well conceived. One journalist described the results: "Anger means confusion, and Van [Wyck] often became confused, forgetting the thread of his argument and what he was there for."[27]

At a presidential level, some state Democratic leaders sought to deprive Harrison of the state's electoral votes by throwing Democratic votes to Weaver, the Populist. Earlier, some had even spoken of withdrawing most of the Democratic state ticket in the hopes that a coalition could be arranged with the Populists. Democrats did not limit their support for Populists to this late-October drive for Weaver. In six of the thirty state senate districts, Democrats made no nominations, and they endorsed the Populist nominee in four others. Bryan based his reelection drive on an appeal to the Populists in his district.[28]

TABLE 9. PERCENTAGE DISTRIBUTION OF SUPPORT FOR MAJOR PARTIES, 1892

Party	Office	Percentage of Total Vote Cast
Republican	President	43.56%
	Governor	39.71
	Other state offices	41.29
Populist	President	41.53
	Governor	34.75
	Other state offices	31.31
Democratic	President	12.46
	Governor	22.38
	Other state offices	24.32
Prohibition	President	2.45
	Governor	3.16
	Other state offices	3.08

Democrats and Populists were again disappointed when the votes were counted; table 9 indicates the percentages received by each major party for president, governor, and other state executive offices, and three congressional seats. Bryan, Kem, and McKeighan were returned to Congress. Republicans held most seats in both houses of the legislature but were short of a majority in both. Democrats apparently lost strength to both the Populists and Republicans.

In 1890, 1891, and 1892, prominent Democratic leaders had made various proposals for cooperation between their party and the Populists but had been uniformly spurned. All "joint" electoral efforts had actually been entirely unilateral in nature; for example, the Democrats' acceptance of McKeighan in 1890, or the withdrawal of all statewide Democratic candidates in 1891, or the support for Weaver in 1892. Similar instances of unilateral Democratic support for the Populists could be found at local and district levels. Up to the opening of the 1893 legislative session there had been no indication that Populists were actively seeking Democratic support, and certainly no indication that Populists were willing to share power with

Democrats as the price for such support. During the 1893 legislative session, however, this one-sided flirtation became a full-scale coalition as Populists and Democrats in the lower house quickly combined to support a Populist for Speaker and to divide other positions between them. Senate cooperation was not so easy, three Democrats helping to elect a Republican as president pro tempore, but Democrats combined with the Populists on other matters of senate organization. Electing a senator took a full month and sixteen ballots. Republicans first supported incumbent Algernon S. Paddock but scattered half their strength to other candidates before uniting behind John M. Thurston, general counsel of the Union Pacific Railroad, on the twelfth ballot. Populists first voted for John Powers but switched to William L. Greene, then to District Judge William V. Allen, a move designed to attract the Democrats. Allen's vote stood at 65, Thurston's at 61; 66 votes could elect. Five conservative Democrats held the balance, and on the sixteenth ballot they all went over to Allen. Close cooperation between silver Democrats and Populists continued through the legislative session, and the coalition forged in the senatorial election became a model for the future.[29]

The Populist state convention of 1893 was the first of the major party gatherings. Reaffirming their dedication to the 1892 Omaha platform, Populists placed first priority on a demand for silver at sixteen to one and denounced the state debt and the corruption of state officials. The platform contained the Populists' first statement on the nativist American Protective Association (APA): "We are opposed to all secret or open political organization based on religious prejudices as contrary to the spirit and genius of our institutions and thoroughly un-American." The nomination for supreme court judge went to Silas A. Holcomb, a district judge from Broken Bow, whose career up to then had been very different from that of Powers, Edgerton, or Van Wyck. He was young, his most prominent pre-1890 political activity had been as delegate to the 1888 county Democratic convention, and he had taken a relatively conservative position in his 1891 campaign for district judge.[30]

The Democrats met nearly a month later and rejected both silver coinage and its supporters. Bryan came near to threatening a bolt—"If the democratic party ratifies your action, I will go out and serve my party and my God under some other name than as a democrat." The platform, stolidly conservative, praised Cleveland, the repeal of silver purchase, and tariff revision. Democrats took the Populists' plank denouncing the APA, added to it in places, and included it virtually word for word in their own platform. The nomination for judge went to Frank Irvine, pro-Cleveland and antisilver.[31]

Republicans prided themselves on having achieved "unexampled industrial and commercial prosperity'' and carefully pointed out that ''stagnation and depression'' had immediately followed Cleveland's accession to the presidency. Recognition of ''the dignity of manhood irrespective of faith, color or nationality''—the only allusion to the APA—was illogically included in a condemnation of Democratic tariff policy. Samuel Maxwell, the incumbent Republican supreme court judge, had made himself unpopular with railroad supporters through a series of decisions unfavorable to the railroads and had alienated regulars by dissents implying that his Republican colleagues had made some crucial decisions primarily on the basis of party loyalty. Maxwell, supported by Rosewater's *Bee*, Governor Crounse, and former judge Reese, appeared to be in the lead until midmorning of the balloting. However, a district judge, T. O. C. Harrison, received the nomination on the fourth ballot. Reese attributed Maxwell's defeat to railroad influences, Maxwell endorsed Holcomb, and the *Bee* refused to support Harrison.[32] Despite the alienation of Republican reformers, Harrison and the Republican candidates for regents were successful.

The Republican convention met first in 1894 and gave its nomination for governor to Thomas J. Majors, lieutenant governor from 1891 to 1895. Personally popular, Majors was an inveterate bloody-shirt waver and a favorite—perhaps even a member—of the APA. National committeeman Rosewater opposed Majors's nomination, resigned his party position when it was announced, and branded it the result of ''wholesale distribution of railroad pass bribes.'' The Republican platform accused the Cleveland administration of disrupting the business community and declared in favor of ''honest money'' and bimetallism.[33]

The Populists convened two days later, overjoyed at Rosewater's bolt and hopeful of their own chances for victory. Rosewater supported the candidacy of Silas Holcomb, and Holcomb won nomination for governor on the first ballot. Of the remaining nominees, only John Powers, candidate for treasurer, had not come to prominence since 1890. The platform affirmed support for the Omaha platform, especially emphasizing silver. At a state level, the Populists demanded more economical administration, a maximum freight rate, the initiative and referendum, and relief for drought sufferers.[34]

Bryan and other prosilver, antiadministration Democrats kept active during the summer preceding the convention. In late June, an Omaha meeting organized the Nebraska Democratic Free Coinage League, complete from state executive committee to precinct captains. The League not only controlled the 1894 state Democratic convention, but included virtually every Democrat who was to achieve a significant party position in the next decade. The convention chairman was a member of the League's executive committee, and the resolutions committee consisted of six League officers and a token Cleveland-appointed postmaster. The convention voted unanimously to support Bryan for senator in 1895 and shouted through an endorsement of free silver. Bryan himself nominated Holcomb for governor, and Holcomb won on the first ballot with a recorded vote of 324 to 188.[35]

Holcomb's success in the Democratic convention seems to have derived from two distinct factors—silver and antinativism. The Nebraska Democratic Free Coinage League and Bryan's personal contacts provided the organizational framework, but Douglas County, casting nearly one-fifth of the total convention votes, was the key to the convention. Without its ninety-two bloc votes, Holcomb would have lost. The longtime hold of the Miller-Boyd group on Omaha voters was broken by an intensive campaign managed by Constantine J. Smyth, a young Irish-born lawyer, assisted by the *World-Herald* and by Rosewater's *Bee*. The nomination of Majors by the Republicans and his high standing with the APA apparently convinced Omaha's Catholics to elect a convention delegation pledged to fusion as the only means of defeating Majors.[36]

Upon the nomination of Holcomb, some fifty to sixty administration supporters withdrew from the convention. The jubilant silverites nominated the Populist candidates for four other state offices, then nominated Free Coinage League activists for treasurer, auditor, and secretary of state. In addition to demanding free silver, the platform denounced the protective tariff, approved the income tax, and urged government operation of the telegraph and foreclosure of the liens upon the Pacific railroads. The platform condemned "any attempt to apply a religious test to the citizen or to the official" and urged all Democrats to remember Jefferson's principles of religious liberty.[37]

Bolting Democrats nominated a full state ticket of administration supporters; many hoped John McShane, the 1888 gubernatorial nominee, would accept the nomination for governor. When McShane refused, the nomination went to Phelps D. Sturdevant, the Democrat who had been elected state treasurer in 1882 with Greenback support. Their resolutions voiced full support for the Cleveland administration, especially Cleveland's interpretation of the money plank of the 1892 national platform. Among the prominent bolters were Euclid Martin, state chairman, and Tobias Castor, national committeeman, both close political associates of J. Sterling Morton, who had become Cleveland's secretary of agriculture in 1893.[38]

Widespread fusion on a county level had preceded that at the state level. Bryan's assistance was implored at times to get local Democratic conventions to endorse Populist candidates. Populists occasionally rejected Democratic overtures, but on other occasions the Democrats and Populists met in the same city at the same time, appointed conference committees to distribute offices between the two parties, and then nominated the same candidates for the various county offices. Some Democratic conventions simply endorsed most Populist candidates, then added a few nominations of their own in the hope that the Populists would withdraw their candidates for those offices.[39]

Republicans based their campaign on the charge that election of a Populist governor would bring financial ruin to the state by stopping all outside investment and decreasing real estate values by 30 to 50 percent. Loan companies wrote scare letters to their debtors, warning of the consequences of a Populist victory. The *State Journal* summarized these arguments:

The issue of the state's material property, of the state's credit, of the employment of labor through the employment of capital, is the paramount issue in this campaign. . . . Shall the election of the entire republican ticket, state and legislative, give assurance to enterprise that the dead-line of populism, the line over which capital refused to step and beyond which destitution and distress haunt the corners of the streets, shall not by the actions of its own citizens be drawn around this state?

Holcomb was portrayed as an opportunistic former usurer and railroad lawyer.[40]

The fusionists campaigned against corruption and extravagance in state government and sought to reassure voters of their reliability. Holcomb was presented as, above all, conservative and honest, promising to cut state spending and maintain the full faith and credit of the state. Majors in particular and the Republican slate in general were attacked as corrupt and dishonest. The *Bee* was especially vitriolic, blasting Majors daily and claiming that the best interests of the Republican party dictated his defeat, for without him the GOP could face the elections of 1896 having "rebuked corruption, shaken off corporate domination and purged itself."[41]

When the votes were counted, Holcomb and Congressman Kem were the only fusionist winners. Republicans took all the state executive offices, five of the six congressional seats, and a clear majority in both houses of the legislature. The percentages received by nominees for the eight statewide offices are shown in table 10. Holcomb averaged about six percentage points above the other fusionist candidates, Majors as much as three points behind the other Republicans. Apparently half or more of the voters who marked a Straight Democratic ballot scratched Sturdevant in favor of Holcomb. The two Democratic parties together had a total of less than 15 percent of the electorate, split roughly evenly between them. Silver Democratic endorsements apparently added about six to seven percentage points to the Populists'

TABLE 10. PERCENTAGE DISTRIBUTION OF TOTAL VOTE CAST, 1894, BY PARTY AND OFFICE

Party	Governor	Lieutenant Governor, Land Commissioner, School Superintendent, and Attoney General (average of four)	Auditor	Secretary of State and Treasurer (average of two)
Republican	46.41%	48.64%	49.40%	48.10%
Populist and (Silver)				
Democratic	47.98	41.54	—	—
Populist	—	—	37.86	34.69
(Silver) Democratic	—	—	—	9.00
Straight (Gold)				
Democratic	3.43%	7.26	9.82	5.67
Prohibition	2.18	2.56	2.91	2.53

totals. Bryan had invoked a little-used provision to enter his name in a preferential vote for United States senator, and his vote approximated that of the fusion candidates for offices other than governor.[42]

The 1895 legislature elected John M. Thurston, attorney for the Union Pacific Railroad, to the United States Senate on the first ballot. The legislature appropriated a quarter of a million dollars for drought relief, reinstated the sugar-beet bounty repealed by the Populists in 1891, and added a chicory bounty. Holcomb vetoed the sugar and chicory bounties, arguing in a lengthy message that it was wrong in principle for the citizen, through taxation, "to support an industry from which he derives no direct benefit," especially at a time when "the burdens of taxation are ... especially onerous, and the people illy able to bear additional burdens." The veto was overturned, with the support of all the Republicans and two Populists. Holcomb vetoed several legislative acts he claimed were unnecessary expenditures of public funds, also an act changing the method of appointment of the Omaha police and fire commission to benefit the Republicans (and allegedly the APA), and an act repealing the state miscegenation law.[43]

Holcomb moved to fill appointive state positions with members of his party. John Powers, party patriarch, was appointed labor commissioner, and J. Harlan Edmisten, state party chairman, was made chief oil inspector. Holcomb's handling of patronage distressed both old Alliancemen and his recent Democratic allies. When Walter F. Wright, longtime Alliance activist, was denied appointment as superintendent of the Institute for the

Blind, one of his friends wrote to the state Alliance secretary: "Old men like him who have done the work & elected a young man to office have got to stand back and see men young in years & young in the party get all the places. . . . I never heard one of them say he [Wright] wasn't honest or truthful, they only say he is an old crank." Wright himself felt that "the Alliance of Nebr is sold out to Lawyers & dudes so far as the Party is concerned." Democrats were also upset about patronage, Smyth complaining that Holcomb failed to recognize the Democrats.[44]

Holcomb's inaugural message had appealed for a nonpartisan approach to the state's problems, asking "the greatest possible economy" in order to minimize "the burdens of taxpayers, which have been rendered especially oppressive by the present distressed conditions" and deploring the "erroneously conceived idea . . . that the interests of the railways and the people of the state are inimical." Holcomb sent appointments to the senate for confirmation even where senate action may not have been constitutionally required "in order . . . not [to] appear to be discourteous to that body." He also took care to select men qualified by ability as well as party loyalty. For example, the eventual appointee as superintendent of the Institute for the Blind, W. A. Jones, had been president of the Indiana State Normal School at Terre Haute from 1870 to 1880 and was the Populist candidate for superintendent of public instruction in 1894. Holcomb reportedly instructed his appointees to avoid "radical changes."[45]

The campaign of 1895 saw five parties, two of them listed on the ballot simply as "Democrat." For supreme court judge, the Republicans nominated the incumbent T. L. Norval, and the Populists nominated Samuel Maxwell, the twenty-year supreme court veteran who had been denied renomination by the Republicans in 1893. Administration Democrats nominated T. J. Mahoney, an Omahan long prominent in party circles; silver Democrats nominated C. J. Phelps, a relative unknown. Bryan reportedly preferred Maxwell but had to establish his wing of the party as the true Nebraska Democracy in preparation for the rapidly approaching national convention. Bryan and Constantine Smyth, his Omaha lieutenant, reportedly agreed not to oppose Maxwell actively, and Maxwell got additional support from his opposition to the APA.[46] Although Republicans won all races, Maxwell showed a strong personal appeal.

The preceding chronological narrative has concentrated on three aspects of the process whereby parties sought to build support among the electorate: issue definition, candidate selection, and actions in office (i.e., policy outputs). From 1890 through 1895, at least half of Nebraska's voters made a conscious party choice rather than simply renewing traditional ties. Under such politically volatile conditions, parties could be expected to define their appeals to attract, as well as reinforce, voters. Of Nebraska's three major parties, two had strong and consistent issue definition over the period from 1890 to 1895. Republicans defined themselves as the party of prosperity, growth, progress, and stability. Their appeal emphasized the role of Republican administrations in furthering these goals through the tariff, Republican currency policies, and the promotion of agriculture. Republicans claimed credit for the spectacular growth Nebraska had experienced under their administration and attacked their opposition as threatening the continuity of Republican-induced growth and prosperity. Populists defined themselves as the champions of the "producing classes"—those who through their labor produced value—and argued that the power of great corporations, especially the railroads, had destroyed the ability of the farmer and worker to realize a just return on their toil. Great capitalists controlled government and used government policy to reinforce their already dominant position. To the Populist, both Republicans and Democrats were to be equally damned for having sold themselves to the money power. At a state level, the Populists attacked the power of the railroads in the old parties and deplored corruption and extravagance in state government.

Democrats confused their self-definition. In 1890 they were the party of opposition to prohibition, but when the salience of that issue was temporarily reduced by the defeat of the prohibition amendment that year, they were unable to define a new issue for themselves. They alternately supported, opposed, and again supported silver coinage. They consistently opposed the protective tariff but had difficulty building a following around that issue. Agreeing with many of the Jeffersonian and Jacksonian tenets of Populism, Democrats found those claims preempted. Attempts to revive the old prohibition cleavage in the electorate and to oppose the anti-Catholicism of the APA found few listeners. The Democrats' shift from prohibition to tariff to currency prevented them from defining a coherent central issue, and their problems were compounded when two Democratic parties in 1894 and 1895 took opposite sides of the silver issue.

The process of candidate selection by Republicans involved the interaction of three factions, the three gubernatorial candidates representing each of the factions in turn—the regulars, the reformers, and the railroad interests.[47] The 1890 convention continued the tradition of the 1880s by selecting a candidate not obviously identified with either the Rosewater reformers or the railroads. In 1892, under pressure from the Populists, the regulars supported Rosewater's choice for the nomination. Rosewater alienated the regulars by his 1893 bolt, and the 1894 convention selected a well-known railroad man.

When possible, Republicans capitalized on their candidates' personalities by holding them up as representative of the wide following they claimed among the state's respectable, successful business community. When they were embarrassed by their candidate, as in 1894, they argued that the issue of continuing prosperity took precedence over personalities.

The Democrats, long dominated by such strong personalities as Morton, Miller, and Boyd, continued to fragment in their selection of candidates. Boyd focused on prohibition in 1890 and courted the wet Populists; in 1892 Morton concentrated on the tariff and attacked the Populists. Boyd favored leaving the judicial ticket vacant in 1891 to aid the Populists but vetoed their railroad rate bill and encouraged the five Democratic holdouts in the 1893 senatorial election. Morton had accepted a Greenback antimonopoly nomination for governor in 1884 and urged coalition in 1890, but he scathingly attacked the Populists in 1892. George Miller opposed aiding the Populists in 1891 but supported the election of a Populist United States senator in 1893. Miller and Morton opposed throwing Democratic votes to Weaver in 1892; Boyd and state chairman Martin organized the effort.[48] In contrast to the opportunistic yawing and tacking of these older men, Bryan not only was young and blessed with an engaging smile and a golden voice, but was also consistent in his willingness to do everything short of leaving his party to cooperate with the Populists. His stand on silver was as consistent as his stand on the tariff and prohibition. His charisma attracted devoted lieutenants wherever he went, especially among young Democrats.

The Populists did not develop strong factions, possibly because of the fervency of the cause, but possibly also because there were too many crosscutting potential lines of fracture—between prohibitionists and anti-prohibitionists, former Republicans and former Democrats, longtime third party activists and post-1890 newcomers, Alliancemen and lawyers, those committed to a radical restructuring of society and those with more limited reformist aims. The many possible lines of division so crisscrossed and overlapped that no strong factions emerged. But the Populists' candidate image did go through a distinct change from 1890 to 1895. The candidates of 1890 were almost all Alliancemen. The selection of Van Wyck in 1892 was a widening of the movement to include antimonopolists and reformers.[49] The election of Allen in 1893 and the nomination of Holcomb in 1893 and 1894 were moves to moderation, with the specific intent of attracting support from both silver Democrats and reform Republicans. This shift did not bring a repudiation of earlier rhetoric but did result in a lowering of volume.

Actions of elected officials, the third way voters' partisan preferences are influenced, did little to change the public images created by the processes of issue definition and candidate selection. The most prominent Democratic officeholders were Boyd, Bryan, and Morton. Boyd vetoed the Newberry bill. Bryan supported the Populists' demands for silver coinage. Morton was secretary of agriculture in the cabinet of the president whose silver policies Bryan so loudly opposed. Populist congressmen Kem and McKeighan gave their full support to Populist proposals in the House and dutifully presented petitions from their districts, but they did little more.[50] Populist legislative leaders in 1891 demonstrated little ability during the election contest, and the defections of a few Populist legislators on key votes embarrassed the party. Populist legislators in 1893 showed much more ability and a greater sense of party unity. Senator Allen soon attracted favorable nationwide publicity as a Populist spokesman.[51] Republican officeholders generally kept to previous patterns of eschewing controversy, administering but not innovating, and supporting their party. These traditional patterns, however, brought a barrage of criticism in the highly competitive early 1890s. The old ways of dealing with construction contracts and state institutions now brought charges of corruption and misuse of public funds. The state supreme court came under special attack for partisanship. Crounse, as governor, was honest and capable, and Republican congressmen and senators generally supported their party's position faithfully without attracting much attention, favorable or otherwise.

Issue definition, candidate selection, and official actions converged to produce party image. The Republicans' self-created image was of stability, growth, and prosperity. Their candidates, for the most part, were blandly capable. The Populists maintained an image as defenders of the producing classes against corporate encroachment and against corrupt and extravagant public officials. Their early candidates had the image of eccentricity and even incompetence, but careful selection of later candidates helped to overcome these handicaps. Populists, unsuccessful in capturing a major Nebraska office until 1893, were ironically hampered by their party's successes in Kansas and Colorado, where Populist governors and senators stamped the party as controversial, chaotic, and crankish. The Democrats' image splintered as they sought issues and fought among themselves over policy and nominations.

If voters were rational and receptive to such political images, those satisfied with the economic status quo should have been attracted to or reinforced in their allegiance to the Republican party. Voters whose economic situation was threatened, whether by high interest payments, high railroad rates, or high taxes, should have been attracted to the Populists. These projections assume that economic determinants would take precedence over ethnocultural determinants for these voters. Both Republicans and Populists avoided cultural issues such as prohibition almost totally throughout the period 1890 to 1895. Democrats' public image through 1890 was ethnoculturally determined, but not thereafter. When the anti-Catholic APA attempted to operate outside Republican conventions, it attracted less than 1 percent of the vote and was probably more useful as a target for Democrats and Populists than as a source of votes for Republicans. The fractured Democratic image might have been expected to encourage the movement of Democratic voters to the more clearly defined parties.

CHAPTER FOUR

Voting Behavior, Leadership, and the Nature of the Political System, 1890–95

We are mortgaged,
All but our votes.
                    Banner on a Populist's wagon, 1890

     The emergence of Populism in 1890, initiating a short-lived three-party political system, coincided with and helped bring to birth a new political system in Nebraska. Before 1890 the Republican party had thoroughly dominated state politics; from 1890 until 1940 Nebraska was one of the most closely competitive states in the Union. The five statewide campaigns between 1890 and 1895 marked a realignment phase during which half of Nebraska's voters broke with their traditional party loyalties. For some the break was permanent. The 1894 election marked the beginning of a return to two-party politics, but the characteristics of the emerging political system were quite different from those of the system that died in 1890. Of course Nebraska was not alone in experiencing a major political realignment in the early 1890s, and the realignment of the 1890s and the political changes that accompanied or followed it have received a good deal of attention from scholars.[1] Although Nebraska shared in some of the larger patterns of realignment, there was a significant difference: at a time when most states were becoming increasingly one-party domains, Nebraska was becoming more closely competitive. This variance from the national tendency is due largely to the coalition between economically motivated Populists and ethnoculturally motivated Democrats, the coalition that was finally brought to such painful birth in 1894. Although Bryan failed in his bid to extend such a coalition to the national level in 1896, he and his allies

53

nonetheless transformed state politics for more than a generation. A full understanding of this political transformation must begin with an intensive analysis of voting behavior and political leadership during the transitional phase, 1890–95.

Voting Behavior

The birth of Populism in 1890 ended almost a quarter-century of Republican dominance, during which both major parties had come to be defined largely in ethnocultural terms, the Democrats appealing to antiprohibition groups, and the Republicans claiming to be the guardians of old-stock American virtue and the successful promoters of growth. Our survey of voting behavior must begin with an analysis of the appeal of Populism.

Perhaps the simplest approach to the voter appeal of Populism is to divide the sixty-one counties analyzed into quartiles on the basis of the three major socioeconomic factors already discussed in chapter 2 (farm income, attitude on prohibition, and percentage of the population living in incorporated areas), then to compute the mean Populist party vote for each quartile and

TABLE 11. POPULIST PARTY STRENGTH INDEXES, FOR COUNTIES, 1890–93, WITH COUNTIES GROUPED BY SOCIOECONOMIC QUARTILES

Independent Variables	Year			
	1890	1891	1892	1893
Vote for prohibition, 1890				
Quartile most opposed	25.50%	46.87%	23.10%	21.25%
Second quartile	32.12	48.20	31.26	29.90
Third quartile	47.33	53.05	40.79	41.44
Quartile most in favor	49.95	53.42	41.06	40.19
Mean income per farm, 1889				
Most prosperous quartile	23.71%	43.25%	23.60%	22.36%
Second quartile	34.04	48.51	31.24	29.56
Third quartile	46.18	52.32	36.81	35.87
Poorest quartile	49.50	56.64	43.52	43.85
Percentage of the population living in incorporated areas, 1890				
Most urban quartile	30.29%	44.36%	26.71%	26.25%
Second quartile	39.93	50.72	35.28	33.57
Third quartile	37.71	51.06	32.58	31.21
Most rural quartile	48.03	55.57	42.04	42.19

TABLE 12. INDEX OF POPULIST STRENGTH AND DIFFERENCE FROM
OVERALL MEAN BY COUNTIES, 1890, WITH COUNTIES DISTRIBUTED BY
ATTITUDE ON PROHIBITION AND BY FARM INCOME

	Farm Income above the Median	Farm Income below the Median
	Prohibition Vote below the Median	
Party index	24.22%	35.70%
Difference from overall mean	−14.69	−3.21
Number of counties	18	12
	Prohibition Vote above the Median	
Party index	36.96%	55.12%
Difference from overall mean	−1.95	+16.21
Number of counties	11	20

compare these quartile means.[2] Table 11 presents this information. We are
most interested in those quartiles with the most extreme variation from the
overall mean, which was 38.9 percent for these sixty-one counties in 1890.
Table 11 suggests that Populism had its strongest appeal in rural areas, in the
least prosperous areas, and in areas that also favored prohibition. We may
attempt to control for interrelationships between independent variables by
constructing a table dividing the counties by both farm income and attitude
on prohibition, then computing the mean Populist vote. This is done in table
12. Again, it appears that Populism was weakest among the most prosperous, most antiprohibition counties, and strongest among the least prosperous, most prohibitionist counties. The relationship between Populism, on
the one hand, and both prosperity and prohibition, on the other, can also be
seen in the coefficients of correlation. Farm income correlates with the
Populist vote in 1890 at −0.53, and the vote in favor of prohibition correlates with the Populist vote at +0.56. The third variable, measuring degree
of urbanization, correlates with the Populist vote at −0.40. A typical
stepwise multiple regression analysis of Populist voting behavior, using
these three independent variables, is summarized in table 13.

These findings suggest that economic status was the major determinant of
Populist voting—certainly in 1892 and 1893, and perhaps in 1890—but that
prohibition sentiment may have been a secondary determinant of considerable importance. Paul Kleppner found a strong relationship between prohibi-

TABLE 13. STEPWISE MULTIPLE REGRESSION SUMMARY TABLE, INDEX OF POPULIST PARTY STRENGTH, 1892

Independent Variables	Multiple R	Multiple R^2	Change in R^2	Simple r
Mean income per farm, 1889	0.58640	0.34386		−0.58640
Vote in favor of prohibition, 1890	0.74095	0.54901	0.20514	+0.58382
Percentage of the population living in incorporated areas, 1890	0.74372	0.55312	0.00411	−0.45400

tion sentiment and Populist voting in his study of the eastern Middle West. How important was this relationship in Nebraska? Intensive analysis suggests that prohibition sentiment was *not* a major factor in the appeal of Populism. A number of observations lead to this conclusion. First, the farm income variable consistently explains 21 to 34 percent of the variation in the Populist vote. The prohibition variable, however, explains between 7 and 34 percent of the variation in the Populist party vote. As may be seen in table 13, adding the prohibition variable to a multiple regression analysis increases the multiple coefficient from 0.59 to 0.74, a rather small increase considering the high simple coefficient between the prohibition variable and the 1892 party vote (+0.58). There is a similarly small increase in the multiple coefficient in every instance. Apparently the interrelationship between these two independent variables (although r = only −0.25) accounts for some considerable part of the relationship that each one has separately with the dependent variable of Populism. Second, a comparison of the coefficient of correlation between Populist voting and prohibition sentiment in different elections reveals a consistent pattern—when the Democrats ran strong campaigns, the correlation between Populism and prohibition is considerably higher (+0.54 to +0.58) than when the Democrats ran weak campaigns or no campaign (+0.27 to +0.30). This observation, together with the analysis of Democratic voting that follows, suggests that the relationship between prohibition sentiment and Populist voting is indirect, deriving from the loyalties the Democrats maintained among the most staunchly anti-prohibition voters. When the Democrats ran a strong campaign, they activated these loyalties and *any* non-Democratic vote consequently tended to have some relationship to prohibition sentiment. When the Democrats ran weak campaigns, or no campaigns, many Democratic voters seem to have divided along economic lines. This conclusion is further reinforced by noting that the coefficients of correlation between farm income and Populist voting are consistently strong and inverse, regardless of the nature of the Democratic campaign, ranging from −0.53 to −0.59. Only a single election, in 1891, saw a coefficient less significant than −0.53, and that election produced a correlation of −0.46.

There is yet a third reason for concluding that the relationship between prohibition sentiment and Populist voting is not significant. A survey of actual voting precincts reveals that precincts strongly antiprohibitionist and economically marginal were typically Populist, but that precincts strongly prohibitionist and more prosperous were typically Republican. A few examples may be cited from 1890, when Nebraska voted on a prohibition amendment to the state constitution. That year the Democratic candidate for governor based his campaign almost solely on opposition to prohibition, and both the Republican and Populist candidates were known to be personally "dry." In 1890 Spalding Precinct, Greeley County, heavily Irish and Catholic, voted only 7 percent in favor of prohibition but 89 percent Populist for governor. Dannevirke Precinct, Howard County, Danish and Polish in ethnicity, voted 11 percent for prohibition and 73 percent Populist for governor. Upper Driftwood Precinct, Hitchcock County (home of John Powers), largely old stock, favored prohibition by only 35 percent but voted unanimously Populist for governor. These voters, all in marginal agricultural regions, saw no conflict in opposing prohibition and supporting a Populist candidate known to be a teetotaler. We may contrast the behavior of two southeastern voting units, both more prosperous: Turkey Creek Precinct, Pawnee County, voted 83 percent in favor of prohibition but only 34 percent Populist for governor; Eureka Precinct, Jefferson County, voted 60 percent in favor of prohibition but 11 percent Populist for governor. The conclusion is unavoidable—Populism was largely a single-interest party, its voters motivated almost entirely by their economic distress.

The Democrats, like the Populists, were a single-interest party in the early 1890s. They had become that earlier, as outlined in chapter 2, and this pattern continued through 1895, even though the *number* of votes cast for Democratic candidates declined by more than half. Dividing the sixty-one counties analyzed into quartiles on the basis of the three population characteristics previously discussed clearly indicates the overriding importance of the prohibition issue for the Democrats. The quartile most opposed to prohibition averaged 45 percent Democratic in 1890, the next quartile 29 percent, the third quartile 17 percent, and the quartile most in favor of prohibition averaged only 14 percent Democratic. Dividing the counties into quartiles based on agricultural prosperity reveals something of an economic dimension to Democratic voting: the poorest quartile averaged 16 percent

Democratic, the second quartile 22 percent, the third quartile 29 percent, and the most prosperous quartile 38 percent. Quartiles based on urbanization show no distinct pattern. Table 14 presents the mean Democratic vote for

TABLE 14. INDEX OF DEMOCRATIC PARTY STRENGTH AND DIFFERENCE FROM OVERALL MEAN BY COUNTIES, 1890, WITH COUNTIES DISTRIBUTED BY ATTITUDE ON PROHIBITION AND BY FARM INCOME

	Farm Income above the Median	Farm Income below the Median
	Prohibition Vote below the Median	
Party index	40.66%	31.73%
Difference from overall mean	+14.67	+5.73
Number of counties	18	12
	Prohibition Vote above the Median	
Party index	21.31%	11.94%
Difference from overall mean	−4.69	−14.06
Number of counties	11	20

four groups of counties, divided on the basis of both prohibition sentiment and prosperity. Democratic strength clearly was concentrated in the most prosperous and most antiprohibition counties. Does this mean that economic status was a major determinant of Democratic voting? The answer must be no, except in an indirect sense. This conclusion stems from the hold Populists acquired on the loyalty of the least prosperous counties; marginal farmers were attracted to Populism regardless of their attitude on prohibition. As a result, Democratic candidates ran most strongly in counties that were both prosperous and opposed to prohibition.

This relationship can also be seen in the correlation coefficients and in the stepwide multiple regression analyses. In the gubernatorial campaigns of 1890 and 1892, and in the party votes of 1890, 1892, and 1893, Democratic voting and opposition to prohibition correlated at a level of +0.75 to +0.81, explaining 56 to 66 percent of the variation in the Democratic vote. Table 15 presents a typical stepwise multiple regression summary table, for Demo-

TABLE 15. STEPWISE MULTIPLE REGRESSION SUMMARY TABLE, INDEX OF
DEMOCRATIC PARTY STRENGTH, 1892

Independent Variables	Multiple R	Multiple R²	Change in R²	Simple r
Vote in favor of prohibition, 1890	0.80048	0.64007		−0.80048
Mean income per farm, 1889	0.86435	0.74710	0.10633	+0.51383
Percentage of the population living in incorporated areas, 1890	0.88304	0.77976	0.03267	+0.28508

cratic party voting in 1892. In each of the five instances mentioned above,
the regression analysis steps in opposition to prohibition as the most significant explanatory variable, and agricultural prosperity as the second variable,
but adding this second variable to the regression equation does not significantly increase the explanatory power of the first variable.

The splintering of the Democratic party in 1894 and 1895 did not substantially change this picture. Opposition to prohibition continued as the major
explanatory variable of Democratic voting for both wings of the party.
Although one might anticipate a significant economic dimension to voting
for the Bryan or Cleveland wings of the Democracy, the coefficients fail to
reveal this. The economic variable continues to be stepped into the regression equations second, adding little to the explanatory power of prohibition.
Nor is there any significant rural-urban cleavage between Silver and Gold
Democratic voting. Voting for both Democratic parties in 1894 and 1895
correlates highly (in the range of +0.7 to +0.9) with Democratic party
voting from 1890 to 1893, and the patterns of vote distribution for the two
Democratic parties correlate highly with each other. Statistical analysis
alone fails to suggest a single significant difference between Silver and Gold
Democratic voters.

Although the profile of Democratic voters in the early 1890s was virtually
unchanged from the late 1880s, the *number* of Democratic voters dropped
precipitously. In 1888 there were some 80,600 Democratic voters, for 40
percent of the total. In 1890 this dropped to 64,000, or 30 percent. In 1893,
the last election before the schism in Democratic ranks, Democrats got about
39,000 votes, or 22 percent of the total. By 1895 the two Democratic parties
combined got only 34,000 votes, or 19 percent of the total. Democratic
losses were disproportionately concentrated in the less prosperous counties;
between 1888 and 1890 the Democratic share of the total party vote dropped

by eight percentage points in more prosperous counties, but by nineteen percentage points in less prosperous counties. This pattern is especially clear at a precinct level. In the rural precincts of Boone, Clay, and Hitchcock counties, Democratic candidates received, on the average, 743 votes out of the 2,419 total votes cast in 1888 (31 percent); in the same precincts in 1890, Democratic candidates averaged only 50 votes out of the total of 2,403 (2 percent). In these three less prosperous counties, the Democratic party virtually disappeared in rural precincts in 1890. By contrast, in the rural precincts of more prosperous Jefferson and Pawnee counties, the Democrats got 561 votes of 1,685 in 1888 (33 percent), and 473 votes of 1,897 in 1890 (25 percent).

The preceding analysis has suggested that both the Populists and the Democrats were fairly clearly defined single-interest parties—the Populist voter motivated largely by economic distress, the Democratic voter by ethnic considerations symbolized by the dispute over prohibition. No such clear picture emerges for the Republican voter. Breaking the counties into quartiles on the basis of social and economic characteristics does not reveal major differences in the Republican vote from one category to another. Coefficients of correlation are almost uniformly low, seldom rising beyond the 0.4 level. Nor does multiple regression analysis help in defining the characteristics of the Republican voter. Although these various analytical techniques are not at all conclusive, some of the findings are suggestive. The various analyses do raise the possibility that Republican voting became more associated with urban residence between 1890 and 1894. The coefficients of correlation rise from -0.2 in 1888 to $+0.1$ in 1890, to $+0.3$ in 1892, $+0.4$ in 1893, and $+0.5$ in 1894. This suggests an increasing tendency for Republican votes to come from more urbanized counties, and the same relationship can be seen in the quartile breakdowns. Breaking the counties into quartiles on the basis of the percentage of the population living in incorporated areas indicates virtually nothing of interest regarding the 1890 Republican vote, but in 1894 there is a clear relationship, albeit a weak one, between the mean Republican vote and urban residence: most urban quartile, 51 percent; second quartile, 48 percent; third quartile, 44 percent; least urban quartile, 43 percent. A similar relationship between urban counties and Republican voting can be discerned in the quartile breakdowns for 1893 and 1895.

It must be emphasized, however, that this analysis does not definitely establish urban areas as the stronghold of the Republican party. First, analysis is by *county,* and all counties included at least some nonurban population. *County*-level analysis suggests that Republican gains between 1890 and 1894 were concentrated in the most urban counties, for the mean Republican vote in the most urban quartile increased from 35 to 51 percent, and the mean Republican vote in the least urban quartile increased only from 34 to 43 percent. Second, analysis of six counties at the *precinct* level reveals a contrary pattern. In eleven precincts more than half urban, the mean Republican vote increased from 49 percent to 54 percent, but in fifty-seven precincts less than 10 percent urban, the mean Republican vote increased from 26 percent to 42 percent. The precinct data do provide some possibility for reconciling this seeming contradiction. Of the counties sampled, the greatest disparity between the mean Republican vote in urban and rural precincts came in the counties with the fewest and smallest urban areas. This disparity was much less pronounced in counties with several urban areas, or in counties with a relatively large urban center. This in turn suggests that Republican recovery between 1890 and 1894 was based upon but not limited to the towns and villages, and that Republican recovery among rural voters was proportionate to their propinquity to a town. We might speculate that the social interaction of a rural area near a town would be focused upon the social institutions of the town (its lodges, churches, etc.) and that this social structure would be more conducive to the town's influence than that of an area distant from town, where social interaction focused on rural social institutions. The former situation would tend to minimize differences between townspeople and farmers, the latter to encourage a feeling of distinctiveness.

The Nature of Fusion: 1894

The well-defined and nonconflicting nature of Nebraska's two single-interest parties, the Democrats and the Populists, should have made cooperation both easy and natural. There is no inherent conflict in the interests of the two parties—Populists were seeking to protect their pocketbooks, Democrats to slake their thirst. The Jacksonian traditions of the Democracy were by no means incompatible with Populist proposals, and Populists sought to unite the producing class regardless of ethnic values. Nonetheless, the path of coalition proved both difficult and painful. Various proposals for cooperation, initiated solely by Democratic leaders failed in 1980, 1891, and 1892. Not until the Democrats actually nominated the Populist candidates in 1894 did coalition occur.

At least some part of the difficulties encountered in promoting coalition came not from the major interests of the two parties, but from the attitudes that tended to accompany those positions. Populism has been described as a uniquely American form of radicalism, and the region of greatest Populist strength in Nebraska was largely populated by old-stock American Protestants, whose cultural baggage included not only a propensity for speculative agricultural investment, but sometimes sympathy for woman suffrage and temperance. While Jacksonian Democratic traditions were not incompatible with Populism, most of Nebraska's Democrats were not the heirs of the Jacksonians but were instead ethnic antiprohibitionists, who often associated reform with prohibition and who were frequently hostile to woman suffrage. Republicans were not put off by Populist sympathies for woman suffrage and prohibition, and Populist demands for strong government were not incompatible with one strain in Republican thought but Populist "calamity howling" ran contrary to Republican boosterism, threatening the GOP image of unfettered growth and prosperity. Populism, distinctly rural, also challenged the political dominance of the small-town elites who had so long controlled the state. Despite these potential conflicts, in 1890 both Republicans and Democrats occasionally endorsed Alliance candidates at the local level.

Republicans after 1890 were willing to accept and even woo Populist support, but they would no longer endorse Populist legislative candidates and would no longer cooperate with—that is, share power with—the radical agrarian leaders. The only Republican leader to do so, Edward Rosewater, first resigned his position on the national committee, and he justified his 1894 bolt on the basis of strengthening the GOP for the 1896 presidential campaign by defeating unsavory Republican candidates. Rosewater's bolt, ·ironically, had the effect of throwing party control to the conservative railroad wing of the party. Republican leaders from 1890 on argued that the Populist goals of economic stability and prosperity could be achieved only through the GOP and, implicitly, under their own leadership. To the dominant Republicans, Populism was a threat to be destroyed. To the out-of-power Democrats, Populism was an opportunity to destroy Republican dominance.

For the Democrats the opportunity was realized in 1894, when the Bryan wing of the party successfully coalesced with the Populists and elected Silas Holcomb governor. What was the nature of this fusion? The following analysis is in two parts: first, the nature of support for fusion within the Democratic party and, second, the nature of voter support for fusion in the general election. As was noted in the previous chapter, Bryan's ability to deliver the Democratic nomination to Holcomb was dependent upon the bloc vote of Douglas County, including Omaha. On 20 September, Omaha

Democrats elected their county convention delegates, who would in turn select state convention delegates. The next day, the organ of the state APA charged that the Bryan victory had been due to the intervention of the Catholic church: "otherwise we cannot account for the presence in this city of a horde of Roman Catholic priests a few days before the democratic primaries, for their secret meeting in the basement of Creighton college last Tuesday evening, or for their going from house to house Thursday afternoon while the democratic primaries were being held." While the validity of these charges is impossible to prove or disprove, a careful examination of that 20 September election in Omaha is revealing as to the nature of Bryan's support. His campaign was headed by Constantine J. Smyth, Irish-born and Catholic; of the eighty-eight delegates on the Bryan ticket, thirty-three had Irish names, ten had German names, six had Czech names, and one was Italian. The list included twelve saloon-keepers; in the third ward, six of the eleven Bryan delegates were saloon-keepers. Observing that "two thirds of the number bear Roman Catholic names," the APA charged that the Bryan victory was one of "saloon loafers and ward heelers."[3]

A ward-by-ward analysis of Bryan's support seems to indicate that the old-line Democratic leaders of the city, while not supporting Bryan, at least were not a source of opposition. In the first and seventh wards, both including large numbers of immigrants, there was no contest, the Bryan and anti-Bryan groups agreeing in advance on a single ticket that divided the positions. In the third ward, containing more than half of all the saloons in the city, notorious as the center for vice operations, there was but one ticket in the field, consisting of nine Bryan delegates and two committed to the opposition. There was, however, a contest for assessor in this ward, and the Bryan faction's candidate received only 35 percent of the vote. As a result of compromise tickets in these three wards where the regular organization should have made a strong showing, Bryan got twenty-three delegates to only fifteen for the opposition. In the remaining six wards, Bryan delegates won sixty-four of the sixty-six positions. Bryan slates swept the fifth, sixth, eighth, and ninth wards with two-thirds or more of the vote. All four wards were roughly 50 percent foreign stock, with German and Scandinavian Lutherans and Protestants prominent in the sixth and eighth wards. Omaha newspapers friendly to Bryan attributed the fifth, sixth, and eighth ward victories to "the laboring element," especially workers from the Union Pacific shops. The ninth ward was almost totally residential and middle class; there the local Democratic organization was actively working for the Bryan slate, although the ward was the home of Euclid Martin, state chairman and leader of the opposition. The closest contests were in the second and fourth wards, where the Bryan slates got just over half the vote. The second ward was working class and the most heavily foreign-stock ward in the city, with Czech and German Catholics most prominent. By contrast, the fourth ward was the most native-stock and Protestant ward, which had been the most fashionable part of the city in the 1880s but was rapidly becoming middle class in the 1890s; it was traditionally the banner Republican ward.[4]

This ward-by-ward survey strongly suggests that the old-line Democratic organization of the city was neutral. In three of the five wards where the organization should have been strongest, there was no contest. Conspicuously absent from accounts of the primary are the names of virtually all prominent Democrats of the city—former governor James Boyd, former congressman John McShane, George Miller, T. J. Mahoney, and others. Euclid Martin, leader of the anti-Bryan forces, was in fact an ally of Secretary of Agriculture J. Sterling Morton rather than a part of leadership of the Omaha wing of the party. If we may trust the accounts of the pro-Bryan newspapers, the brunt of the anti-Bryan campaign was carried by federal patronage appointees from the Agriculture Department, by those who hoped for post office appointments from the Cleveland administration, and by Republicans.[5] The erstwhile leaders of the Omaha Democracy apparently found themselves in an uncomfortable dilemma—on one side was Thomas Majors, Republican candidate for governor, with his APA connections, and on the other side was William Jennings Bryan, advocate of free silver and of fusion with the Populists as the only alternative to a Majors governorship. They seem to have resolved the dilemma by staying home. In that vacuum, Bryan's lieutenants mobilized their organization, selected a carefully balanced ticket, and waged a campaign so successful that on election day the opposition resorted to circulating bogus tickets listing anti-Bryan delegates as being committed to Bryan. Whether or not there were priests going door to door is less important than the issue of the APA and of Majors's supposed sympathy for it.

The same pattern persisted into the general election. Prominent Democrats—most obviously John McShane—spurned the proposals of administration Democrats that they accept the Gold Democratic nomination for governor, and the nomination finally went to a relative unknown. In the eleven counties with the highest proportion of Catholics, the Gold Democrats got 10 to 15 percent of the vote for minor state executive offices, yet only 5 percent of the vote for governor. In all sixty-one counties, the Gold Democrats averaged 5 to 7 percent of the vote for minor state executive offices, but only 3 percent for governor. The coefficients of correlation, while all quite low, do suggest a shift in the direction of the relationship between proportion of Catholics and the percentage of the vote cast for the Populist candidate for governor—in 1890 the coefficient was −0.21, in 1892 it was −0.14, and in 1894 it became positive, +0.14.

The evidence strongly suggests that Bryan, in fact, simply took the party structure in the same direction many Democratic voters had already gone. No totally reliable analysis of party switching is possible using county totals, for the three major parties (plus the Prohibitionists) allow for too many possible directions for party switching. If we begin with certain assumptions about the direction of party switching, however, some analysis becomes possible. If we assume that losses for the old parties represent gains for the Populists in 1890 and 1892, if we assume that losses for the Populists between 1890 and 1892 represent a return to former parties, and if we assume that no Republicans became Democrats and that no Democrats switched to Republican, we may then begin to evaluate the nature of the Populist voter in terms of his former party allegiance. Applying these assumptions to the thirty most rural counties produces the following picture of Populist voters in 1890: 49 percent were former Republicans, 36 percent were former Democrats, 7 percent were former Union Laborites, and 7 percent were former Prohibitionists. By 1892, however, applying these assumptions indicates that the Populist electorate was composed of 42 percent former Republicans, 45 percent former Democrats, 8 percent former Union Laborites, and 5 percent former Prohibitionists. If the same assumptions are applied to study those who voted Republican in 1888, it appears that 40 percent of them voted Populist in 1890 but only 29 percent voted Populist in 1892. Of those who voted Democratic in 1888, the assumptions suggest that 39 percent voted Populist in 1890 and 43 percent in 1892. If these assumptions have any validity whatsoever, they indicate that Democratic voters were increasingly attracted to the new party but that the Republican voters were already returning to their former allegiances by 1892.[6]

[handwritten margin note: agreed with Frank]

The disproportionate appeal of Populism to formerly Democratic voters is even more apparent if we examine only the fifteen most rural counties. Applying the previous assumptions, in 1890 and 1892, 53 percent of the 1888 Democrats were voting Populist, compared with 40 percent of the Republicans in 1890 and 32 percent in 1892. In these fifteen counties, in 1890, the Populist electorate was composed of 46 percent former Republicans and 40 percent former Democrats, and in 1892 of 42 percent former Republicans and 47 percent former Democrats. Former Prohibitionists accounted for 7 percent of the Populist vote in 1890 and for 4 percent in 1892. These conclusions—which, it must be emphasized, are only as reliable as the assumptions upon which they are based—nonetheless coincide with the observations of contemporaries in locations as distant as Cherry County (north central Nebraska) and Richardson County (extreme southeast Nebraska), who felt the Alliance and subsequently the Populists had more appeal to Democratic farmers than to neighboring Republicans. In the rural precincts of Boone, Clay, and Hitchcock counties between 1888 and 1892, the Democratic vote had fallen by 70 percent, the Republican vote by only 37 percent.

By 1892 Populists were also making some inroads into the Democratic vote in urban areas. In Omaha's first and second wards, both very Catholic, immigrant, and working class, the Democrats averaged 65 percent of the two-party vote in 1888, but only 44 percent of the three-party vote in 1892. The Republican share of the major-party vote did not change appreciably, from 35 percent in 1888 to 38 percent in 1892. But in 1892 the Populists averaged 19 percent in those two former Democratic strongholds. Applying the previous assumptions about party switching to the thirty-one most urban counties suggests that, in 1890, 36 percent of the former Republicans were voting Populist and, in 1892, 22 percent. By contrast, in 1890, 28 percent of the former Democrats were voting Populist and, in 1892, 39 percent. In 1892 the Populist voters in these relatively urban counties would seem to have been composed of 38 percent former Republicans, 49 percent former Democrats, 6 percent former Prohibitionists, and 7 percent former Union Laborites.

If the assumptions which have governed this analysis of party switching are correct—and both precinct data and the observations of contemporary observers suggest that they are reasonably correct—then it appears that, by 1892, a third of Democratic voters in urban, immigrant, working-class areas and as many as three-fourths of Democratic voters in rural, economically marginal areas had gone over to the Populists. And it also appears that the Populists captured virtually none of the Republican voters in urban areas and no more than 40 percent in rural, economically marginal areas. If this analysis is correct, then Bryan was not leading Nebraska Democrats into an unprecedented coalition with the Populists—he was instead taking the formal party structure down the same path that had already been traveled by nearly half the Democratic voters of the state. The presence of so many former Democrats in Populist ranks, including Silas Holcomb himself, must have helped allay the suspicions of Democratic leaders regarding the wisdom of fusion. In 1894 the final nudge was provided by the APA leanings of the Republican gubernatorial candidate. Some old-line leaders, unable to overcome their revulsion for free silver, simply sat out the election on the sidelines. Others, especially those with strong ties to the Cleveland administration—most of them from the Morton wing of the party—formed the Gold Democrats, aided by those few Democrats for whom free silver posed a greater danger than did the APA. Most voters who had stuck by the Democrats in 1892 (24 percent of the total) and in 1893 (22 percent) followed the now well-traveled path to the Populists; the Gold Democratic candidate for governor got only 3 percent of the total, even though Gold Democratic candidates for other state offices averaged 6 to 10 percent.

Political Leadership

Voting behavior illustrates only a part of the nature of the political system. To examine the political leadership, biographical data was collected for more than 400 Nebraska political leaders prominent between 1890 and 1895.[7] Date of birth, place of birth, and occupation were located for 457 leaders, and more detailed information for 402 of them. The group contains virtually all major party candidates for statewide office, virtually all major party officials, the editors of important party organs, and all members of the state legislature. Data on occupation and place of birth are summarized in table 16. Several other biographical characteristics are summarized in table 17.

The composite Republican who emerges from these data is not very different from the Republican leader of the 1880s. He was between forty and fifty years old in 1890, was likely a Union Army veteran, had probably been born in the upper Middle West, in the Middle Atlantic area, or in New England, and was better educated than the average Nebraskan. He had equal chances of being a professional, a businessman, or a farmer, and he was very likely a Mason, a member of the GAR, and a member of commercial or professional associations. Data on church affiliation are available for only 20 percent of the group of Republican leaders, but three-quarters of those for whom church membership is known belonged to an old-stock Protestant church, with the Methodist church claiming a third of the total and the Presbyterian church one-fifth. There were no known Catholics in the Republican leadership. In a word, the composite Republican was a member of the small-town elite, well known in his community, with a web of interpersonal relationships based upon church, associations, and business or professional relationships.

The average Democratic leader may have been well educated, a Mason, an Episcopalian (a third of the Democratic leaders for whom church mem-

TABLE 16. PERCENTAGE DISTRIBUTION OF NEBRASKA POLITICAL LEADERS
BY OCCUPATION AND PLACE OF BIRTH, 1890–95

Characteristics	Republicans	Populists	Democrats
Occupation	N=198	N=173	N=86
Agriculture	33.3%	76.9%	18.6%
The professions			
Law	23.2	6.9	20.9
Journalism	9.3	5.8	12.8
Total, professions	34.3	15.6	39.5
Business			
Merchandising	12.1	5.2	4.7
Finance	14.1	0.0	20.9
Total, business	28.8	6.9	36.1
All other occupations	3.5	0.6	5.8
Place of birth	N=198	N=173	N=86
Born in U.S.			
New England	7.6%	5:2%	2.3%
Middle Atlantic	20.7	16.2	17.4
Middle West	50.5	43.9	34.9
Border	4.5	12.1	4.7
Confederate South	1.5	2.3	5.8
Total born in U.S.	84.8	80.9	66.3
Foreign-born			
Germany	6.6	1.7	9.3
Ireland	1.0	2.9	5.8
Total foreign-born	15.2	18.5	31.4
Unspecified	0.0	0.6	2.3

Note: Columns may not add to 100 owing to rounding.

bership is known belonged to the Episcopalian church), and a lawyer or
financier—that is, the stereotype Bourbon. Or he may have been an immigrant, less well educated, probably a Lutheran or Catholic (those two
churches account for another third of the Democratic leaders for whom
church membership is known), and a small merchant, artisan, or farmer.
Whether Bourbon or immigrant, he had probably not served in the Civil War
and may—like J. Sterling Morton or Dr. George Miller—have opposed
resorting to war to preserve the Union. Democrats were more foreign-born,
more southern, more ritualistic in church membership, more evenly distributed by age than Republicans, but Democratic and Republican composites
were more alike than different with regard to occupation, education, and
associational memberships.

TABLE 17. PERCENTAGE DISTRIBUTION OF NEBRASKA POLITICAL LEADERS
BY VARIOUS BIOGRAPHICAL CHARACTERISTICS, 1890–95

Biographical Characteristics	Republicans	Populists	Democrats
Date of birth	N=198	N=173	N=86
Born before 1841	14.6%	24.3%	23.3%
Born 1841–50	46.5	43.9	25.6
Born 1851–60	29.8	19.7	37.2
Born after 1860	8.6	11.0	12.8
Unspecified	0.5	1.2	1.2
Union Army service among			
Leaders born 1836–45	88.2%	50.0%	27.3%
Educational level	N=176	N=148	N=78
None or unspecified	31.8%	48.0%	51.3%
Apprenticeship	0.0	0.7	3.9
Eighth grade or less	8.0	10.8	3.9
Some secondary	13.6	11.5	6.4
Read law, no college	10.2	4.0	0.0
Some college	23.9	19.6	12.8
Law, medical, or other			
professional school	12.5	5.4	21.8
Total college	36.4	25.0	34.6
Associational memberships	N=64	N=59	N=21
Grand Army of the Republic	29.7%	17.0%	4.8%
Masons	51.6	13.6	38.1
Commercial and professional			
organizations	26.6	1.7	38.1
Farmer's Alliance	7.8	72.9	4.8
Knights of Labor	0.0	11.9	0.0
Labor unions	0.0	3.4	0.0

Note: Data for date of birth and education may not add to 100 owing to rounding. Percentages for associational memberships are based on the number indicating memberships rather than on total number of subjects and columns do not add to 100 because of multiple memberships.

The Populists' composite biography shows ethnocultural characteristics that generally fall between the poles represented by the two older parties, although tending somewhat more to the Republican. If Republican and Democratic affiliation was, in fact, largely ethnoculturally determined, it is not surprising that the Populists should display ethnocultural characteristics less extreme than either, for the new party drew its leadership from adherents of both of the old parties. Information exists on the previous party affiliation of 70 percent of the Populist leadership, and of this group 52 percent had once been Republicans, 37 percent had once been Democrats, 2 percent had been both at various times, and 9 percent had had only third-party affiliations before becoming Populists. This distribution closely approximates the division of the popular vote in 1888, when the Republicans got 53 percent and the Democrats 40 percent.

Although Populists were not ethnoculturally distinctive, they were highly distinctive in terms of occupation, with very nearly all the Populist leaders drawn from agriculture. During 1890–91, in fact, 92 percent of Populist leaders were farmers. This high level declined somewhat in 1892 and after, as nonfarmers—especially lawyers, editors, and merchants—began to take a more prominent role in the party. This shift corresponds to a shift away from the leadership of the leaders of the Alliance to a more broadly based leadership. By 1894–95, two-thirds of the Populist leadership were farmers, 11 percent were lawyers, 7 percent were journalists, 5 percent were other professionals, and 5 percent were merchants. This shift from near-total farmer dominance of party leadership to a broader leadership group caused concern for some old-line Alliancemen, who wrote their fears for the future of their party to the state Alliance secretary:

Lawyers and professional Men in office *do not represent* productive labor I fear we are going to slide into the old party groove. [1894]

The better element is being rapidly forced to the rear, the lawyers, professionals and their knavish helpers effectually dominate the party movements. [1894]

Rally the Farmers to the danger that the party has encountered by allowing the towns & Lawyers & Shysters to get control of our party. [1894]

Everything will be run by a lot of cigarette smoking dudes in a little while. [1896][8]

Despite the intensity of these jeremiads, it is necessary to recall that the Populist leadership remained two-thirds agricultural, more than double the proportion of farmers in the leadership of either of the other two major parties. The same is true of the most significant party leaders for the period 1890–95: 43 percent of the Populists were farmers, compared with none of the Democrats and only 2 percent of the Republicans.

Populist leaders were distinctive not only in terms of their occupations, but also in terms of the indicators of social status. Populists' educational levels, the type of college attended, if any, membership in the high-status Masonic lodge, or participation in commercial or professional organizations were all quite different from those of the Republicans or Democrats and suggest that the Populist leadership came from a different—and lower—social level. The skimpy data on church membership further reinforce this conclusion, with Republicans and Democrats more likely than Populists to belong to the Presbyterian or Episcopal church, and Populists more likely than Republicans or Democrats to belong to denominations usually associated with lower social status.

This collective portrait of the political leadership of Nebraska in 1890–95 reveals many of the same factors that were of high significance for voting behavior. The most significant determinant of Democratic voting was antiprohibition sentiment; Democratic leaders were more often foreign-born and ritualistic than were leaders of either of the other two parties, but they were not vocationally or socially distinct from the Republicans. Populist voting behavior was most significantly related to marginal agriculture, and Populist leadership was distinctly agrarian but not ethnoculturally distinct. Republican voting was related to residence in or near an incorporated area, and the characteristics of the Republican leadership clearly placed them in the small-town elite.

The Political System, 1890–95

Nebraska's political system in these years was in rapid transition. The relatively stable system of the 1880s was destroyed by the rise of Populism. Populism, initiator of change, was itself in flux, as its leadership shifted from almost totally agrarian to a mix of farmers, professionals, and a few businessmen. The Nebraska Democracy reacted by running first one way, then the other, and finally tearing itself in two. Control in the state GOP shifted from the regulars to the reformers to the railroad-supporting conservatives. No party achieved a majority of the vote between 1890 and 1895, and control of the state legislature was uncertain. The Populists and Democrats entered into a series of ad hoc coalitions, almost always through unilateral action by the Democrats. Both Populist and Democratic parties contained supporters and opponents of fusion. Leadership fluctuations reflected attempts by shifting factions to maximize their party's position—and their own.

Legislative behavior changed significantly from that of the 1880s. The Republican legislatures of the 1880s had concentrated on promoting the state's growth through constructing state buildings, establishing state institutions, and, in 1889, enacting a sugar-beet bounty. Railroad rate regulation was deftly sidestepped by most of these legislatures, some memorializing Congress and others referring the question to the voters for constitutional amendment or to a state board of transportation that never acted to regulate rates. The one non-Republican legislature, that of 1883, acted no differently. Occasional investigations of state officials ended inconclusively. However, the legislatures of 1891 and 1893, the former Populist-controlled, the latter organized by a coalition of Populists and Democrats, tackled the railroad rate question head on, and both passed rate bills. The first was vetoed and the second was overturned by the courts, but the legislature had taken up the problem. These two legislatures also passed a number of other measures long advocated by reformers. By contrast, the 1895 Republican-controlled legislature's most lasting contributions were selecting an official state flower and choosing a state nickname. Squabbling over new state institutions, especially normal schools, a favorite device to promote community growth, continued through all three legislatures.[9] These differing legislative actions reflect more general party attitudes, with Populists attempting to legislate solutions to the economic and political grievances of their agrarian constituents, Republicans avoiding controversy and attempting to encourage a general prosperity through boosterism and bounties.

None of the three governors elected between 1890 and 1895 carried with them majorities in either legislative house. Democratic Governor Boyd faced Populist majorities in both houses in the 1891 session, Republican Governor Crounse faced Populist-Democratic coalitions in each house in 1893, and Populist Governor Holcomb was opposed by large Republican majorities in both houses in 1895. Thus none could exert effective party pressure on the legislators. But there is no indication that Boyd or Crounse would have done so had they had the opportunity. Boyd's inaugural message to the legislature urged economy, an Australian ballot law, and carefully considered action on the railroad rate problem, but it suggested nothing more specific than a constitutional amendment to provide for a nonpartisan elective rate-setting commission. Boyd vetoed two bills: one, setting railroad rates, on the basis that it embodied "inflictions of injustice" on the railroads; the other was a minor bill duplicating a bill already approved. Governor Crounse's inaugural address urged economy and took note of the agitation for railroad regulation but made no specific recommendations at all. Crounse vetoed one bill, to add an additional judgeship, for reasons of economy.[10]

Populist Governor Holcomb departed from a number of precedents. His inaugural message called for the establishment of a state railroad commission by constitutional amendment and the abolition of railroad passes. Holcomb vetoed twelve bills in 1895, more than any previous governor.[11] Holcomb, the moderate Populist, was one of the most active governors

Nebraska had experienced up to that time, but he avoided the abrasiveness of Populist administrators in Kansas and Colorado. In his vetoes, Holcomb showed the same tendencies the Populist legislators had shown, the same willingness to use the power of office in support of his perceived constituency even though such actions aroused controversy. In doing so, he broke with the traditional Whiggish pattern of gubernatorial deference to the legislature.

The political system as of 1895 contained many elements deriving from the 1880s but also many that would come to full development only in 1896 and after. In 1894 the Democratic state convention rejected the men who had led the party from its birth in the territory in 1854 and embraced the leadership of Bryan and his associates. Bryan led his wing of the now-divided party into accepting most Populist candidates for state office. The pattern coalition would take from 1896 through 1906 was already established in some counties, with Populist and Democratic county conventions meeting at the same time, in the same city, and nominating the same men for office.[12] The Republican convention in 1894 rebuked the party's reform wing and turned to candidates sympathetic to the railroads, a pattern that continued until 1906. Populists were less agrarian, less strident, less eccentric in 1894 than they had been in 1890, but they were not ostensibly less radical. Ad hoc coalitions between Populists and Democrats had elected William V. Allen to the United States Senate in 1893 and Silas Holcomb to the governorship in 1894; in 1896 and after, state-level fusion of economic radicals, the Populists, and antiprohibition Democrats would become permanent and structured.

CHAPTER FIVE

Fusion Victory and
Republican Redemption, 1896–1904

> The average democrat will insist that the democrats are swallowing the populists, while the most enthusiastic fusion populists will claim that . . . the fusion compact has grafted populistic ideas upon the democratic tree until all that is left is the root hidden beneath the surface.
>
> *Omaha Bee*, 1902

Building on the fusion of 1894, Nebraska's Democrats and Populists swept to near-total victory in 1896. Bryan carried Nebraska with 52 percent of the vote, and Holcomb won reelection with 53 percent, the highest percentage polled by any gubernatorial candidate in a decade. They carried with them a majority of both houses of the state legislature and the entire fusion statewide slate of six Populists and one Democrat. Fusionists won four congressional seats, leaving the Republicans with two. In 1897 fusion elected a Democrat to the supreme court and a Populist and a Silver Republican to the University of Nebraska board of regents. Holcomb did not seek a third term as governor in 1898; nonetheless, fusionists won all statewide offices in 1898 and four fusionists returned to Congress, but control of the state legislature went to the Republicans. In 1899 fusion elected former Governor Holcomb to the state supreme court and a Democrat and a Silver Republican to the board of regents, giving fusionists a majority on both bodies. These repeated fusion victories were always by relatively narrow margins; no fusion candidate for governor or judge topped the 54 percent Holcomb received in 1899.[1]

The Republicans "redeemed" Nebraska in 1900 and widened their margins over the next three elections. Bryan lost his own state in 1900 by nearly 8,000 votes, fusionists lost all statewide offices and both houses of the state legislature, retaining only their four congressional seats. The fusionists lost these congressional seats in 1902 but won a formerly Republican seat when Edward Rosewater and the *Bee* bolted the incumbent. In 1904 Roosevelt carried Nebraska by the largest percentage polled by any presidential candidate since Grant in 1868, and he carried with him the entire statewide slate, the state legislature, and all six congressional seats. Republican candidates for minor statewide offices received only a tenuous 49.5 percent of the vote in 1900, but they increased this to 55 percent in 1904. No Republican gubernatorial nominee received a majority of the vote, however, and their winning margins varied from fewer than 900 votes in 1900 to just over 9,000 in 1904. Table 18 indicates party strength in the legislature from 1897 through 1903.[2]

TABLE 18. PARTY LEGISLATIVE STRENGTHS, 1897–1903

| Legis-lative Body | Year of Session | Repub-licans | Fusion Parties | | | | Total Legis-lators |
			Demo-crats	Popu-lists	Silver Repub-licans	Total Fusion[a]	
House	1897	32[b]	21	49	2	72[b]	104[b]
	1899	54[c]	14	28	2	48[c]	102[c]
	1901	53	16	26	—	47	100
	1903	76	8	8	—	24	100
Senate	1897	8[d]	7	17	2	26[d]	34[d]
	1899	21	3	8	—	12	33
	1901	19	7	5	2	14	33
	1903	29	—	1	—	4	33

[a]Including the following members identified only as Fusion: 1899 house, 4; 1899 senate, 1; 1901 house, 8; 1903 senate, 3.
[b]The 1897 house unseated four Republicans and replaced them with the Fusion contestants.
[c]The 1899 house unseated two Fusionists and replaced them with the Republican contestants.
[d]The 1897 senate unseated a Republican and replaced him with the Fusion contestant.

Although historians have given detailed attention to the events of 1890–96, they have been less interested in the period between the consummation of fusion and the emergence of an active state progressive movement within the Republican party in 1905–6.[3] Most recent studies seem to assume that after 1896 Populism died a rapid death and that the fusion campaigns of 1896 through 1904 were dominated by the Democrats. The analysis that follows indicates that Populism remained a significant political force after

1896, although it was declining after 1900. The fusion administrations of 1895–1901 were largely Populist, and voting behavior through 1904 showed the continuing, albeit decreasing, influence of the Populist movement. Although some studies have posited a significant change in the nature of the Democratic party with the advent of Bryan,[4] the Nebraska Democracy, while committed to Bryan, remained essentially what it had been in the 1880s—antiprohibition, antinativist, proimmigrant—to which was added a veneer of economic radicalism. Progressivism did not come to the state

TABLE 19. APPROPRIATIONS, NUMBER OF PATRONAGE APPOINTEES, AND PARTY DISTRIBUTION OF FUSION NOMINEES FOR STATEHOUSE OFFICES, 1896–1904

Office	Appro-priation, 1897–99[a]	Number of Appointees, 1897–99[b]	Party Affiliation of Fusion Nominee[c]				
			1896	1898	1900	1902	1904
Auditor	$32,025	7	Pop.	Pop.	Pop.	Pop.	Pop.
Commissioner of public lands and buildings	29,550	10	Pop.	Pop.	Pop.	Dem.	Pop.
Superintendent of public instruction	19,760	2	Pop.	Pop.	Pop.	Pop.	Pop.
Secretary of state	18,300	5	Pop.	Pop.	Pop.	Pop.	Dem.
Treasurer	17,300	4	Pop.	Pop.	Pop.	Pop.	Pop.
Attorney general	12,125	2	Dem.	Dem.	Dem.	Dem.	Dem.
Lieutenant governor	1,000[d]	—[d]	Pop.	S.R.	S.R.	Pop.	Dem.

[a]Includes the salary of the officer, salaries of patronage apppointees, and office supplies. Appropriations in 1899 and 1901 were comparable; see *Laws, Joint Resolutions, and Memorials Passed by the Legislative Assembly of the State of Nebraska at the Twenty-fifth Session* (Lincoln: State Journal Co., 1897), pp. 423–42; *Laws . . . at the Twenty-sixth Session* (Lincoln: Jacob North, 1899), pp. 370–414; *Laws . . . at the Twenty-seventh Session* (York: Nebraska Newspaper Union, 1901), pp. 533–72.

[b]Ibid.; the auditor had seven appointees in 1899, ten in 1901; the attorney general had three in 1899 and in 1901.

[c]Pop.=Populist, Dem.=Democrat, S.R.=Silver Republican.

[d]The lieutenant governor's salary was fixed by the state constitution at twice that of a state senator, and that in turn was based on the number of days of legislative session; $1,000 is the constitutional maximum for the lieutenant governor, plus mileage. The lieutenant governor was usually allowed a personal secretary and perhaps a page during the legislative session; the salary and office expenses came out of the general legislative appropriation and are not listed separately.

Republican party until 1905–6; throughout the period 1896–1904 the GOP remained basically what it had been in the early 1890s: the self-proclaimed party of growth and prosperity, noncontroversial and economically conservative.

The contemporary description of the alliance of Democrats, Populists, and Silver Republicans as "fusion" was actually a misnomer, for the parties never merged into one. Each election year saw the "fusion" parties renegotiate a coalition. Typically all three parties—Populists, Democrats, and Silver Republicans—would meet in the same city at the same time, and a conference committee would recommend how nominations should be divided among the parties. The separate conventions would then accept or reject the conference committee report and set about the difficult process of finding a candidate for each office who could achieve a majority in each of the three conventions. After the dissolution of the Silver Republicans' state organization in 1901, the "three-ring circus" was reduced to two.[5] This convention system operated for nine state elections. Certain recurring patterns suggest generalizations regarding the basis of coalition. First, and foremost, Populists received the nominations for most state offices, especially those with the largest patronage. Table 19 indicates this situation. Of five gubernatorial nominations made between 1896 and 1904, only one went to a Democrat. The Democrats received a share in the gubernatorial patronage and support for Bryan's presidential ambitions. They also had a veto on Populist nominees, for no nomination was declared final until the same person received a majority in all the conventions. Democrats apparently used their veto only to guarantee that nominees were not prohibitionists. In 1898 the Democratic convention balked at accepting William A. Poynter for governor until he came before the convention and pledged that, though personally temperate, he was not a prohibitionist. In 1898 congressional nominations went to the largest fusion party in the district; Populists had the nominations for the three western districts, Democrats for the three eastern districts. In 1900 the fusion conventions in the first district, an eastern district, settled on a Populist, whereupon Democrats in the fifth district, a western district, argued that a Democrat should be nominated there so that congressional nominations would remain evenly divided between the two parties, each getting three. In 1902 the nomination in the first district went back to the Democrats, who managed to retain that in the fifth as well. All congressional nominations in 1904 went to Democrats.[6]

Coalition was never easily accomplished. In 1898 the Democratic convention's first choice for governor was an Irish-born Catholic, Constantine J. Smyth, who had given control of the party to Bryan by successfully carrying the Omaha primaries in 1894 and had been elected attorney general in 1896. Smyth easily carried the first three convention ballots, then withdrew when the Democrats were notified that the Populist convention had given a majority to Poynter. The Silver Republican convention thereupon nominated Poynter, but the Democrats held back, a majority favoring Edgar Howard, an editor of Virginia parentage. Leading Democrats, including prominent Bryan lieutenants James C. Dahlman and William H. Thompson, pleaded with the Democratic convention to nominate Poynter. Evening stretched into night, but the Democratic delegates held fast and did not nominate Poynter until 6:00 A.M., after his pledge on the prohibition issue. Opposition to Poynter's renomination in 1900 surfaced within all three parties, but no one candidate united the opposition, and Poynter was renominated. In 1902 the Democratic convention first supported Constantine J. Smyth, and the Populists backed Michael F. Harrington, also a Catholic of Irish descent. Bryan preferred William H. Thompson, but it took until 3:00 A.M. for the Populist convention, perhaps out of exhaustion, to accept Thompson, a Democrat, as their standard-bearer. Democrats in 1904 were disturbed not only that the Populists' approach to coalition that year smacked of ultimatum, but also that George W. Berge was forced upon them as their nominee for governor.[7]

Gilbert M. Hitchcock's *Omaha World-Herald* was the most prominent Democratic daily in the state. In 1896 the paper concentrated on silver and trusts nationally and on the need for honesty and economy in state government. The currency issue still received prominent attention in 1898, but in 1900 the national focus was on the twin dangers of imperialism abroad and trusts at home. Throughout the period the *World-Herald* claimed that Republican nominees were controlled by the railroads and corporations and thus were incapable of providing honest, economical administration. In 1902, and more intensively in 1904, Hitchcock editorially attacked John H. Mickey, the GOP candidate for governor, as bringing prohibition into the state campaign as a cover for his corporate ties. The *World-Herald* denounced Mickey, a prominent Methodist layman and a trustee of the state Anti-Saloon League, for his "insufferable egotism and unbearable Phariseeism." A special German-language article in 1902 termed him "ein Fiend persönlicher Freiheiten und Rechte"—an enemy of personal freedom and rights. By branding Mickey a puritan, the *World-Herald* sought the votes of antiprohibitionists, and by denouncing his puritanism as a cover for corporate subservience it sought the support of temperate economic radicals.[8]Democratic platforms almost totally avoided cultural issues, concentrating on currency, corporate abuses, and imperialism; advocating the direct election of United States senators, an income tax, arbitration of labor disputes, the initiative and referendum, lower tariffs, and direct primaries; and opposing labor injunctions, a large standing army, and the prevailing national bank system.[9]

The (Lincoln) *Nebraska Independent*, the most prominent Populist organ in the state, was edited throughout most of this period by Thomas Tibbles, the 1904 Populist vice-presidential nominee. The *Independent*'s editorial policy was similar to the *World-Herald*'s in 1896. In 1898 and 1900 it gave very heavy emphasis to the issue of imperialism. Although jingoist before the declaration of war, *Independent* editorials approached pacificism before the war's end. In 1900 the paper indicted McKinley for having engaged in a war that was brutalizing American society and assailed Theodore Roosevelt as a militarist. By 1902 both the *Independent* and the *World-Herald* pronounced tax assessment the most significant state issue, and in 1904 they continued to focus on taxes, Republican extravagance, and the recently passed revenue law as leading state issues. In 1904 the *Independent*, as a supposed public service, printed instructions on ticket-splitting, using as an example voting for Roosevelt but not for Mickey. The Populist paper did not attack Mickey's temperance views.[10] Populist platforms took most of the same positions, opposed labor injunctions and railroad passes, advocated the initiative and referendum, employer liability, and railroad rate laws, and sympathized with striking coal miners and the Boers of South Africa.[11]

Most of the important Democratic fusionists had come to statewide prominence between 1890 and 1896. Bryan was unchallenged master of the state party; most other leading Democrats—notably Thompson, Smyth, and Dahlman—had been leaders of the Nebraska Democratic Free Coinage League, the organization through which the forces in favor of fusion and silver had gained control of the 1894 state convention. Gilbert Hitchcock of the *World-Herald* had urged cooperation with the Populists as early as 1890. Edgar Howard had not found the Populists and the silver crusade attractive, but he was captivated by Bryan's personal charm. Only three leading fusion Democrats had not been active in the movement that brought Bryan to power—James Manahan, Ashton C. Shallenberger, and Philip L. Hall. Manahan, a young Irish Catholic lawyer, came to Lincoln in 1894, was caught up in the silver crusade of 1896, and sought election to Congress from Bryan's old district in 1898. Shallenberger came to Nebraska in 1881, became a bank president in Alma in 1893, and was, like Manahan, caught up in the silver fever of 1896; state organizer for the Nebraska Bi-metallic

Union in 1897, he was elected to Congress in 1900 and lost his bid for reelection to George W. Norris in 1902. Hall, of Irish descent, had been educated as a physician, was appointed secretary of the state banking board in 1897, and was state party chairman from 1898 through 1904.[12]

The most important fusion Populists included both some of the party's earliest leaders and a number who became significant only after the fusion victory of 1894. Holcomb and Allen, by virtue of their offices, remained prominent in the Populist leadership group, but such early leaders as John Powers and Charles Van Wyck did not. J. Harlan Edmisten, a Texas-born former Democrat, became state party chairman in 1894 and remained extremely powerful through 1904. Michael F. Harrington, an Irish-Canadian Catholic lawyer from O'Neill and—like Edmisten—a former Democrat, developed a strong following in Populist conventions after 1896 but refused all nominations except that for elector in 1896. George W. Berge, a former Republican of German parentage, unsuccessfully sought the first district congressional nomination in 1898, received it in 1900, and was the fusion candidate for governor in 1904. William A. Poynter, elected governor in 1898 and unsuccessful candidate for reelection in 1900, had a long history of third-party activity—he had been elected to the lower house of the state legislature in 1884 as an antimonopolist and to the state senate in 1890 as a Populist and had been nominated for Congress in 1892. James N. Gaffin, state chairman in 1898, had been elected to the lower house of the legislature in 1890, 1892, and 1896, had been Speaker of the 1893 and 1897 sessions, had been the nominee for lieutenant governor in 1894, and had been state chairman in 1893. John Powers accepted rather insignificant appointments from Governors Holcomb and Poynter, was fusion nominee for secretary of state in 1902, and was a delegate to the Populist national convention in 1904. Van Wyck spent much of his time in Washington between his defeat for governor in 1892 and his death in 1895.[13]

In 1897 fusionists held full control of two branches of the state government—the executive and the legislative—but the 1897 legislative session disappointed many of their supporters. Bills to prohibit railroad passes and to regulate passenger rates were indefinitely postponed. A bill regulating stockyards passed but with an obvious defect in title that caused it to be struck down by the courts. The only lasting reforms were acts extending the initiative and referendum to municipalities, prohibiting street railway passes to municipal officials, repealing the sugar-beet bounty, and prohibiting political contributions by corporations. Attorney General Constantine Smyth secured the conviction of the former state treasurer, Joseph Bartley, on charges of defalcation. Governor Holcomb in 1897 again exercised the previously little-used item veto of appropriations to keep state expenses low. Governor Poynter faced a Republican legislature in 1899, but he nonetheless urged a railroad rate law as an interim measure pending government owner- ship, urged that the state labor commissioner be given the power to arbitrate labor disputes, and advised the abolition of railroad passes, a revision of the method of tax assessment, and rigid economy. Poynter vetoed five bills, including a senate resolution commending the First Nebraska Volunteers for "defending in the far off Philippines the principles of our government and adding new glory to our flag"; Poynter acknowledged the troops' "bravery and gallantry" but regretted "that circumstances have compelled them to give their services and sacrifice their lives in a conflict at utter variance to the very fundamental principles of our government" and vetoed the resolution rather than approve "the statement that the war of conquest. . . is in defense of the principles of our government and is adding new glory to our flag." Poynter was faced with filling the senate seat left open by the death of Monroe Hayward, and he opened a rift within the Nebraska Democracy by encouraging the aspirations of *World-Herald* publisher Hitchcock and of William H. Thompson, then writing to Bryan for advice, and finally ap- pointing William V. Allen and shifting the credit—or blame—to Bryan.[14]

Republican rhetoric from 1896 through 1904 continued to stress that the GOP was the party of prosperity and growth. In 1896 they repeatedly tied the silver issue to the tariff, the *Bee* declaring that "free silver is only a mask for free trade." In 1900 the GOP claimed imperialism was a false issue, "their straw man," to cover a Democratic desire to tinker with—and destroy— Republican prosperity. Labeling Democrats the party of low prices and low wages, Republicans claimed they alone could insure "the safety of the business interests of the state and nation." When fusionists revealed that Republican state treasurer Bartley was more than half a million dollars short upon surrendering office in 1897, the GOP retaliated by collecting and publishing statistics purporting to show that Populist county officials throughout the state had defaulted to the collective extent of nearly a quarter of a million dollars. GOP leaders portrayed Populist officials as political manipulators and "a rapacious free pass brigade." After 1900, when fusionists pointed to the state's deficit, Republicans marshaled statistics to prove the deficit stemmed from fusion administrations. They charged that anti-imperialism was unpatriotic, as were all who espoused that cause. Governor Poynter especially came under attack as being unpatriotic for his veto of the senate resolution praising Nebraska troops. Fusionists also came under attack for not having delivered on their promises of reform when they had the opportunity to do so.[15]

Although these issues of the economy, foreign policy, and state administration were given first prominence, a consistent cultural subtheme runs through the GOP campaign rhetoric, expressed by the *State Journal* in 1896 when it termed the fusionists "degenerate, mattoid and morally crippled" and accused Bryan of being opposed to prohibition and charged fusion congressional candidate William L. Greene with being a public drunkard. In 1900 Republicans damned Governor Poynter, a teetotaler, for accepting support from liquor and saloon interests in his reelection bid, and in 1902 they proudly claimed to be free from influence by the liquor interests, bemoaning the way gubernatorial candidate Mickey's "good character" caused him to be impugned by the Democrats. The *Bee* gave less play to these cultural issues; Rosewater himself was a leading opponent of prohibition and the *Bee* had its largest circulation in Omaha, an antiprohibition stronghold. The *Bee*, in 1896, charged that Bryan was *not* opposed to prohibition and was, in fact, an APA sympathizer. Republican platforms totally avoided any mention of cultural issues.[16]

The four men nominated for governor by Nebraska Republicans between 1896 and 1904 were cut from similar cloth. As in the period from the mid-1870s through 1890, the GOP selected successful small-town businessmen with little political experience. John H. "Jack" MacColl, the 1896 nominee, was a Scots-Canadian who had come to Nebraska in 1869 and worked as a Union Pacific woodcutter, eventually acquiring more than three thousand acres of farmland as well as interests in several commercial ventures. Associated with the Union Pacific throughout his political career, he had been county clerk for thirteen years, served in the 1877 legislative session, been a delegate to the 1884 national convention, and sought the nomination for governor in 1890 and 1894. Monroe L. Hayward, the 1898 candidate, was a New York–born Union veteran, a lawyer, and local attorney for the Burlington railroad. His only public offices had been delegate to the 1875 constitutional convention and district judge, but he had attended the 1885 and 1896 state conventions and had held party positions. Charles Dietrich, son of a German forty-eighter, had been a successful Black Hills gold prospector before coming to Hastings in 1878. A prosperous merchant and banker, he had not held any significant public office before his election to the governorship in 1900. The nominee in 1902 and 1904, John H. Mickey, a Civil War veteran and active Methodist, came to Nebraska in 1868, farmed until 1872, served ten years as county treasurer, then became a

bank cashier and subsequently bank president and built up large landhold-
ings. Aside from county treasurer and local school board offices, his only
previous involvement in government was as a member of the 1881 legislature. Neither MacColl in 1896 nor Hayward in 1898 put much of a personal
stamp on his campaign. Dietrich in 1900, however, tried to capitalize on his
German parentage by running a "beer and sauerkraut" campaign in German
areas, emphasizing his own tolerance and his opponent's personal temperance. Mickey reversed this in 1902 and 1904; staunchly moral, he emphasized his independence of the liquor interests and, above all, his incor-
ruptibility. Mickey's unquestioned honesty was a boon to the GOP, plagued
by revelations of corruption, by the spectacularly disastrous 1901 United
States senatorial elections (see below), and by constant allegations of railroad and corporate influence in party councils.[17]

Republicans had secure majorities in the legislative sessions of 1899,
1901, and 1903. Given the closely competitive political situation in the state,
they might have been expected to move to attract their former partisans who
had been voting fusionist. In 1899, however, the legislature did little aside
from electing Monroe Hayward to the United States Senate, and that only
after two full months of acrimonious intraparty battling. Hayward died
before taking office, and the other incumbent senator, John M. Thurston,
had come under heavy attack for continuing to draw a large salary from the
Union Pacific while serving in the Senate; he was not considered "available" for a second term, so the 1901 legislature had two seats to fill. The
leading contenders were *Bee* editor Edward Rosewater, Assistant Secretary
of War George Meiklejohn, and D. E. Thompson, a Lincoln utilities and
insurance magnate and former Burlington railroad superintendent. Eight
Republican legislators refused to enter the caucus until Thompson withdrew.
He eventually did so, but his associates were able to dictate the election of
Governor Dietrich, known to be close to the Burlington, and Joseph H.
Millard, an Omaha banker supposed to be acceptable to the Union Pacific.
Thompson was rewarded by an appointment as minister to Brazil. With
Dietrich in the Senate, Lieutenant Governor Ezra Savage became governor;
the only significant act of his term was the pardon of Joseph Bartley, the
defaulting state treasurer. Savage had apparently been assured that a pardon
for Bartley would gain him support for the 1902 nomination for governor,
but instead it precipitated a storm of criticism and allegations of a "deal." In
mid-1902, charges of embezzlement were brought against the Republican
state treasurer, William Stuefer. The election of Mickey in 1902 helped the
GOP overcome some of the onus of corruption and railroad influence arising
from these events, and the 1903 legislature moved to increase state revenue

by revising the state tax assessment law. Popularly elected precinct assessors were replaced by an elected county assessor, and penalties were enacted for concealment of personal property. Although the law did increase revenue, it was highly unpopular; fusionists charged that it allowed railroads to evade their fair proportion of taxes but raised taxes for farmers.[18]

Before the 1904 convention, Senator Dietrich was indicted for allegedly selling postoffice appointments, for having the Hastings postoffice moved to a building he owned, and for having drawn salaries both as governor and as senator for a few months. The 1904 convention was therefore again faced with the necessity of sanitizing the party image. In 1902 the convention had nominated the regular, but clean, Mickey for governor. In 1904 the convention renominated Mickey and invoked a little-used provision of state law to nominate Congressman Elmer Burkett for the United States Senate, thereby putting a ''clean'' and popular nominee in a prominent position on the ballot and eliminating the possibility of another bruising legislative battle over the Senate in 1905.[19]

Between 1896 and 1904, each of Nebraska's three major parties—Democrats, Republicans, and Populists—spun off schismatics who claimed to be the true carriers of party principles and traditions and who aligned themselves with the opposition against their misguided brethren. The three splinter parties—Gold Democrats, Silver Republicans, and Middle-of-the-Road Populists—were all small and short-lived; many of their leaders seemed to have been rejected by their old parties before they had left those parties.

Fusion of Democrats and Populists in 1894 produced the first of these splinter parties, the Gold Democrats. Described on the ballot variously as Straight Democrats, National Democrats, or Democrats, they ran full tickets in the state elections of 1894, 1895, 1896, and 1897. After 1897 there were no more state tickets, and prominent Gold Democrats went various ways. Even in 1896, when there was a Gold Democrat presidential ticket, a number of prominent former Democrats declared for McKinley, including former national committeemen Tobias Castor and Dr. George Miller. J. Sterling Morton, who had been promoted in some quarters as the Gold Democratic presidential nominee in 1896, retired to his Nebraska City home in 1897 to edit a newspaper, the *Conservative*, a conservative prototype for Bryan's *Commoner*, and to promote a new national party, based on Jeffersonian principles and conservative economics. He was a national vice-president of the Anti-Imperialist League but took no active part in promoting its aims in Nebraska; his hatred of Bryan was stronger than his anti-imperialism, and he voted Republican in 1900.[20]A few prominent Gold Democrats did become Republicans—including Frank Irvine, candidate for supreme court judge in 1893 and 1896, and Daniel Cook, chairman of the 1894 splinter convention—but most seem to have eventually returned to the Democracy. Dr. Miller supported McKinley in 1896 and 1900 but by 1904 was again involved in local Democratic politics. Former Governor Boyd remained politically inactive until 1902, but in 1904 he sought the Democratic nomination for governor. Phelps D. Sturdevant, state treasurer in 1883–85 and Gold Democratic candidate for governor in 1894, had returned to the party by 1910 and sought the Democratic nomination for state treasurer in the primary that year. Robert S. Bibb, 1896 gubernatorial candidate, endorsed Bryan in 1900. Euclid Martin, state chairman in 1894, had resumed participation in local Democratic politics by 1906. T. J. Mahoney, candidate for supreme court judge in 1895 and state chairman in 1896, had returned by 1912, as had John McShane, the 1888 candidate for governor. John Mattes, Jr., candidate for secretary of state in 1896, was a Democratic leader in the legislative sessions of 1915 and 1917. A McKinley organizer in 1900 estimated that three-quarters of the Nebraska Gold Democrats were supporting Bryan.[21]

The Gold Democrats were never very successful at the polls, ranging from 12 percent for university regents in 1895 to less than 1 percent for supreme court judge in 1897. Their best showing, in 1895, came when both the Gold and the Silver Democrats were identified on the ballot only as "Democrat," and the Gold Democrats were listed first because candidates were listed alphabetically; in the 1894 race for auditor, their next best showing, the Silver Democrat withdrew in favor of the Populist candidate and the Gold Democrat was the only candidate for that office identified as a Democrat. Gold Democratic candidates for major offices—governor and judge—consistently ran behind party nominees for other offices, especially in 1894 and 1895, when the Populist candidates for those offices emphasized their opposition to the anti-Catholicism of the American Protective Association.[22]

Third parties have sometimes been described as way stations for persons moving from one major party to the other. The Gold Democratic party obviously did serve this function for a few of its adherents, but for most its function may be compared to a safe observation point. Gold Democrats, opposed to the Populist currency panacea and suspicious of Populist sympathies for prohibition and woman suffrage, but equally unwilling to join with the APA-tinged Republicans, used the party as an honorable, if futile, alternative to both.[23] When they saw that the Populists, in power, did not agitate temperance or suffrage issues, and when Bryan emerged as clearly the most prominent Democrat nationally, most Gold Democrats apparently returned to the party fold.

The Silver Republicans formally came into existence in 1897, were dissolved by their executive committee in August 1901, and were never large.[24] Their leadership included a number of men who had held elective offices in the state as Republicans. Samuel Maxwell, elected to Congress in 1896 as a Silver Republican fusionist, had served on the state supreme court from 1873 to 1894, was denied renomination by the state Republican convention in 1893, and was the Populist nominee for supreme court judge in 1895. He was not renominated for Congress in 1898. Gilbert L. Laws was appointed state party chairman in 1896 and was appointed a secretary of the state Board of Transportation in 1897, serving until 1901. Laws had been elected secretary of state in 1886 and reelected in 1888, and he resigned in 1889 to seek, successfully, election to a vacant congressional seat. Antimonopoly Republicans charged that the congressional nomination had been bought by the railroads, and Laws was not renominated in 1890. Neither Maxwell, after 1899, nor Laws, after 1901, took an active part in state politics. John N. Lyman, Silver Republican state chairman in 1899, had been elected county treasurer in 1895 as a Republican, reelected in 1897 as a fusionist, and elected to the state senate in 1900; after 1901 he became a Populist, was nominated for state treasurer in 1902, and was a member of the Populist state executive committee in 1904. Edward A. Gilbert, lieutenant governor in 1899–1901 and candidate for that office in 1900, had served as a Republican in the 1889 legislature and remained a Republican until 1896; after 1901, he too became a Populist and was again nominated for lieutenant governor in 1902. Charles O. Lobeck had been elected to the state senate in 1893 as a Republican, was a fusion candidate for elector in 1900, was Omaha city controller from 1903 to 1911, and was elected to Congress as a Democrat, serving until defeated in 1918. Charles Wooster had been an antimonopoly Republican in the 1880s, had publicly attacked the Populist movement in 1890, was elected to the 1896 legislature as a Silver Republican fusionist and unsuccessfully sought reelection in 1898; he sought election as a Democrat in 1910 and again in 1912. Wooster had become a Republican again by 1919, in the hopes of taking over the GOP by the Non-Partisan League, and was an NPL-endorsed candidate for the 1919 constitutional convention. Arthur J. Weaver, son of Republican congressman Archibald Weaver, was elected to the 1898 legislature, became a Democrat after 1901, again became a Republican some time before 1920, was elected governor in 1928, was defeated for reelection in 1930 by Charles Bryan, and unsuccessfully sought the Republican nomination for the United

States Senate in 1940 as the favorite of George W. Norris and, apparently, President Roosevelt.[25]

Middle-of-the-Road (antifusion) Populists fielded a full state ticket only once, in 1900, but the faction made its influence felt in the 1898 and 1904 state conventions of the Populist party. Mid-road sentiment in 1896 took the form of campaigning for the Bryan-Watson ticket rather than the Bryan-Sewall one; such campaigning was basically pointless, for no Bryan-Watson ticket appeared on the ballot. A few antifusionists, such as Samuel Elder, the blundering Speaker of the 1891 house who had been denied that position in 1893, declared for McKinley. Mid-road sentiment centered on the remnants of the Alliance in 1898. Lucien Stebbins, a Populist legislator, called for an antifusion state convention but yielded to a plan by the Buffalo County Alliance to take over the existing party organization. The nomination of Poynter for governor and the selection of Gaffin for state chairman—rather than Edmisten—were seen as victories for the antifusion forces. Even so, a few prominent Populists campaigned against the ticket, notably Mart Howe, a former state party secretary who had been removed from a patronage position by Holcomb, and Paul Vandervoort, an APA sympathizer who had been denied appointment as Omaha fire and police commissioner by Holcomb.[26] By 1900, an organization complete with a newspaper, the *True Populist*, had developed, led by D. Clem Deaver, state chairman in 1893, who had been denied a patronage position by Poynter. A full Mid-road ticket was nominated and given considerable assistance by the Republicans. The Mid-road campaign leveled a strong attack on the fusion nominees and the fusion record but virtually ignored the GOP. Charges of Republican sponsorship of the Mid-road movement, together with McKinley's subsequent appointment of Deaver to a patronage position, thoroughly discredited the Mid-road movement, and after 1900 there was no serious threat to the position of the state's established, fusionist, Populist leadership. In 1904 it was these established leaders—William V. Allen, Michael F. Harrington, and Thomas Tibbles—who led the movement for a separate national ticket. A strong element in the 1904 state convention wanted a separate state ticket as well but were satisfied with the nomination for governor and most state offices.[27]

Political rhetoric, campaigning, and issues from 1896 to 1904 continued to show the impact of the events of the early 1890s. Fusion of Democrats and Populists produced a coalition in which each party retained its basic identity, the Populists as agrarian radical reformers, the Democrats as ethnic anti-prohibitionists, willing to barter domination of state government for pledges not to agitate the liquor issue. Republican rhetoric largely avoided controversial state issues to focus on the question of prosperity, to claim credit for it, and to indict the Democrats for threatening it. Imperialism was a prominent issue for only a few years; few Republicans—no prominent ones by 1900—opposed the course of empire. Populists were the most vociferous opponents, followed closely by their Democratic allies. By the end of the period, state campaigns were being fought more and more on such local issues as railroad passes and taxation. Both Republican and Democratic rhetoric, at the same time, began to show distinct tinges of ethnic-prohibition coloring.

Critical election

89

CHAPTER SIX

Voting Behavior and Political Leadership, 1896–1904

The campaign of 1896 . . . fused the old-line Democrat and the new-line Populist in a common cause. It broke the Western Republicans into two elements, and brought the more daring into the new coalition. . . . Through more than forty years its essential principles . . . have been the basis of American liberalism.

Arthur F. Mullen, late 1930s

Analysts of American politics have long described the election of 1896 as of crucial significance. Recent theorists have seen the presidential election of 1896 as completing a realignment process catalyzed by the depression of 1893 and as thereby initiating the fourth electoral system, a system characterized by a normally secure Republican majority at the national level and by departisanization, a decline in voter participation, and a change in policies at a federal level. Historians and political scientists have accordingly paid close attention to the nature of the realignment of 1896 and have produced three major hypotheses regarding its nature.[1] One portrays the realignment as pitting urban voters against those of the rural countryside, with McKinley building a Republican majority on the votes of the cities and Bryan leading a party of farmers. A second hypothesis suggests that voters divided along an economic dimension, with McKinley securing the support of the wealthy and the upper middle classes and Bryan winning the poor and the lower middle classes. Still a third view sees the basic voter movement as ethnoculturally motivated, suggesting that Bryan made over the Democracy into "a new entity, with a new leadership crusading in the name of evangelical Protestantism for the creation of a moral society," and that, as a result, ritualistic groups (Catholics and Lutherans) moved to McKinley and pietistic groups became Bryan Democrats.[2] To these three hypotheses may be added a fourth, derived from the analysis of party rhetoric in the preceding chapter: In Nebraska, the party of Bryan was a coalition of marginal farmers who had previously been Populists and traditionally Democratic ritualistic ethnic groups, and the Republican party was but little changed from what it had been before 1890 save for the losses it suffered among marginal farmers. An examination of voting behavior will help determine which of these hypotheses most closely accords with the behavior of Nebraska voters.

Voting Behavior: General Patterns

The election of 1898 is a good example of most general voting patterns during this period because there was no presidential election to "pull" voters out of party patterns; because both major gubernatorial candidates conducted party campaigns rather than personal ones and their votes correlate highly with the party vote; and because minor parties were more insignificant than at any other time during the period from 1896 to 1904.[3] Three population attributes derived from the 1900 census were selected as independent variables to test the various hypotheses: (1) the percentage of the population living in incorporated areas, a measure of the extent to which a county was rural and agricultural, or urban and commercial or industrial; (2) the mean dollar income per farm, a measure of the prosperity of agriculture; and (3) the percentage of the population born in Germany, Bohemia, Ireland, or Poland, a measure of the ethnocultural value structure of a county, with a high value indicating the presence of many residents with a ritualistic perspective and a low value indicating the absence of ritualists. Pearson coefficients of correlation are not particularly helpful in revealing the extent to which these three variables are statistically related to voting for the two major parties. The low values of Pearson coefficients, and similarly low values for a multiple regression, suggest that none of the three variables is related to party voting in a linear pattern. The absence of a linear pattern is confirmed if we break down the sixty-one counties into groups based upon the three independent variables and calculate the mean party vote for these smaller, more homogeneous groups. Table 20 summarizes these data and suggests that the fusionists were strongest in low-income counties, in ritualistic counties, and in rural counties. Yet none of the breakdowns reveals a clear linear pattern.

We may begin to represent the interrelationships among the various population characteristics in combinations of two. Each of the three vari-

TABLE 20. PARTY STRENGTH INDEXES, FOR COUNTIES, 1898, WITH
COUNTIES GROUPED BY SOCIOECONOMIC QUARTILES

Independent Variables	Index of Fusion Party Strength	Index of Republican Party Strength
Percentage of the population born in Germany, Bohemia, Ireland, and Poland, 1900		
Highest quartile	53.55%	45.49%
Second quartile	52.72	46.34
Third quartile	49.27	49.63
Lowest quartile	51.90	46.96
Mean income per farm, 1899		
Most prosperous quartile	50.89%	48.26%
Second quartile	51.68	47.30
Third quartile	50.51	48.40
Poorest quartile	54.25	44.54
Percentage of the population living in incorporated areas, 1900		
Most urban quartile	48.04%	50.77%
Second quartile	49.99%	49.10
Third quartile	54.05	44.94
Most rural quartile	55.31	43.64

ables in table 20 is divided into quartiles. If we construct a table with ethnicity and farm income as its two dimensions, we produce sixteen cells ordered from the most ritualistic to the most pietistic along one dimension and from the highest mean farm income to the lowest among the other dimension. When the sixty-one counties analyzed are distributed into the appropriate cells and the mean party vote calculated for each cell, we find—not surprisingly—that the fusion party vote was strongest in the counties which were both most ritualistic and of lowest farm income. The entire table may be represented as a square, each corner of which represents a different combination of the extreme values of the two population attributes. Cells with similar patterns of political behavior may be combined and major dividing lines drawn between different patterns of political behavior; figure 1 presents the results. The horizontal dimension represents ethnicity, and the vertical dimension represents mean farm income. If voting behavior broke along a single dimension, the major dividing line would be either vertical or horizontal. As may be seen from figure 1, the major dividing lines are neither vertical nor horizontal, but diagonal. The figure is a striking

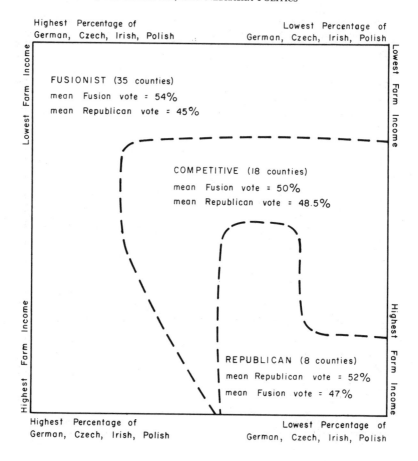

FIGURE 1. Voting behavior, 1898, counties distributed by ethnicity and farm income.

depiction of the coalitional nature of the fusion vote—fusionist strength includes all cells in the most ritualistic column, and also all the cells in the lowest farm income row. The Republican vote is more contained, concentrated among counties of high farm income and a high degree of pietism.

Although it might be desirable to add a third dimension to this figure, extending it into a cube to represent a third population attribute, such an exercise is beyond the capacity of the printed page. We shall have to be content with another two-dimensional table, figure 2. Ethnicity remains the

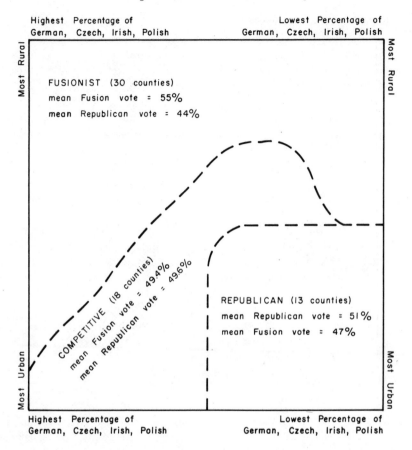

FIGURE 2. Voting behavior, 1898, counties distributed by ethnicity and degree of urbanization.

horizontal dimension, but the vertical dimension has been changed to the urban-rural scale. As in the previous figure, the major dividing lines are neither horizontal nor vertical, but diagonal. Fusion strength is concentrated in the most rural and most ritualistic counties, and Republican strength in the opposite corner, the most urban and most pietistic counties.

Both of these figures are important in understanding the nature of the fusion coalition in the electorate. As may be seen from both figures—and, if your imagination will cooperate, from a cube you must construct by combining the two—the fusion electorate was stretched over considerable distances, from most ritualistic to most pietistic, from highest mean farm income to lowest, from urban to rural. To be sure, there is a center to the coalition in the most rural and most ritualistic and lowest farm income corner of the cube, but continued fusion victory required the maintenance of the "arms" reaching out to other parts of the population.

Precinct level returns exist for the entire state for the 1900 presidential and gubernatorial elections and allow for a more intensive look at the reaction of precincts largely of one ethnic group. According to one hypothesis that seeks to explain the nature of the realignment of 1896, ritualistic groups would be expected to react strongly against the "evangelical Protestantism" represented by Bryan, the head of the fusion ticket, and by William Poynter, the incumbent fusion governor, who was known to be personally temperate. If such a thesis applies to Nebraska, one would expect the most ritualistic areas to back McKinley and Charles Dietrich, the Republicans' "beer and sauerkraut" candidate for governor; the most pietistic areas would be expected to support Bryan and Poynter. This clearly was not the case. Six Irish precincts in Greeley, Holt, and Dakota counties supported Bryan with between 82 and 89 percent of their votes and gave Poynter about the same margin. Five Czech precincts in east central and southeastern Nebraska averaged 77 percent for Bryan. Two precincts with large concentrations of Poles, one in Platte County and one in Howard County, gave Bryan 69 and 83 percent, respectively, and gave similar percentages to Poynter.[4]

Urban areas tended to be less ethnically homogeneous and more subject to crosscutting pressures. However, Wilber, largely Czech, voted for Bryan by 59 percent. O'Neill, Irish, gave him 55 percent. Columbus, containing many Germans and other Catholics, supported Bryan with 51 percent. Omaha's Second Ward, the home of many Czechs and smaller numbers of Poles and Germans, gave Bryan 58 percent, and the First Ward, with somewhat smaller concentrations of these groups, gave him 55 percent. South Omaha, a meat-packing center with large numbers of Czechs, Poles, Germans, and Irish, voted for Bryan by 60 percent. The significance of these Bryan victories in urban areas increases when one realizes that these were the *only* incorporated areas with more than a thousand people that McKinley did not carry. *Every* urban Bryan majority came in a city or town with significant numbers of Catholics, Irish, Czechs, Poles, or Germans.[5]

Clearly the Irish, Czechs, and Poles of Nebraska did not desert the Bryanized Democracy. Many of Nebraska's Germans retained similarly strong Democratic preferences. Four German Catholic precincts in Cuming and Platte counties gave Bryan between 72 and 90 percent of their vote, averaging 79 percent, and Poynter received a similar margin, varying from 73 to 88 percent. Of six Missouri Synod Lutheran precincts, only one failed to give Bryan a majority, his vote ranging from 49 to 79 percent, averaging 60 percent. Support for Bryan in four precincts predominantly of other Lutheran synods or non-Lutheran and non-Catholic in religion ranged from 39 to 55 percent, averaging 44 percent. It appears that German Catholics supported Bryan nearly as strongly as their coreligionists among the Irish and Slavic groups, that archconservative Lutheran groups like the Missouri Synod were only slightly less enthusiastic in their support, and that fusion found the least support among Germans toward the pietistic end of the spectrum.[6]

We may finally turn our attention to the Scandinavians. Danes had shown no strong tendency to vote as a bloc before this period, and this continued. Three largely Danish precincts in central Nebraska gave Bryan between 54 and 82 percent of their vote, but a rural Danish precinct in eastern Nebraska gave him only 40 percent. Swedes and Norwegians tended to behave similarly, regardless of location. Five strongly Swedish precincts, two in eastern Nebraska and three in the south central part of the state, gave Bryan an average of 31 percent of their vote, ranging from 22 to 38 percent. Two Norwegian precincts in Madison and Boone counties averaged 24 percent for Bryan, ranging from 23 to 25 percent. One other group, the Dutch, fit into the same political pattern as the Swedes and Norwegians. South Pass precinct, Lancaster County, two-thirds Dutch, cast 21 percent of its vote for Bryan in 1900.[7]

These data allow for a projection of the extent of fusion support among various ethnic groups in Nebraska:

Irish	80–90%
Czechs	75–85%
Poles	70–80%
German Catholics	70–90%
German Lutherans, Missouri Synod	50–80%
Germans, other religious groups	40–55%
Danes	40–80%
Swedes	20–40%
Norwegians	20–25%
Dutch	20–25%

In Nebraska, Catholics remained the most solidly Democratic group in the electorate, followed by conservative Lutherans. Swedish, Norwegian, and Dutch pietists did not support Bryan to any significant extent. Insofar as the data allow for projection, the same pattern (if not the same proportions) held true for urban as well as for rural areas.

Thus far, this survey of voting behavior has pointed to the genuinely coalitional nature of the Democratic-Populist fusion. Fusion candidates drew most strongly in rural areas of low farm income (the Populist factor) and in ritualistic areas (the Democratic factor). Not surprisingly, the fusion strongholds were in those counties where these multiple factors coincided—eight rural, low-income, ritualistic counties that averaged nearly 58 percent for fusion in 1898. Republican candidates ran most strongly where the opposite complex of characteristics coincided—in four urban, high-income, pietistic counties that cast nearly 55 percent of their vote for Republicans in 1898. The two parties were most closely competitive where these multiple characteristics conflicted rather than coincided.[8]

The presidential election of 1904 provides a good illustration of the nature of voting for the fusion coalition. That year the coalition was ruptured at the presidential level, with the Nebraska Democracy supporting the candidacy of Alton B. Parker, and Nebraska Populists that of Tom Watson. Analysis of voting for these two candidates reveals quite clearly the very different voter composition of the two fusion parties. The vote for Parker correlates highly with the Democratic party vote from 1888 through 1893, ranging from a low of +0.75 (for the 1888 party vote) to a high of +0.90 (for that of 1893). Similarly, the vote for Watson correlates highly with the Populist party vote during the early 1890s, varying from a low of +0.89 for the 1890 party vote to a high of +0.93 for that of 1893. As might be expected from these relationships, both the Parker vote and the vote for Watson show strong linear correlations with the independent variables previously found to be related to Democratic and Populist voting in the 1890s. Stepwise multiple regressions further confirm the largely single-issue nature of voting for Parker and Watson and are summarized in tables 21 and 22. Note that adding

TABLE 21. STEPWISE MULTIPLE REGRESSION SUMMARY TABLE, DEMOCRATIC VOTE FOR PRESIDENT, 1904

Independent Variables	Multiple R	Multiple R^2	Change in R^2	Simple r
Percentage of the population born in Germany, Bohemia, Ireland, or Poland, 1900	0.66992	0.44879		+0.66992
Mean income per farm, 1899	0.74315	0.55228	0.10349	+0.52279
Percentage of the population living in incorporated areas, 1900	0.74331	0.55251	0.00023	+0.12484

TABLE 22. STEPWISE MULTIPLE REGRESSION SUMMARY TABLE, POPULIST VOTE FOR PRESIDENT, 1904

Independent Variables	Multiple R	Multiple R^2	Change in R^2	Simple
Mean income per farm, 1899	0.64951	0.42187		−0.64951
Percentage of the population living in incorporated areas, 1900	0.71596	0.51260	0.09074	−0.45968
Percentage of the population born in Germany, Bohemia, Ireland, or Poland, 1900	0.75449	0.56925	0.05665	−0.43907

a second and third variable to the regression equations does not substantially alter the multiple correlation in either case.

Voting Behavior: Ticket-splitting and Party-switching

The election of 1904 saw widespread ticket-splitting for both president and governor, to an extent unparalleled over the previous twenty years. Table 23 summarizes patterns of ticket-splitting from 1888 to 1904. Three instances of ticket-splitting stand out in this table—the presidential election of 1892 and the presidential and gubernatorial elections of 1904. Although ticket-splitting in the 1892 presidential election was a ploy by Democratic leaders to deprive Harrison of Nebraska's electoral votes by throwing Democratic votes to Weaver, in 1904 the initiative came not from party leaders but from the voters.

This trend toward ticket-splitting seems to derive both from a decline in the intensity of party commitments and from the multiple, crosscutting determinants of party preference. Between 1890 and 1896, as many as half of Nebraska's voters broke loose from previous commitments. The new Populist party garnered up to 40 percent of the vote, and the two old parties both developed schismatic wings, then regrouped. The process of disintegration was actually encouraged by those party leaders who urged their constituents to cross party boundaries—Governor Boyd in 1892 and Edward Rosewater in 1893 and 1894, to mention only two prominent examples. This loosening of party loyalties, as has been observed by political analysts, is a necessary precondition for realignment, as voters first are shaken loose from one party, then move to the other.[9] For some voters, however, the loosening of the early 1890s was never followed by the reestablishment of loyalties as

TABLE 23. TICKET-SPLITTING IN PRESIDENTIAL AND GUBERNATORIAL ELECTIONS, 1886–1904

Office	Year	Number of Votes Difference between Vote for Party Candidate for Office Specified and Index of Party Strength[a]				Percentage of Split Tickets[b]			
		Republican	Democrat	Populist	All Parties	Republican	Democrat	Populist	All Parties
President	1888	+2,507	-56	—	+2,853	+2.3	-0.0	—	+1.4
	1892	+6,345	-22,688	+21,807	+4,331	+7.2	-47.6	+26.2	+2.2
	1896	+5,974	+7,299		+8,993	+5.8	+6.3		+4.0
	1900	+6,403	+2,471		+8,133	+5.3	+2.2		+3.4
	1904	+15,669	-15,771[c]		+981	+11.3	-16.7[c]		+0.4
Governor	1886	+726	-668	—	-601	+0.9	-1.2	—	-0.4
	1888	-1,935	+4,822		-354	-1.8	+5.6		-0.2
	1890	-5,226	+7,300	-467	+724	-7.1	+10.2	-0.7	+0.3
	1892	-2,456	-3,436	+7,290	+1,598	-3.0	-7.2	+2.6	+0.8
	1894	-1,934	+14,692		+3,672	-2.0	+15.0		+1.8
	1896	-2,367	+7,715		+2,582	-2.4	+6.6		+1.2
	1898	+1,230	+1,117		+2,223	+1.3	+1.2		+1.2
	1900	-1,553	+1,476		-316	-1.3	+1.3		-0.1
	1902	-2,822	+6,085		+1,876	-2.8	+6.7		+1.0
	1904	-11,178	+14,358		+1,144	-9.1	+14.0		+0.6

[a]The index of party strength is calculated by taking the mean of the votes cast for the following statewide offices: lieutenant governor, secretary of state, treasurer, auditor, attorney general, superintendent of public instruction, and commissioner of public lands and buildings.

[b]The percentage of split tickets is derived by expressing the difference between the index of party strength and the vote for the party's candidate for the office specified as a proportion of the larger of the two. Thus a positive percentage indicates the proportion of the presidential (or gubernatorial) candidate's voters who presumably did not support his party's candidates for less significant offices. A negative percentage indicates the proportion of voters for minor offices who scratched the head of the ticket. This is actually a minimal measure of ticket-splitting, for it assumes that those voters who support the head of the ticket will normally support that party's candidates for minor offices, or that the voters who support a party ticket for minor offices will normally vote for the head of the ticket. This method measures only deviations from that basic assumption.

[c]Based upon the combined vote for both Parker (Democrat) and Watson (Populist).

durable as those that had been broken. This general weakening of party commitments may well have been the end result of the intensity of multiple, crosscutting political determinants.

In the late 1880s, voters divided largely along the single axis of the ethnocultural struggle over prohibition. The emergence of Populism in 1890 added economic and urban-rural lines of cleavage, but the individual voter seems to have still been guided by a single determinant: low-income farmers voted Populist, antiprohibitionists voted Democratic, and most of the others voted Republican. Fusion changed this by producing a set of candidates embodying two or three dimensions, and as a result, some voters were increasingly susceptible to cross-pressures. These voters would be the most likely possibilities for ticket-splitting, perhaps being attracted to a candidate on the basis of one issue, but to a party on the basis of another. At a presidential level, between 1896 and 1904, it was the charismatic candidates—Bryan in 1896 and Roosevelt in 1904—who most clearly exerted this pull on voters.

Although the 1904 presidential election saw far more ticket-splitting than did that of 1896, the 1896 results do illustrate exactly the pattern described—counties where key determinants of voting behavior coincided were least likely to exhibit ticket-splitting, and those where determinants showed the greatest potential conflict were likely to have larger numbers of split tickets. In 1896 both Bryan and McKinley ran ahead of their tickets, drawing from the vote of the minor party presidential candidates in high-income ritualistic areas—exactly the sort of area where determinants conflicted and voters were caught by cross-pressures. Apparently Gold Democrats bolted the head of their ticket to support McKinley in urban areas and Bryan in rural ones. McKinley ran least ahead of his ticket in low-income counties, and Bryan ran least ahead of his ticket both in rural low-income counties and in urban pietistic counties—areas where determinants coincided for most voters.

Before examining the ticket-splitting of 1904, we must turn our attention to another symptom of multiple, crosscutting determinants of party preferences—the decay of the fusion coalition. Among the sixty-one counties examined, the fusion party vote in 1896 averaged 52 percent and the Republican party vote 44 percent; by 1904 this had more than reversed, with fusionists averaging 41 percent and Republicans getting 54 percent. Even though the sturdy coattails of Roosevelt somewhat skewed the 1904 election, the pattern that year was only an intensification of what had been occurring over the previous eight years, as is illustrated by the mean fusion party vote among the sixty-one counties:

1896	52.3%
1898	51.8%
1900	49.2%
1902	45.5%
1904	41.3%

One major factor in the decay of the fusion coalition is the gradual reduction of the importance of both farm income and the urban-rural dimension as major dividing lines of voter preference, and some gradual return to ethnicity as the primary determinant. This pattern can be seen if we compile a crude significance measure for each independent variable by subtracting the mean party vote in the counties measuring highest in that attribute from the mean party vote in the counties measuring lowest in that attribute. The more closely this measure approaches zero, the less significant that attribute seems to be in determining party affiliation; the further the difference departs from zero, the more significant. Table 24 presents these results for each party vote between 1896 and 1904 and for the 1904 presidential vote.[10]

The same pattern—increased salience for the ethnic variable, reduced salience for the rural-urban dimension, greatly reduced salience for farm income—can be clearly seen by employing the approach introduced with figures 1 and 2. Figure 3 shows Republican gains and fusion losses on the same sort of square grid employed in figures 1 and 2. We see that Republican gains (and fusion losses) were concentrated in the most rural/most pietistic quadrant; the dividing line between changing and more stable cells is a diagonal almost perpendicular to the band dividing the two parties in 1898 (see figs. 1 and 2). Exactly the same sort of pattern exists when farm income is substituted for the urban-rural dimension. Republican campaign strategists, it seems, concentrated their attention upon rural pietists as the most vulnerable part of the fusion coalition. In rolling back the fusion support there, the GOP was willing to accept a stable situation among urban ritualists—in fact, to accept slight losses in urban areas.

All these different forms of analysis point to the same conclusion: Republican gains and fusion losses were most pronounced among rural, low-income pietists. Why should this be so? Why did Republicans fail to extend their gains in urban areas from the 1890s? In part the answer seems to lie in the reduction of urban-rural tensions that accompanied the generally improved situation of agriculture after 1896. Prices were up, though the legacy of the 1890s remained in the form of extremely high rates of farm tenancy in many parts of the state. Data on indebtedness and mortgage rates were not collected by McKinley's Census Bureau in 1900, and so we do not know if

TABLE 24. SIGNIFICANCE MEASURES, THREE INDEPENDENT VARIABLES, 1896–1904

Dependent Variables	Ethnicity[a]		Urban-Rural Dimension[b]		Farm Income[c]	
	Fusion	Republican	Fusion	Republican	Fusion	Republican
Index of party strength						
1896	+0.3	−2.5	−9.2	+8.7	−5.5	+3.9
1898	+1.6	−1.5	−7.3	+7.1	−3.4	+3.7
1900	+3.1	−2.3	−5.0	+5.7	−2.5	+2.3
1902	+3.2	−3.1	−5.4	+4.8	−1.4	+2.9
1904	+5.4	−4.2	−5.5	+4.4	+0.3	+1.0
Presidential vote in 1904	+14.2[d]		+3.3[d]		+13.0[d]	
		−3.8		+3.9		+1.1
	−9.5[e]		−8.6[e]		−12.9[e]	

Note: This measure of the significance of each varable is derived by (1) dividing the total number of counties into quartiles for each independent variable and calculating the mean index of party strength or presidential vote for each quartile, then (2) subtracting the mean index of party strength (or presidential vote) in the lowest quartile from that in the highest quartile. The *sign* of the result indicates the direction of the relationship; that is, a positive sign indicates that the party (or presidential) vote is highest in the highest quartile and a negative sign indicates that the vote is highest in the lowest quartile. The *size* of the result indicates the relative importance of the independent variable in explaining variation in voting behavior; that is the larger the result, the more important that independent variable is. The *direction* of the result over time indicates the changing importance of the particular independent variable; for example, if the sign of the result remains constant and the size of the result increases over time, then that particular variable is of increasing importance for understanding voting behavior.

[a]"Ethnicity" is based upon the percentage of the population born in Germany, Bohemia, Ireland, or Poland, in 1900. A positive result indicates that the party was stronger among ritualistic groups.

[b]"Urban-rural dimension" is based upon the percentage of the population living in incorporated areas in 1900. A positive result indicates that the party was stronger in more urban areas.

[c]"Farm income" is based upon the mean farm income in 1899. A positive result indicates that the party was stronger in more prosperous areas.

[d]Vote for Alton B. Parker, the Democratic candidate.

[e]Vote for Tom Watson, the Populist candidate.

there was any significant improvement in that area.[11] At any rate, this improvement in the situation of agriculture was likely a necessary precondition for Republican gains in rural areas, aided perhaps by such dramatic Rooseveltian actions as the Northern Securities case of early 1902.

The reduction of urban-rural tensions coincided with an increase in the agitation of the prohibition issue. The state Anti-Saloon League, founded in

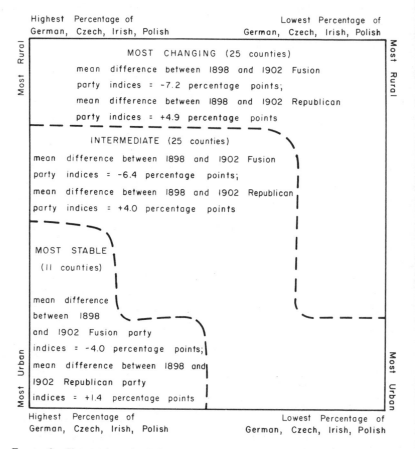

FIGURE 3. Changes in voting behavior, 1898–1902, counties distributed by ethnicity and degree of urbanization.

1897, was trumpeting its cause up and down the state, and Governor Mickey's membership in the League was well known. Mickey, who canceled the 1903 inaugural ball because he disapproved of dancing, was also well known in Methodist lay circles, and his supporters felt that they gained voter support through advertising these church and temperance connections; one of his supporters in 1902 attributed Mickey's victory to "the Lord and the Methodists."[12] At the same time the GOP was emphasizing the personal righteousness of its leading candidate, fusionists in 1902 selected as their gubernatorial candidate the first Democrat to receive that honor since the consummation of fusion in 1894. Populists sympathetic to temperance were now thrust on the horns of a dilemma—should they vote for Mickey, the Republican, whose religion and personal views on temperance coincided with their own, or should they vote for a candidate handpicked by Bryan but known to oppose the cold water reform? Enough voters chose the former to change certain patterns of gubernatorial voting. In 1900 the fusion candidate for governor had run most strongly in rural, ritualistic counties and next most strongly in rural, pietistic counties. In 1902 Mickey, with the help of the Lord and the Methodists, picked up enough support from rural pietistic areas to reorder this and to push the mean Republican vote for governor in those areas ahead of that in urban, ritualistic counties. In these rural, pietistic counties, Mickey's gains were concentrated in low-income areas—areas that had been a major source of support for Populism and that had been most resistant to Republican inroads since 1894. Although the mean Republican vote for governor over all sixty-one counties increased from 47.6 percent in 1900 to 49.7 percent in 1902, the vote in five urban, ritualistic counties actually *fell* slightly, from a mean of 49.9 percent in 1900 to a mean of 47.3 percent in 1902.

We now turn our attention to the election of 1904 and the ticket-splitting that took place then. Roosevelt ran strongly ahead of his party ticket in all areas, but the distribution of the Republican presidential vote closely parallels the distribution of the Republican party vote. Roosevelt ran best in the urban, high-income, pietistic counties that had been the center of Republican strength over the previous decade; he ran most poorly in the rural, ritualistic counties that had been the fusion bedrock. But ticket-splitting ran in exactly the opposite direction—Roosevelt ran most ahead of his ticket in the most rural and most ritualistic counties. And, controlling for both the urban-rural and the ethnic values dimensions, Roosevelt ran more strongly in low-income rural counties than in high-income rural counties. His coattails were sufficiently broad to shift the party vote in these low-income rural counties as well. Apparently Roosevelt's much-publicized trust-busting and such measures as the Elkins Act convinced some marginal farmers to switch to the GOP. George Berge, the personally temperate German-American whom the Populists forced upon the Democrats as the fusion gubernatorial candidate in 1904, conducted his campaign largely on the issue of railroad influence in state politics and ran considerably ahead of his ticket in most areas. There is virtually no relationship between the ticket-splitting that aided Berge and that which pushed the Roosevelt vote above the Republican ticket—the coefficient of correlation between Berge's margin over the 1904 fusion party vote and Roosevelt's edge over his 1904 party vote is a low +0.26.

We must now turn from the voters at the grassroots to the political leaders before attempting a summary of the key characteristics of the political system.

Political Leadership

Data were collected for 661 political leaders who were prominent at a state level from 1896 through 1904: 346 Republicans and 315 fusionists, of whom 160 were Populists, 125 were Democrats, 13 were Silver Republicans, and 17 were identified only as fusionists. Table 25 summarizes data on occupation and place of origin for Republicans, Populists, and Democrats. Table 26 summarizes various other biographical information for the same groups.[13] As in the earlier periods, the collective characteristics of this leadership group show Republicans and Democrats most sharply different with regard to such variables as place of origin, religion, and Union Army service. Populists, in collective profile, tend to fall between the characteristics of the two older parties on these measures and to differ most sharply from both with regard to occupation.

The typical Republican who emerges from this data looked very much like his predecessors in the 1880s and early 1890s—he was about forty-five years of age, a lawyer or banker or merchant, a Methodist or Presbyterian or Congregationalist, had probably attended a state university, was a Mason, and likely belonged to local commercial or booster associations. His occupation, religion, education, and Masonic membership would clearly place him in the top levels of the socioeconomic structure of his community. (And he was most definitely a "he." Both women in the sample were Populists.) The typical Democrat also looked rather much like his predecessors in the 1880s and early 1890s—he was about forty years old, likely of Irish or German descent and perhaps a Catholic, was a lawyer or banker or merchant, had attended college, belonged to a fraternal lodge, and took part in professional and commercial associations in the community. His religion, ethnicity, lodge memberships, and other activities might put him in a level below the social standing of his Republican counterpart in some communities in the state, although certainly not in the communities where his ethnicity and religion were not atypical. The typical Populist was about forty-five years old, was a farmer, may have been either Methodist, Presbyterian, Baptist, or Catholic, and had probably attended a small church college or a normal school if he had any college at all; his associational affiliations tended to farm groups or perhaps a fraternal lodge. His charac-

TABLE 25. PERCENTAGE DISTRIBUTION OF NEBRASKA POLITICAL LEADERS
BY OCCUPATION AND PLACE OF BIRTH, 1896–1904

Characteristics	Republicans	Populists	Democrats
Occupation	N=346	N=160	N=125
Agriculture	26.6%	64.4%	23.2%
The professions			
Law	22.0	11.3	19.2
Journalism	3.2	6.9	8.8
Total, professions	30.6	23.1	33.6
Business			
Merchandising	12.7	5.6	13.6
Finance	19.4	0.0	16.8
Total, business	39.0	7.5	36.8
All other occupations	3.8	5.0	6.4
Place of origin[a]			
Regions of U.S.	N=346	N=160	N=125
New England	4.1%	3.8%	1.6%
Middle Atlantic	16.5	17.5	8.0
Middle West	46.8	43.7	32.8
Border	2.0	5.0	5.6
Confederate South	1.7	3.8	5.6
Total U.S.	71.1	73.8	53.6
Outside U.S.			
Germany	6.7	8.1	16.8
Ireland	4.0	6.3	17.6
Scandinavia	5.5	3.1	3.2
British	9.8	5.0	2.4
Total, outside U.S.	28.9	25.6	44.0
Unspecified	0.0	0.6	2.4

[a]Based on place of birth, parent's place of birth, and surname.

teristics would place him well below the top levels of the social structure of
most communities.

The Political System, 1896–1904

The characteristics of the Nebraska political system from 1896 through 1904
continued to be determined largely by the events of the early 1890s. The
coalition of Democrats and Populists produced a fusion in which each party
retained its basic identity, the Populists as agrarian reformers representing
the marginal farmer, the Democrats as ethnic antiprohibitionists, willing to
barter domination of state government for pledges not to agitate the liquor

TABLE 26. PERCENTAGE DISTRIBUTION OF NEBRASKA POLITICAL LEADERS BY VARIOUS BIOGRAPHICAL CHARACTERISTICS, 1896–1904

Biographical Characteristics	Republicans	Populists	Democrats
Date of birth	N=346	N=160	N=125
Born before 1841	6.6%	15.0%	7.2%
Born 1841–50	31.8	20.0	18.4
Born 1851–60	38.4	35.0	33.6
Born 1861–70	17.3	24.4	32.8
Born after 1870	3.5	4.4	4.8
Unspecified	2.3	1.2	3.2
Union Army service among			
leaders born 1836–45	65.7%	46.2%	16.7%
Attendance at or graduation from			
college or normal school	37.0%	28.1%	43.2%
Associational memberships	N=126	N=55	N=47
Grand Army of the Republic	14.3%	9.1%	0.0%
Mason	60.3	16.4	31.9
Other fraternal lodges	65.9	43.6	55.3
Professional and commercial			
organizations	23.8	10.9	40.4
Agricultural societies	4.0	14.5	0.0
Farmer's Alliance	0.8	50.9	2.1
Religious affiliations	N=85	N=41	N=25
Baptist	4.7%	12.2%	4.0%
Disciples of Christ	0.0	9.8	0.0
Methodist	27.1	19.5	12.0
Presbyterian	21.2	14.6	12.0
Congregational	16.5	4.9	8.0
Episcopal	4.7	2.4	8.0
Lutheran	8.2	0.0	12.0
Roman Catholic	1.1	14.6	36.0
All others	16.5	21.9	8.0

Note: Data for date of birth and religious affiliations may not add to 100 owing to rounding. Percentages for associational memberships and for religious affiliations are based on the number of people indicating memberships or affiliations rather than on total number of subjects. Percentages for associational memberships will not add to 100 because of multiple memberships.

issue. Republican party rhetoric largely avoided controversial issues to focus on the question of prosperity—to claim credit for it and to indict the fusionists for threatening it. Imperialism was a prominent issue for only a short time. Few Republicans—no prominent ones by 1900—opposed the course of empire; Populists were the most vociferous opponents, followed closely by their Democratic allies.

Fusionists used the powers of the attorney general's office to attempt to make operative the maximum freight rates passed in 1893, and they also sought—for the most part without success—to extend regulation to stockyards, grain elevators, telephone and telegraph companies, express companies, hail insurance companies, and meat-packing companies. Populists favored state ownership of the stockyards, and both fusion parties agreed on municipal ownership of public utilities. Both parties likewise agreed on support for the initiative and referendum, the direct primary, and the direct election of United States senators. Republicans said little about regulation aside from occasional diatribes against the evils of monopoly, and, though Republican legislatures did enact a few minor regulatory measures, most fusion proposals along those lines were met with bloc Republican opposition. Republicans, instead, focused their major attention on tax reform, and in 1903 they produced a measure that replaced locally elected tax assessors with county officials. Fusionists consistently railed against corporations' granting of special privileges to public officials—especially free railroad passes—but Republicans maintained a discreet silence on that subject.[14]

The fusion coalition, forecast by widespread Democratic voter desertion to the Populists before 1894, became increasingly difficult to maintain in state conventions at the same time that voters were shifting their loyalties. The general pattern of voting behavior through the period 1896–1904 was for fusion loyalties to be most secure in rural and ritualistic counties and Republican strength to be concentrated in urban and pietistic counties. As political rhetoric came to focus more on ethnic issues in 1902 and 1904, voters in regions with conflicting political determinants—especially in rural pietistic counties—slowly shifted their party preferences. By 1904 the Republicans seemed to have the loyalty of most voters, although the Republican leadership was frequently wracked by power disputes and scandals.

By the end of 1904 most of the leaders of Nebraska's first progressive era had emerged—Bryan, Ashton C. Shallenberger, and James Dahlman for the Democrats, and Elmer Burkett, George W. Norris, Norris Brown, and George L. Sheldon for the Republicans. At the same time, the Civil War generation seemed to have finally passed from the political scene. Charles Gere of the *State Journal* died in 1904, and Edward Rosewater was to die two years later; Senators Paddock and Manderson were dead or retired; Church Howe and Tom Majors were gone; John H. Mickey was the last Civil War veteran to occupy the governor's mansion. The handful of Democrats who had nurtured the party from territorial days—Morton, Miller, Boyd, Vifquain, and their fellows—were dead or in retirement. The presidential election of 1904, and the pitifully attended Populist state conventions of 1902 and 1903, seemed to convince many Democrats that they were the strongest partner in the fusion coalition. Likewise, the ticket-splitting of 1904, working to the advantage of Roosevelt at a presidential level and anti–free pass crusader George Berge at a gubernatorial level, could not have helped but persuade political leaders of the extent to which the electorate was increasingly receptive to strong personal campaigns dedicated to ''progressive'' reforms.

CHAPTER SEVEN

Nebraska Progressivism, 1905–15:
Campaigns, Issues, and Personalities

All the candidates of all parties if we
may believe them, are progressive. . . .
All stand for doing mighty things,
Despising tricks and trades;
The most of them are sprouting wings
Upon their shoulder blades.
                    J. L. Bixby, 1912

Beginning about 1905, Nebraska politics entered what
may be called its first progressive period. Campaign rhetoric became
oriented more to specific state issues and, at the same time, more to the
personalities of leading candidates. In the four statewide contests of 1906,
1908, 1910, and 1912, Republican party strength (based on the vote for
minor statewide candidates) averaged 50.5 percent, and Democratic
strength averaged 45.8 percent. Republican and Democratic candidates for
governor both averaged exactly 49.4 percent. No incumbent governor or
United States senator was reelected during these years, though every incumbent sought reelection. Republicans controlled both legislative houses in
1905 and 1907, Democrats had majorities in both houses in 1909 and
1911, and the 1913 session was split, Republicans controlling the senate,
Democrats the house. Intraparty competition was equally intense. After
1906, party nominations resulted from primary elections, and only once
between 1907 and 1914 was a major party nomination for governor or United
States senator uncontested. The incumbent Democratic governor was denied
renomination in the 1910 primary, and the incumbent Republican United
States senator was defeated in the 1912 primary. The 1912 presidential
primary saw three serious contenders in each party—Roosevelt, La Follette,

and Taft in the Republican primary, Wilson, Clark, and Harmon in the Democratic.[1]

During this period, state politics came to focus on the regulation of business practices and of personal morality. Measures extending popular democracy—the direct primary, popular election of United States senators, the initiative and referendum—were embraced by most political leaders. Most leaders were similarly agreed on the necessity for at least some business regulation; the state legislature established employer liability, prohibited the use of railroad passes by public officials, regulated railroad rates (all in 1907), guaranteed bank deposits and established food inspection (both in 1909), and passed other measures regulating business in the interests of employees, consumers, and the general public.[2]

Efforts to regulate morality focused on restricting the liquor traffic. Other so-called moral issues—the prohibition of cigarettes, the tightening of divorce laws, or the forbidding of Sunday baseball games—were agitated in some circles, but the liquor issue came increasingly to the fore. The state Anti-Saloon League was founded in 1897. Denigrated by a Prohibition party leader in 1899 as "a namby-pamby-republican affair," within ten years the League developed more political power than the Prohibition party had ever exercised. By 1908, some 450 of Nebraska's towns and villages had "gone dry" under the provisions of the state local option law, and the Anti-Saloon League and other temperance advocates began to devote their considerable talents to the enactment of a county option law as a step to statewide prohibition. The growing temperance thrust provoked a counterreaction on the part of the liquor interests and other opponents of prohibition. A state Personal Liberty League was formed, followed by the establishment of a state German-American Alliance in 1910. The battle over alcohol raged through the state's politics for a decade, with the issue of county option increasingly prominent from 1907, when Governor Sheldon called for passage of such a law, through 1910, when that issue dominated state elections. Rejection of county option by the 1911 legislature prompted temperance forces to turn their efforts to securing statewide prohibition, a drive that culminated in the passage of a prohibition amendment to the state constitution in 1916.[3]

The prohibition drive spawned and encouraged other conflicts. In 1910 a constitutional amendment was proposed to limit the suffrage to fully naturalized citizens; at that time any alien with his first papers could vote, and many of these voting aliens opposed prohibition. When voters estab-lished the statewide initiative and referendum in 1912, it had wide support as an extension of direct democracy, but some opponents saw it as a device to secure temperance reforms. Woman suffrage came before the voters in 1914, and both supporters and opponents saw it as a device to increase the pro-prohibition electorate.[4]

In 1906, Republicans embraced the candidacy of George L. Sheldon for governor and Norris Brown for United States senator, and with them their antirailroad campaign. Sheldon and Brown had stumped the state beginning in early spring, lambasting railroad control of state politics. Never before had preconvention candidates taken their cause so directly to the people; Republicans seeking a nomination had traveled the state before but had limited their talking to local party leaders. The 1906 state Republican nominating convention became, in effect, a statewide popular referendum on Sheldon and Brown. Brown's chief opponent was Edward Rosewater, leader of the GOP antimonopolists throughout the 1880s but generally regular since the late 1890s. Brown won nomination on the sixth ballot and Sheldon on the second, with their support essentially the same. The Republican platform came from the mold used by the GOP in Wisconsin and Iowa, demanding a stringent antipass law, the direct primary, direct election of United States senators, an elective state railroad commission, an employer-liability law, and a new method of assessing railroad property for tax purposes.[5] The Nebraska GOP had, somewhat belatedly, joined the antirailroad crusade.

The Republican campaign of 1906 built upon the antirailroad orientation of the convention. Sheldon and Brown made extensive speaking tours, claiming that the election of Sheldon and of the Republican legislature necessary to elect Brown would mean the elimination of railroad influence in state politics. Republican newspapers compared Sheldon to La Follette and, late in the campaign, charged that the railroads were issuing passes in support of Sheldon's opponent. Sheldon, Brown, the Republican statehouse ticket, and Republican majorities in both legislative houses swept to victory. The new legislature approved the direct primary, a child labor act, an antipass act, a two cent per mile railroad passenger fare, a railroad antidiscrimination act, a railroad employer-liability act, and a state board of pardons. Republican newspapers were jubilant in their praise of the legislature's accomplishments. Even the Democratic *World-Herald* joined the praise with the opinion that it was the best legislature in the history of the state.[6]

Sheldon carried the banner of Republican progressivism into the 1908 election. Unopposed in the primary, he nonetheless found the state convention unwilling to draft a platform in full accord with his wishes. The

Democrats and their candidate for governor, Ashton C. Shallenberger, favored a state law establishing a bank deposit guaranty system. Sheldon also favored such a law, but the Republican state convention refused to endorse his proposal. Opposition spokesmen took care to point out that bankers had been very active in the convention and that, of the seven members of the resolutions committee, three were bank presidents and the other four were bank directors or stockholders. Leading Republican newspapers opposed the guaranty plan, though Sheldon continued to endorse it. Republicans based their campaign largely on the record of the Roosevelt administration and on the accomplishments of the 1907 legislature, with some Republicans also claiming that the Democrats in general, and Shallenberger in particular, were dominated by liquor and saloon interests.[7]

In 1910 some Republicans, including Victor Rosewater (who controlled the *Bee* after his father's death in 1906) and Senator Elmer Burkett, apparently undertook to return the party to regular control. The two leading candidates for the nomination for governor, Chester A. Aldrich and A. E. Cady, progressive and regular, were also, respectively, for and against county option. The Republican convention added to their platform, from the floor, endorsements of county option and of Republican congressional insurgency, and Aldrich won the primary. When James C. Dahlman won the Democratic primary and continued his wringing wet campaign for governor into the general election, Aldrich and the Republicans concentrated more and more on the liquor issue. Republican identification with the cause of county option extended through the legislative contests. Of 133 Republican legislative nominees, 91 (68 percent) announced in favor of county option and only 20 (15 percent) announced in opposition; outside Douglas County (including Omaha), only 8 of 113 Republican legislative candidates opposed county option. Republican campaigners focused almost solely on the liquor issue and on the personality of Dahlman. The *State Journal* described him as ''an ignorant man . . . carousing, poker playing, gun playing . . . inherently lawless'' and as ''an unbalanced ignoramus.'' Other Republicans delighted in noting that Dahlman had originally come to Nebraska under an assumed name, fleeing Texas after a shooting. In the 1911 legislature, the identification of the GOP with temperance was reinforced when fifty-three of the sixty-six votes for county option and only six of the sixty-five opposing votes came from Republicans.[8]

Progressive Republicans had dominated the party since 1906, and this continued in 1912, but the effort by the regulars to regain control culminated in two rival state organizations that year. Sentiment for La Follette surfaced early, with the establishment of a La Follette League in September 1911, led by former congressman J. J. McCarthy and including Charles O. Whedon, who had sought to replace Burkett as the Republican senatorial nominee in 1910, and J. R. McCarl, Congressman George W. Norris's administrative assistant. Governor Aldrich initially declared for La Follette, but in February of 1912 he joined six other Republican governors in appealing to Roosevelt to enter the primaries. Roosevelt won the presidential primary, Aldrich was renominated for governor over a regular opponent, Congressman Norris defeated Senator Brown for the senatorial nomination, and R. Beecher Howell, a Roosevelt supporter, was elected national committeeman over Victor Rosewater, supporting Taft. Rosewater was chairman of the national convention, but most Nebraska delegates bolted to Roosevelt. Offered a position on the Progressive party committee on organization, Aldrich declined any such formal identification with the new party, preferring to operate within the state Republican organization. Under his chairmanship, the state Republican convention nominated six electors pledged to Roosevelt and two to Taft. A number of delegates bolted, led by Victor Rosewater, lame-duck senator Norris Brown, and the other ninety Douglas County delegates. Taft supporters held their own state convention, and a separate Progressive state convention was also held. The GOP national committee recognized the Taft bolters, and the Progressive national committee channeled its efforts through the Progressive party, whose state chairman, F. P. Corrick, had been secretary of the La Follette League and had been narrowly defeated for the chairmanship of the Aldrich branch of the state GOP. All three state organizations approved the Republican nominees for state offices, although five of them, including Aldrich and Norris, supported Roosevelt and five supported Taft. The Progressives also endorsed the six Roosevelt electors nominated by the Aldrich branch of the Republican state convention and added two Roosevelt electors of their own. In the end, the state supreme court resolved the problem of electors by awarding the designation "Republican" to the Taft electors and specifying that the Roosevelt electors could not use that name; they went on the ballot as Progressives. All state-level GOP primary winners were designated on the ballot as Republican and Progressive, but separate Progressive congressional candidates ran in the first and second districts; Progressives occasionally endorsed Democratic candidates for the state legislature. The campaign focused almost solely on national issues, though Aldrich came under attack for being too preoccupied with national politics to tend to the business of the state.[9]

The defeats of Roosevelt and Aldrich in 1912 helped to end Nebraska's first progressive era. The Progressive party fielded a full state ticket in 1914, endorsed leading Republican nominees in 1916, then quietly disappeared.

Some Republican progressive leaders remained, notably George W. Norris and R. Beecher Howell, but when Nebraska entered its second progressive period, in about 1922, it was under different leadership, with different goals and a different organizational structure. The state GOP, however, did not suddenly turn conservative—indeed, Republican conservatives did not regain full control until the exodus of leading progressives into the camp of the second Roosevelt in the 1930s.[10]

Most of the reforms labeled "progressive" had been promoted by the Bryan Democrats and their Populist allies for well over a decade before 1906. Nebraska Democrats were united on progressivism; conservatives had lost power, and some had left the party in 1894. In 1906 and 1908 all leading state Democrats united behind Bryan and Bryanite reforms. By 1912, however, the party had divided into a number of competing factions, Bryan had been repudiated by a large element of his own state party, and he had in turn repudiated the gubernatorial candidacy of one of his oldest and most active supporters, James C. Dahlman.

The 1906 Democratic convention marked the assertion of Democratic dominance within the fusion coalition. George W. Berge, the Populist who had been the 1904 fusion candidate for governor, sought the 1906 nomination and had strong support in the Democratic convention, most notably from Christian Gruenther and the Platte County delegation. A majority of the Democratic delegates, however, preferred to place one of their own at the head of the ticket, and Ashton C. Shallenberger, a Bryan activist from 1896 and a former congressman, was nominated on the first ballot. The Populists balked at accepting Shallenberger until, after an all-night session, agreement was reached at 8:30 A.M., after many Populist delegates had gone home. Populist representation on the ticket was limited to nominees for auditor, land commissioner, and two of the three railroad commissioners. William H. Thompson, Democrat and longtime Bryan enthusiast, was nominated for the United States Senate. The fusion campaign urged that Shallenberger and the other fusion nominees were better able to carry out the reform measures espoused by both parties, and it parodied Republican conversion to reform principles: " 'Reform' must be left to that party which, throughout its years of power, has fastened the burdensome evils upon us. The tariff must be revised by friends of the tariff; the trusts must be regulated only by the friends of the trusts; the cure of corruption must be entrusted to the authors of corruption."[11]

Democrats enthusiastically praised the work of the 1907 legislature but at the same time set out upon a thorough statewide organization drive that would eventually bring them to power. Key roles fell to Christian Gruenther and Arthur F. Mullen. Gruenther had led the Berge forces in the 1906 Democratic convention. Mullen was a former Populist who switched to the Democratic party sometime between 1904 and 1906; he had established his political credentials by successfully organizing the sprawling ten-county Fifteenth Judical District in 1907. Of this, he later boasted: "The Populists had not gone back into the Republican Party. In Valley County I found every man in the courthouse anti-Republican, but not yet Democratic. I moved them, lock, stock and barrel, over into the Democratic party. To a less degree this condition held through the district. Election day was moving day." Mullen's efforts elected the two district judges, seven county treasurers, nine sheriffs, and all ten county clerks. Two months later Bryan requested him to undertake a similar organization effort state-wide. In establishing the Bryan Volunteers, Mullen spent nine months, traveled thirty thousand miles, and went into all but six of the state's ninety counties. In about a third of these counties there had been no Democratic organization or candidates for years; Mullen organized or reorganized, in all, seventy counties. His technique, according to his autobiography, "was repetition of what I had done in the Fifteenth Judical District . . .take over the Populists." Gruenther superintended administrative details, initially from Columbus, later from Lincoln.[12]

In the 1908 primaries, Shallenberger won the Democratic nomination for governor, and George W. Berge won that of the Populists. Berge declined to run without the Democratic nomination, and the Populist state committee nominated Shallenberger. The same procedure allowed all the Democratic nominees for state offices to go on the ballot as Democratic and People's Independent. Bryan received the full support of all prominent state Democrats in his third presidential bid, and "Shall the People Rule?" became the campaign watchword. Shallenberger and the Democratic convention urged a state bank guaranty system. It was claimed that, in some rural counties, Democratic organization was so thorough that all Bryan-Shallenberger voters were known and all Democrats' automobiles committed to ferrying voters to the polls. The Mullen organization and the bank guaranty issue carried the day as Bryan, Shallenberger, three of six congressional nominees, and majorities in both legislative houses swept to victory. Mullen became state oil inspector, the chief patronage post in the new administration, and also acted as Shallenberger's liaison to the 1909 legislature.[13]

Shallenberger and Mullen, his "special advisor on legislation," secured passage of the bank guaranty law in a near-straight party vote:

	House Yea Nay	Senate Yea Nay	Total Yea Nay
Republicans	7 23	— 12	7 35
Democrats and fusionists	65 —	19 —	84 —

The new law established a system of compulsory insurance payments by all state-chartered banks, creating a fund to reimburse depositors in any failed state-chartered bank. Other bills established sanitary inspection of food and food sellers, an open primary, and the "Oregon Pledge Law." The Oregon Pledge Law, by which candidates for the state legislature could pledge to vote for the popular preference winner for United States senator and have that pledge printed on the ballot, was, like the bank guaranty law, a party measure:

	House Yea Nay	Senate Yea Nay	Total Yea Nay
Republicans	2 28	1 12	3 40
Democrats and fusionists	66 1	19 1	85 2

By these achievements, Democrats laid the foundation for claiming to be the true leaders of the progressive movement in Nebraska.[14]

Shallenberger and Mullen evidently determined to go one step further, to tread the delicate line between disarming the increasingly potent county option drive (and simultaneously laying to rest Republican charges that liquor interests ran the Democratic party) and keeping the support of anti-prohibition Democratic voters. The plan finally drawn up was ingenious—it would not deny any Nebraskan the right to buy liquor, but it would require all saloons to close at 8:00 P.M. Mullen, operating out of the Speaker's office, forced the measure through the legislature with the aid of temperance-minded Republicans:

	House Yea Nay	Senate Yea Nay	Total Yea Nay
Republicans	21 2	12 1	33 3
Democrats and fusionists	31 35	7 12	38 47

Shallenberger emphasized his key role by delaying approval for several days, giving great publicity to the pressure to veto placed on him by the liquor interests, then finally approving the bill.[15]

Shallenberger had hoped to consolidate all the progressive voters in the state behind his leadership by the impressive record of the 1909 legislature and by disarming the potentially divisive liquor issue, but the eight o'clock law splintered his own party. James C. Dahlman, mayor of Omaha and Bryan's choice for national committeeman from 1900 to 1908, refused to enforce the law in Omaha and won reelection as mayor in a campaign in which nonenforcement was the major issue. He then entered the Democratic gubernatorial primary of 1910 in opposition to Shallenberger. Bryan, convinced that the liquor interests had helped defeat him in 1908, came out for county option and urged Shallenberger to call a special legislative session to pass the measure; Shallenberger, aware that it could not pass and that it would be political suicide for him even to propose it, refused. Bryan took his campaign to the state convention and sought to place a county option plank in the state platform, thereby shattering the party. In an emotional session, Bryan lost the support of many of his earliest and most active supporters, including Dahlman, Willis D. Oldham, the chairman of the 1894 state convention that had given control of the party to Bryan, Populist leader Michael F. Harrington, who had always been among the foremost fusion advocates, and William V. Allen, former Populist United States senator. Bryan's proposal was defeated overwhelmingly, 647 to 198. A motion to oppose county option was just as decisively defeated, 638 to 202. A platform plank approving the eight o'clock law and commending Shallenberger for signing it passed 701 to 163. The Shallenberger-Mullen forces were in full control, riding the center between the county optionists on one side and the wringing wets on the other.[16]

The result, however, was to be a Pyrrhic victory for both Bryan and Dahlman. After his rejection by the state convention, Bryan withdrew from active participation in the primary. For some time, he may have considered supporting the primary candidacy of a third person for governor, but apparently an arrangement was made whereby Bryan would stay out of the gubernatorial primary, supporting neither Shallenberger nor Dahlman nor some third candidate, and in return for this neutrality Shallenberger and Mullen would support Richard Metcalfe, Bryan's choice for the nomination for the United States Senate. This in turn forced Dahlman into an alliance with Gilbert M. Hitchcock, publisher of the *World-Herald* and also a candidate for the senatorial nomination. Dahlman and Hitchcock both won, Dahlman narrowly and Hitchcock overwhelmingly.[17] The outcome of the primary meant that Shallenberger's delicate balancing act between the county optionists and the wets had all been for naught. He did win the Populist gubernatorial primary, and many Democrats urged him to make the general election a three-way race. Although there were intimations that he would receive Bryan's support in such a third-party venture, Shallenberger declined the Populist nomination. The Populist state committee, appalled at

Dahlman's outspoken views on temperance, did not fill the vacancy. With the choice between Aldrich and Dahlman, liquor overshadowed all other issues. Bryan, Metcalfe, and other leading temperance Democrats announced they could not support Dahlman. Dahlman promised his supporters a huge free beer party on the capitol lawn to celebrate his election, and with Dahlman as its standard-bearer the Democratic party became the unquestioned opponent of all new restrictions on the sale of alcoholic beverages. Of 133 Democratic candidates for the legislature, 73 (55 percent) announced in opposition to county option and only 33 (25 percent) in favor. Dahlman lost but Hitchcock won, and Democrats won control of the state legislature and took three of the six congressional seats.[18]

The Democrats in the 1911 legislature promoted two institutional reforms designed to eliminate partisanship in certain aspects of state government, one (HR 132) to make the judiciary nonpartisan and the other (SF 324) to place state institutions under a nonpartisan board of control.[19] Both were distinctly party measures:

Vote on HR 132, House	*To Pass*		*To Reconsider*	
	Yea	*Nay*	*Yea*	*Nay*
Republicans	1	42	2	40
Democrats and fusionists	52	1	52	—

Vote on SF 324	*House*		*Senate*		*Total*	
	Yea	*Nay*	*Yea*	*Nay*	*Yea*	*Nay*
Republicans	3	39	4	8	7	47
Democrats and fusionists	52	—	18	—	70	—

The animosity that had developed among the Bryanites, the Shallenberger-Mullen group, and the Hitchcock-Omaha group continued into the 1912 primaries. Bryan's closest lieutenants, his brother Charles and his brother-in-law Thomas S. Allen, began early to promote Wilson's presidential candidacy. Senator Hitchcock and Christian Gruenther organized for Judson Harmon. Shallenberger sought the nomination for the United States Senate, as did William H. Thompson, a longtime Bryan ally. Richard Metcalfe, associate editor of Bryan's *Commoner*, filed for the gubernatorial nomination and was opposed by John H. Morehead, a Falls City banker not associated with either the Bryan or the Hitchcock wing. Morehead's Richardson County associates filed a petition to place Champ Clark in the presidential primary, and, urged by Shallenberger, Arthur Mullen agreed to become Clark's Nebraska manager. Mullen and Shallenberger reasoned that a strong Clark campaign would so divert Bryan's attention from state races that Thompson and Metcalfe would be deprived of Bryan's active support. The strategy succeeded—Clark, Shallenberger, and Morehead all won handily. Mullen had not had time to put together a slate of Clark delegates to run in the primary, but he had extracted from all candidates for delegate except Bryan and one other a pledge to consider the primary outcome binding; after the primary the state committee instructed the delegation for Clark. Bryan's dramatic switch from Clark to Wilson on the thirteenth convention ballot provoked an angry reaction from many Nebraska Democrats, but the state convention, after acrimonious debate, approved a platform plank endorsing Bryan's conduct.[20]

Despite this bitter intraparty fighting, Democrats managed to forge a united front for the general election. Only one prominent Democrat—former Populist Michael F. Harrington—bolted to Roosevelt and the Bull Moose. Democrats who had not taken an active part in party affairs since 1894 contributed to the Wilson campaign, among them John McShane, the 1888 candidate for governor, and T. J. Mahoney, 1895 Gold Democratic candidate for the supreme court. Morehead's campaign generally focused on the need for a full-time businesslike administration of state affairs and for prison reform. Most Democrats saw the Republican schism as an opportunity that must not be lost through intraparty wrangling. Wilson carried Nebraska and Morehead was elected governor, but Shallenberger lost to Norris in the senatorial election.[21]

The most prominent officeholding Democrats in 1912 and after— Hitchcock, Morehead, and the three congressmen—were not members of the Bryan wing of the party, and the Democratic legislatures of 1913, 1915, and 1917 were dominated by the Mullen-Shallenberger-Morehead wing of the party. Morehead won reelection in 1914, and Shallenberger was elected to Congress that year. Bryan's slate was defeated in the 1916 primary, and Mullen was elected national committeeman. Bryan himself lost a bid for election as delegate to the 1916 national convention and thereafter spent less and less time in Nebraska, failing even to vote in 1918 and eventually moving his legal residence to Florida.[22]

The selection of George W. Berge as the fusion candidate for governor in 1904 and his strong showing in the face of the Roosevelt landslide of that year marked the last surge of Populism as an independent political entity. Watson's poor showing in the presidential race and sparse attendance at Populist state conventions convinced many Democrats that they had greatly overestimated Populist strength. Only fifty delegates attended the 1905 state convention, and they accepted a state ticket headed by a Democratic candidate for supreme court and including one Democrat and one Populist nominee for regent. Some 200 to 350 Populists, including many old-time Populist leaders who had not been active for some time, attended the 1906 state convention, the last significant state gathering. The rejection of Berge and the nomination of Shallenberger by the Democrats was a bitter dose for them to swallow. When they demanded all the other spots on the ticket as compensation, the Democrats refused. The angry Populists continued in session all night until the pleading of prominent Populists and Democrats, including Berge himself, convinced them not to nominate a straight Populist ticket and to give a reluctant approval to Shallenberger in return for the nominees for auditor, land commissioner, and two of the three railroad commissioners.[23]

The introduction of the direct primary furthered Populist disintegration. Because the same candidate only rarely won both the Democratic and Populist primaries for statewide office, the years after 1907 saw the repeated enactment of an embarrassing ritual whereby the winner of the Populist primary would decline the nomination and the state committee would then fill the vacancy with the Democratic candidate for that office. The only exceptions to this pattern occurred in 1910. Dahlman did not enter the Populist primary; when Shallenberger, winner of the Populist nomination for governor, declined to run on that ticket alone, the state executive committee voted, 14 to 9, to leave the head of the ticket vacant. In 1910, also, the Democratic nominee for attorney general had not entered the Populist primary and expressed no interest in receiving the party's nomination. The winner of the Populist primary did not decline and made the race as a Populist. In both 1908 and 1912, the Populist state organization gave their party nominations for elector to candidates pledged to Bryan and Wilson, respectively, disregarding actions by Populist national conventions.[24]

A number of leading Populists bolted their party during this period of decline. In 1906 former Populist governor William A. Poynter endorsed Sheldon, as did such formerly Populist newspapers as the Greeley *Citizen* and the Schuyler *Quill*. In 1908 most prominent Populists united behind Bryan and backed the state ticket as a show of support for the Peerless Leader. General James Weaver and James H. "Cyclone" Davis spoke for Bryan in Nebraska. Between 1908 and 1910, Bryan's increasing attraction to temperance legislation brought several leading Populists, including Michael F. Harrington and William H. Dech, into the Democratic party to oppose Bryan's temperance thrust. Harrington had been active in Populist politics for many years and had been a candidate for elector in 1896 and 1908; Dech was the 1890 Populist candidate for lieutenant governor and a candidate for Congress in 1892. Both Harrington and Dech were delegates to the 1910 Democratic state convention. The 1910 Populist state convention approved county option; among those in attendance were John H. Powers, 1890 candidate for governor, party patriarch, and member of the state County Option League, and former Senator William V. Allen, who opposed the endorsement of county option and declared that it "simply puts an end to the populist party." Some leading Populists, including Elmer E. Thomas, a prominent prohibitionist, state party chairman Cassius B. Manuel, and former state senator W. F. Dale, sought to give their party's 1910 nomination for governor to Aldrich. Although there was no official endorsement of Aldrich, Manuel personally urged Populists to vote for Aldrich and was joined by Powers, Jacob V. Wolfe, and DeWitt Eager, all leaders from the early 1890s. Between fifty and seventy-five delegates representing fifteen counties attended the 1912 state convention. Former party leaders George W. Berge and Otto Mutz now affiliated openly with the Democratic party. Several prominent Populists and former Populists joined Roosevelt's battle for the Lord, including Harrington, Manuel, and W. F. Porter, Populist secretary of state from 1897 to 1901. The party last appeared on the ballot in 1914 and 1916, endorsing all Democratic candidates. During its final years the party was kept alive by an unnamed prominent Democrat, probably a Bryan lieutenant, who paid party expenses and salaries in an effort to hold the few thousand Populist votes for the Democrats.[25]

The Progressive party in Nebraska came into existence because of Roosevelt, existed to support him, and quickly sank into oblivion without him. Most of its leaders came from the progressive wing of the GOP and soon returned to the party fold. Most leading progressive Republicans, notably Aldrich and Norris, never affiliated with the new party, and the former Populists and Democrats who joined the party rarely achieved positions of prominence. In 1912 and 1916 the party endorsed all statewide Republican candidates. A separate state ticket in 1914 drew only about 5 percent of the vote statewide.[26]

Nebraska's first progressive era closed with the polls on 5 November 1912. Republican progressives lost the governorship and failed to carry the state for Roosevelt. Democratic moderates won the governorship and the legislature and would hold both until the election of 1918. The Bryan wing of the Democracy, reduced to a minority, would remain so until 1922 when "Brother Charley" would capture the governorship. The moribund Populist party would soon disappear even from the ballot. The Progressive party would never become more than a feeble appendage of the GOP. But the results of this progressive interlude would outlive progressive dominance of the political system. New dimensions had been added to state politics—regulation, departisanization, and an emphasis on such consumer issues as the protection of bank deposits. These new dimensions did not replace previous political concerns but came in addition to them. Temperance acquired a political prominence it had not seen since 1890. Republicans continued to emphasize, as they had long since done, that theirs was the party of stability and prosperity. Democrats, since the fusion of 1894, consistently combined demands for reform with opposition to prohibition and nativism.

CHAPTER 8

Voting Behavior and Political Leadership in the Progressive Era, 1906–14

Out of the work of the Bryan Volunteers
came the elections of Governor John
Morehead and of Governor Keith Neville,
and United States Senator Gilbert M.
Hitchcock. Out of it came Democratic
legislatures from 1908 to 1918. The
Democrats controlled Nebraska . . .
during that time.

                                        Arthur F. Mullen

        Historical analyses of the nature of progressivism in the
early twentieth century tend to fall into three major schools. The first of these
groups, progressive historians like Vernon Parrington, John D. Hicks,
Chester McA. Destler, and Russel Nye, saw the progressive movement as
the lineal descendant of Populism and Bryanism ("the same ideas traveling
in the same direction, with new leaders, new vitality, and new weapons,
against the old forces of privilege and corruption") and stressed the
economic basis of progressivism's appeal. The second school, by contrast,
tended to distinguish between the two movements, finding progressivism to
have been a coalition of various groups. Richard Hofstadter, in *The Age of
Reform*, stressed the coalitional nature of progressivism by surveying a
series of separate groups including a displaced genteel upper class, lawyers,
ministers, and social workers. Where he had found the Populists largely "of
one mind on most broad social issues, and that mind . . . rather narrow and
predictable," the progressives by contrast were "more likely to be aware of
the complexities of social issues and more divided among themselves."
Despite the coalitional nature of progressivism, Hofstadter noted that most
of its leadership seemed to come from a white, Protestant, old-stock American middle class, motivated by status anxieties, and that its voting strength
sprang from consumer issues.[1]

A group of more recent historians has given still a third view of the nature of progressivism. Samuel P. Hays has presented it as a movement led by a cosmopolitan elite, interested in moving decision-making up the federal ladder and in selecting decision-makers from higher on the socioeconomic scale. The dominant thrust of progressivism, according to Hays, came from the upper class, and its voting support sprang from that group and the middle class. Opposition to progressive reform was most likely to be concentrated in working-class neighborhoods. Gabriel Kolko argues in a somewhat similar vein that the moving force behind the reforms of the Roosevelt and Wilson administrations was a desire by the business leaders of the nation to use the government to do what they had not been able to accomplish on their own—rationalize the economic structure. Progressive reforms at the federal level had the effect, according to Kolko, of holding "nascent radicalism" at a state level in check by deceiving its leaders, "who could not tell the difference between federal regulation *of* business and federal regulation *for* business."[2]

We may extract from these analyses several hypotheses that would allow for testing. The progressive historians' model of progressivism would feature voting behavior tied largely to issues of farm economics and would likely show a direct and continuing relationship to the voting behavior of the 1890s. The second model would have progressive voting sentiment strongest among the white Protestant old-stock American middle class, especially in urban areas. The third model would be characterized by a direct relationship between progressive voting behavior and wealth and urbanness. We may test these models by extracting from the 1910 census independent variables similar to those employed previously: the percentage of the population in each county living in incorporated areas, the mean annual income per farm, and the percentage of the population born in or having parents born in Germany, Austria, (largely Czech), or Ireland. To these we may also add a scale of Populist proclivities, based on the Populist party vote in 1890, 1892, and 1893, and the Populist presidential vote in 1904.[3] The treatment of voting behavior that follows is in three parts: patterns in general elections, patterns in primary elections, and a profile of "progressive" voters.

Voting Behavior: General Elections

All methods of analyzing voting behavior in general elections, whether based on the regression approach (scatter diagrams, correlation, or multiple regression) or on clustering, point to ethnicity as the most important deter-

TABLE 27. PEARSON COEFFICIENTS OF CORRELATION BETWEEN INDEXES OF PARTY VOTING STRENGTH AND INDEPENDENT VARIABLES, 1906–14

Dependent Variables		Independent Variables			
Party	Year	Percentage of the Population Born in or Having Parents Born in Germany, Austria, or Ireland, 1910	Mean Income per Farm, 1909	Percentage of the Population Living in Incorporated Areas, 1910	Distribution of Support for Populist Candidates, 1890, 1892, 1893, 1904
Democratic and People's Independent	1906	+0.5990	+0.1790	−0.2148	−0.0455
	1908	+0.5212	+0.0127	−0.0968	+0.0798
	1910	+0.7997	+0.1956	−0.0652	−0.3684
	1912	+0.4501	+0.0410	−0.1117	−0.1176
	1914	+0.6690	+0.1896	−0.2899	−0.1230
Republican	1906	−0.4305	−0.0909	+0.2714	−0.1603
	1908	−0.4458	+0.0303	+0.1154	−0.1798
	1910	−0.7598	−0.0954	+0.0615	+0.2652
	1912[a]	−0.3271	+0.1605	−0.0004	−0.0165
	1914	−0.4660	+0.0409	+0.2186	−0.1074

[a] Officially Republican and Progressive.

TABLE 28. MEAN INDEXES OF PARTY STRENGTH, FOR 1906–14, WITH
COUNTIES GROUPED BY SOCIOECONOMIC QUARTILES

Independent Variables	Mean Index of Democratic Party Strength, 1906–14	Mean Index of Republican Party Strength, 1906–14
Percentage of the population born in, or having parents born in, Germany, Austria, or Ireland, 1910		
Highest quartile	51.06%	45.57%
Second quartile	47.48	48.01
Third quartile	44.44	50.84
Lowest quartile	43.99	50.30
Mean income per farm, 1909		
Most prosperous quartile	46.68%	49.49%
Second quartile	47.87	47.71
Third quartile	45.94	49.03
Poorest quartile	46.22	48.65
Percentage of the population living in incorporated areas, 1910		
Most urban quartile	45.21%	49.74%
Second quartile	47.27%	49.98
Third quartile	46.00	49.38
Most rural quartile	48.41	46.64

minant of party preference.[4] Coefficients of correlation, presented in table
27, show Democratic party voting and ethnicity to correlate at about +0.45
to +0.80, and Republican party voting and ethnicity at about −0.33 to
−0.76. The election of 1910 is clearly unique in the strength of the relationship; that was the year James Dahlman, Democratic nominee for governor,
promised a beer party on the capitol lawn if he won, and Chester Aldrich, the
Republican candidate, campaigned on a pledge of county option. No other
clear or consistent relationship emerges from the other coefficients, which
are so low as to be almost entirely nonsignificant. Stepwise multiple regression allows the combination of these independent variables in a correlational
analysis. As we would anticipate from the simple coefficients, ethnicity is
the first variable to be stepped into the regression in each instance. Using the
party vote as the dependent variable and the three independent variables of
second independent variable increases the R^2 by more than 0.075.[5] Table 28
presents summaries by quartiles and, once again, ethnicity appears as the

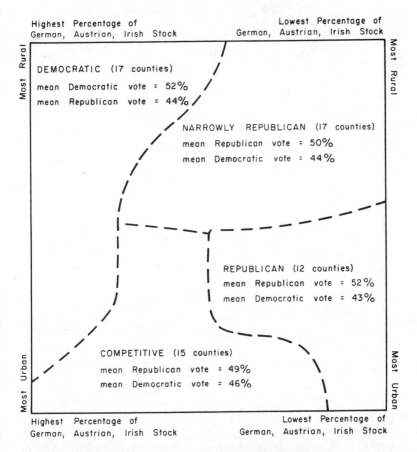

FIGURE 4. Voting behavior, 1906–14, counties distributed by ethnicity and degree of urbanization.

most significant determinant and the rural-urban dimension shows a rather weak relationship.

The relationship between party voting behavior, ethnicity, and the urban-rural dimension may be represented by a figure like that already presented for the period 1896–1904 (see figs. 1 and 2). Once again we begin with a table of sixteen cells (four each way), with ethnicity ranged along the horizontal dimension and the rural-urban dimension along the vertical axis. Figure 4 presents the result and clearly indicates how the line of division between the two parties had become considerably more "vertical" (i.e., tied

TABLE 29. ETHNIC CHARACTERISTICS OF TWELVE COUNTIES

County	Percentage Distribution of Party Vote, 1906–14		Percentage Distribution of the Population by Parents' Place of Birth					Percentage of Adult Males Native Stock	Percentage Distribution of the Population by Religious Affiliation	
	Democratic	Republican	German	Austrian	Irish	Danish	Swedish		Roman Catholic	Old-Stock Protestant
Platte	59.3	37.8	23.1	11.0	2.7	2.5	4.6	22.2	35.2	12.0
Greeley	57.2	38.4	8.0	1.3	12.7	3.2	3.4	40.8	29.9	9.0
Cuming	57.2	41.1	37.0	5.9	1.2	2.3	5.3	16.1	16.7	5.8
Howard	56.1	39.6	13.8	9.7	0.8	21.7	3.2	24.0	34.7	9.3
Butler	56.0	41.3	9.2	26.1	1.3	0.2	0.3	40.1	35.4	21.2
Colfax	53.1	42.8	13.2	35.6	2.1	0.7	0.4	19.7	31.8	12.8
Burt	36.7	60.0	5.1	0.2	1.1	3.7	18.9	47.7	2.1	23.0
Nance	41.0	56.0	5.5	7.0	1.0	2.0	5.3	58.8	8.7	19.9
Pawnee	40.3	55.8	6.8	8.8	1.1	0.0	0.2	59.9	6.7	36.9
Lancaster	39.9	54.7	8.8	1.2	2.1	1.1	2.9	53.8	10.8	24.2
Antelope	42.0	54.1	11.3	0.3	1.5	3.2	3.3	53.0	5.5	16.3
York	42.2	53.6	10.6	0.1	1.8	0.9	3.1	56.2	4.8	29.2
State	45.6	49.4	12.7	4.5	2.1	2.3	4.2	47.7	9.9	17.6

Note: Sources of data for this table are outlined in detail in Appendix A.

more closely to a single variable) than in the late 1890s. A comparison of figure 4 with figure 2 illustrates that, between the late 1890s and 1906–14, the Republicans made significant gains in the upper right quadrant (the most rural and most pietistic counties) and suffered some erosion of their 1898 strength in the most urban counties (the lower tier of the figure). Democrats retained their support in the upper left quadrant (the most rural and most ritualistic counties) and added some strength in urban ritualistic areas. The net result of these changes was to shift the major axis of division between the two parties from a diagonal running from lower left to upper right (the 1898 pattern) to a nearly vertical line.

An examination of the six banner counties for each party affirms the signal importance of the ethnic dimension. Table 29 summarizes ethnic data for these twelve counties. The two groups of counties are most clearly different with regard to the proportion of Germans, Austrians (Czechs in Butler and Colfax counties, Czechs and Poles in Howard County), Irish, and Catholics, and in the proportion of adult males who were native-born of native parentage. In fact, the five most Catholic counties in the state are included in the six Democratic counties. Non-ethnic variables show no such sharp differences. The Democratic counties ranged from 23 to 40 percent urban, the Republican counties were somewhat higher, ranging from 31–38 percent for Antelope, Burt, Nance, and Pawnee to 61 percent for York and 76 percent for Lancaster. The mean annual farm income was somewhat higher for the Democratic counties than for the Republican ones, varying from a low of $2,700 for Howard County to a high of $3,500 for Cuming. The Republican counties ranged from a low of $2,400 for Pawnee County to a high of $3,200 for Burt.

This analysis so far has concentrated on party voting. Although individual candidates in presidential, senatorial, and gubernatorial elections attracted a good deal of attention and sometimes ran campaigns separate from their parties, voting behavior in these elections nonetheless tended to follow the general patterns of party voting. Ethnicity is the independent variable most significantly related to voting for these offices in nearly every instance, but the coefficients of correlation tend, as a rule, to be somewhat lower than for party voting, suggesting that some voters were pulled out of ethnically determined patterns by individual candidates. Gubernatorial elections, especially, saw extensive ticket-splitting. In both 1912 and 1914, for example, 12 to 13 percent of those who voted for Morehead for governor did not vote for Democratic candidates for other statewide offices.

Aside from the 1912 split in the Republican party, the 1910 gubernatorial election saw the most interesting ticket-splitting of the period. That year the Democratic candidate for governor, James C. Dahlman, ran his campaign so exclusively on the basis of his opposition to any further temperance legislation that many temperance-minded Democrats scratched him. His opponent, Chester Aldrich, drew nearly 9,000 more votes than any other Republican candidate and over 20,000 more votes than the Republican senatorial candidate, Elmer Burkett. The result was to align voters more closely along the ethnic values axis than in any other election of the period. Although Dahlman's sopping-wet campaign actually gained a few votes over the normal Democratic party vote in the most ritualistic and most antiprohibition counties of northeastern Nebraska, these gains were more than offset by massive losses among the erstwhile Populist counties of central Nebraska. In Furnas County, for example, Dahlman lost two of every five normally Democratic voters, and he lost three of every ten in Custer and Hitchcock counties. In five old-stock precincts where the Populists had drawn more than 90 percent of the vote in 1890, and where the Populist vote for attorney general in 1910 averaged 16 percent of the vote, Dahlman lost between a third and three-fourths of the normally Democratic vote.[6]

One of the striking characteristics of voting behavior in the period from 1908 through 1916 is the revived strength of the Democratic party, which won the governorship four times out of five, won two of the three elections for the United States Senate, and carried all three presidential elections. This strength is all the more surprising given the extremely poor showing the party made in the elections of 1904 and 1906. What happened during the years 1906 to 1908? Arthur F. Mullen claims that his organizing efforts moved unconverted Populists into the Democratic fold and that these voters supplied the Democrats with their margins of victory from 1908 through 1916. Calculating the coefficient of correlation between Democratic party gains from 1906 to 1908 and the mean Populist vote in 1890, 1892, 1893, and 1904 yields a very low value, only +0.2. Examining the relationship between these Democratic gains and independent population variables also yields rather low coefficients of correlation, but these coefficients do suggest that there was a difference between these voters and those who had voted Democratic consistently since the 1880s. Whereas the core strength of the Democratic party was ethnic and opposed to prohibition, with a tendency to be situated in the more prosperous agricultural areas, the coefficients of correlation suggest that Democratic gains between 1906 and 1908 tended to come from other areas:

Percentage of the population German, Austrian,
        or Irish stock, 1910 . . . . −0.20
Percentage of the vote in favor of prohibition, 1916 . . . . +0.38
Mean annual farm income, 1909 . . . . −0.32

Insofar as any projections may be made from such data, the new Democratic voters seem to have been from marginal areas and rather pietistic in their values.

In retaining Mullen to organize the Bryan Volunteers in 1908, Bryan seems to have made the classic blunder of creating an organization whose primary loyalties were to the organizer rather than to the ostensible leader. Mullen built his political career upon the organization he first developed in 1908, becoming chief patronage officer in the Shallenberger administration and later serving as national committeeman or state party chairman until the late 1930s. Mullen broke with Bryan in 1909, allying himself with Bryan's opponents within the party—first with Shallenberger, then with Morehead and Hitchcock. If we take the increase in the Democratic vote between 1906 and 1908 as a rough measure of Mullen's organization, we can find some traces of it in the voting behavior of at least the next several elections.[7]

Before examining voting behavior in primary elections, we must examine the strength of the Populist party and assess the degree of voter loyalty it retained. There was only one candidate who appeared on the ballot solely as a Populist during the period 1906 to 1914—Menzo Terry, candidate for attorney general in 1910. Terry won the Populist nomination in the primary that year and did not follow the usual practice of declining when the Democratic primary winner expressed no interest whatsoever in receiving the Populist nomination. Terry did poorly statewide but did show a few centers of strength, receiving as much as 15 percent of the vote in some counties. By and large his vote came from the old centers of Populist strength. And by and large he cut into the vote of the Democratic candidate without much affecting that of the Republican. In twenty-five central Nebraska counties, Democratic candidates for other statewide offices averaged 45 percent of the vote, but the candidate for attorney general averaged only 38 percent and Terry pulled 9 percent. This in turn suggests that about one out of every five Democratic voters in central Nebraska still considered himself a Populist as late as 1910. In a few counties the proportion seems much higher. In the old Populist strongholds of Sherman, Loup, and Custer counties, for example, one of three Democrats had a higher loyalty to the old Populist cause than to the Democratic banner. It is even possible to find a few isolated rural precincts, like Grant in Hitchcock County, where fully half the Democratic voters bolted to Terry.

How many voters in Nebraska retained latent loyalties to the Populist party? Estimates are difficult. The number of Populist voters in the primary elections declined from nearly 4,000 in 1906 to 1,000 in 1912 to only 433 in 1916, the last year the party appeared in the primary. The 1907 and 1909 elections for university regents provide a different indication of Populist strength: each year, the two fusion parties coalesced on candidates by each withdrawing one of their primary winners but not formally giving their nomination to the other candidate. Thus, each year, candidates appeared on the ballot as either Democrat or People's Independent, but not as both. It was expected that the fusion voter would support both, and this seems to have happened in 1907, when the Democrat got 66,000 votes and the Populist got 72,000. In 1909, however, many Democrats seem to have voted only for their candidate, who got 71,400 votes. The Populist got only 25,000. This was apparently the datum upon which Arthur Mullen drew when he wrote in 1912 that "there are twenty-five or thirty thousand Populists in this state, and most of them vote the Democratic ticket when it suits them."[8] The 1910 vote for Terry would dispute this figure, his statewide total coming to only about 10,000 votes, about 4 percent of the total.

Voting Behavior: Primary Elections

The establishment of the direct primary by the 1907 legislature introduced a new dimension into Nebraska electoral politics. To be sure, there had been occasions before 1907 when the election of delegates to state party conventions had operated somewhat like a direct primary, most especially for the Democrats in 1894 and for the Republicans in 1906. After 1907 the typical pattern became a contest for every major office every year. In 1908 three major contenders sought the Democratic gubernatorial nomination, and in 1910 incumbent Democratic governor Shallenberger lost his own party's primary. The year 1910 also saw spirited multicandidate contests in the Republican gubernatorial primary and in both parties' senatorial primaries. In 1912 three major candidates contested each party's presidential primary, two candidates sought each gubernatorial nomination, and both senatorial primaries were closely fought.

Throughout the period, both parties contained a crowd of self-proclaimed "progressives," and primary elections often saw candidates vying with each other in expressing their devotion to the principles of "progressivism." In 1908 Democrats Berge and Shallenberger both sought to convince the Democratic voters of their devotion to reform, and Democrat Dahlman pointed to his long record of service as Bryan's handpicked national committeeman. In the 1910 Democratic senatorial primary, Bryan lieutenant Richard Metcalfe claimed to be more progressive than *World-Herald* publisher Gilbert Hitchcock, a claim Hitchcock denied. In the Republican senatorial primary of that year, Charles O. Whedon accused incumbent

Elmer Burkett of not being sufficiently enthusiastic in support of the progressive cause, but Burkett could, in fact, point to a long record of support for Rooseveltian legislation. The gubernatorial primaries of both parties in 1910 revolved around the issue of liquor, with incumbent governor Shallenberger defending his daylight saloon bill against Omaha mayor James Dahlman and Republican Chester Aldrich promoting the cause of county option against several opponents. The 1910 Republican state convention also saw the forging of a coalition between the supporters of county option and the friends of insurgent congressman George W. Norris. The 1912 Republican presidential primary involved all three major candidates, Roosevelt, Taft, and La Follette, though the La Follette campaign faltered after the candidate's breakdown. The Democratic presidential primary witnessed a bitter battle among Wilson, who had Bryan's support, Champ Clark, backed by both the Mullen organization and gubernatorial candidate John Morehead, and Judson Harmon, supported by Senator Hitchcock. In the Republican senatorial primary, Congressman George W. Norris challenged the progressivism of incumbent senator Norris Brown, who sought to deflect such charges by pointing to his record, which included sponsorship of the income tax amendment. The Democratic senatorial primary featured several candidates, the strongest of them former governor Shallenberger and longtime Bryan ally William H. Thompson. The Democratic gubernatorial primary pitted Bryanite Richard Metcalfe against Clark supporter John Morehead, but the incumbent Republican governor, Aldrich, had only minimal opposition.

On the basis of the coalitions formed by the candidates in the primaries, we would anticipate finding evidence of some statistical relationship in voting for Democrats Shallenberger and Metcalfe in 1910; Shallenberger, Clark, and Morehead in 1912; Wilson, Thompson, and Metcalfe in 1912; and perhaps for Hitchcock in 1910 and Harmon in 1912. Among the Republicans, we would anticipate some statistical relationship in voting for Norris and La Follette in 1912; for Brown and Taft in 1912; and perhaps for Aldrich in 1910 and Norris in 1912. If we calculate the Pearson coefficients of correlation for the distribution of support for each pair of candidates, we may begin to explore the possible interrelationships. Doing so makes it clear that coalitions engineered among candidates or their campaign managers did not necessarily extend to the electorate.

Among the Democrats, there appear two weakly defined blocs of candidates, the first consisting of Shallenberger, Clark, and Metcalfe, the second including Dahlman, Harmon, Hitchcock, and Morehead. Within the first bloc, the key relationships revolve about Shallenberger (fig. 5).

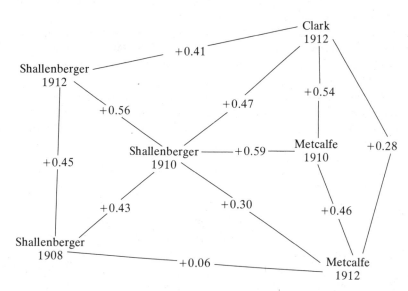

FIGURE 5. Coefficients of correlation between voting support for Clark, Metcalfe, and Shallenberger in Democratic primaries, 1908–12.

Within the second bloc, there is no figure quite so central as Shallenberger, but Dahlman's vote in 1910 is a better index than any other (fig. 6).

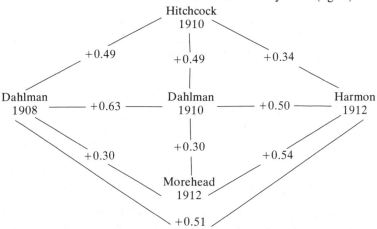

FIGURE 6. Coefficients of correlation between voting support for Dahlman, Harmon, Hitchcock, and Moorhead in Democratic primaries, 1908–12.

Although some of the coefficients are rather low, the *direction* of all relationships is consistent—coefficients are positive *within* each bloc and negative *between* blocs. The vote for Wilson in the 1912 presidential primary has no strong or consistent relationship to either bloc; the most significant correlations are with the Clark vote (−0.41), the Harmon vote (−0.35), and the Morehead vote (−0.30).

Two blocs also exist among the Republican candidates, one consisting of Brown, Burkett, Taft, and Cady (the 1910 gubernatorial candidate who opposed county option), the other including Norris, La Follette, Aldrich, and Whedon. Within the first of these, the relationships center on the vote for Norris Brown (fig. 7).

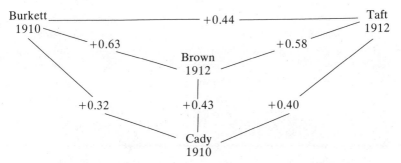

FIGURE 7. Coefficients of correlation between voting support for Brown, Burkett, Cady, and Taft in Republican primaries, 1910 and 1912.

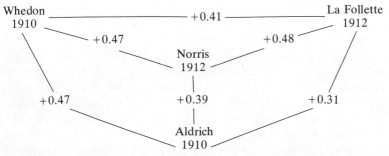

FIGURE 8. Coefficients of correlation between voting support for Aldrich, La Follette, Norris. and Whedon in Republican primaries, 1910 and 1912.

The coefficients are less significant for the second bloc (fig. 8). However low the coefficients may be in some instances, just as with the Democratic blocs, the direction of all relationships is consistent—coefficients are positive *within* each bloc and negative *between* blocs. There is no strong or consistent relationship in the coefficients for Roosevelt in 1910 or for Aldrich that same year. The Roosevelt vote correlates at −0.66 with the La Follette vote, at −0.26 with the Taft vote, and at +0.29 with the 1912 Aldrich vote. Examining the correlations between voting for various primary candidates and independent population variables suggests the nature of the differences between the two blocs within each party. Although coefficients of correlation are often low, the signs are consistent within and between blocs. Distribution of support for Democratic candidates Shallenberger, Metcalfe, and Clarke correlates inversely with ethnicity in each case (*r* ranges from −0.32 to −0.60), suggesting a tendency for these candidates to appeal more strongly in counties with higher proportions of pietistic voters. Voting for this group also correlates inversely with the mean annual farm income (*r* ranges from −0.15 to −0.33) and with the percentage of the population living in incorporated areas (*r* ranges from −0.05 to −0.43). Voting for the other group of Democratic candidates, Dahlman, Hitchcock, Harmon, and Morehead, correlates positively with ethnicity (*r* ranges from +0.12 to +0.66), farm income (*r* ranges from +0.00 to +0.36), and the percentage living in incorporated areas (*r* ranges from +0.05 to +0.43). Similar patterns exist within the Republican blocs: voting for Norris, La Follette, Whedon, and Aldrich correlates inversely with both ethnicity (*r* ranges from −0.28 to −0.44) and farm income (−0.22 to −0.44). Voting patterns for Brown, Taft, Burkett, and Cady are the reverse (*r* ranging from +0.26 to +0.48 for ethnicity, and from +0.22 to +0.44 for farm income). There is no consistent relationship between Republican primary voting and the percentage of the population living in incorporated areas.

These patterns of support, which are only suggested by the coefficients of correlation, are reflected when the sixty-one counties studied are broken into homogeneous clusters. Table 30 summarizes these data and again suggests that Shallenberger, Metcalfe, and Clark had their greatest strength in rural, pietistic counties with below-average farm income and that Dahlman, Harmon, Hitchcock, and Morehead ran better in urban and ritualistic counties. Among Republican candidates, Norris, La Folette, Aldrich, and Whedon were stronger in rural, pietistic counties with below-average farm income, and Brown, Taft, Burkett, and Cady ran better in counties with the opposite characteristics. Counties likely to support Democratic primary candidates like Shallenberger, Metcalfe, or Clark had population characteristics similar to those most likely to support Republican primary candidates like Norris, La Follette, Whedon, or Aldrich.

Voting Behavior: A Profile of the "Progressive" Voter

The survey just completed of both general election and primary election voting behavior has suggested some of the characteristics of the "progressive" voter. We now need to draw those suggestions together into a description of the "progressive" voter and the relationship between such voters and the majority of each party. We may begin with some observations on the statistical relationship between voting behavior in the primary elections and in the general elections, arrived at by calculating the difference between the normal party vote and the vote for those candidates who were the victims or beneficiaries of ticket-splitting, and then correlate that difference with primary election behavior. The results suggest that the Democrats who bolted Dahlman in 1910 were likely to have come from the same areas as Democrats who supported Metcalfe in the 1910 and 1912 primaries, or Shallenberger in the 1910 primary, or Wilson in the 1912 primary. Calculating the difference between the vote for Aldrich and the normal Republican party vote, and then correlating this difference with the results of Democratic primaries, suggests the same conclusion. The coefficients also suggest relationships between Hitchcock's margin over the normal Democratic party vote in 1910 and the vote for Whedon in the Republican primary, and between Morehead's margin over the normal Democratic vote in 1912 and the vote for Newton in the Republican primary. Similarly, Morehead's margin over the normal Democratic party vote in both 1912 and 1914 seems related to the vote for Taft. Finally, the difference between the combined vote for Roosevelt and Taft in 1912 and the Republican party vote for that year seems related to the primary vote for La Follette, as does the increase in the Democratic party vote between 1910 and 1912.[9]

We may now begin to develop a picture of the nature of both major parties, with our attention first focused on the Democrats. The Democratic party, it seems, was composed of a "core" and a "periphery" (fig. 9). The core consists of ethnic Democrats, the groups who had provided the bulk of Democratic votes since the 1880s: Germans, Czechs, Irish, Poles; Catholics and conservative Lutherans; adamant opponents of prohibition who tended to be situated in the more prosperous agricultural areas of eastern Nebraska or in Omaha. The periphery consists of voters with a rather different profile, more likely to be old-stock and Protestant, more likely to be situated in areas of less prosperous agriculture, quite similar in their composite characteristics to the Populists of the 1890s. Indeed, the data from the 1910 elections suggest that in the old-time Populist regions of the state, the normal Demo-

TABLE 30. VOTE FOR CANDIDATES IN PARTY PRIMARIES, FOR COUNTIES, 1908, 1910, AND 1912, WITH COUNTIES GROUPED INTO HOMOGENEOUS SOCIOECONOMIC CLUSTERS

Dependent Variables (Name of candidate, nomination sought, and year)	Mean Vote, All Counties (N = 61)	Independent Variable Clusters					
		More Ritualistic Counties[a]			More Pietistic Counties[a]		
		More Urban Counties[b] (N = 14)	More Rural Counties[b]		More Urban Counties[b] (N = 17)	More Rural Counties[b]	
			Lower Farm Income Counties[c] (N = 7)	Higher Farm Income Counties[c] (N = 9)		Lower Farm Income Counties[c] (N = 8)	Higher Farm Income Counties[c] (N = 6)
Democratic Primaries							
Shallenberger, governor, 1910	57.15%	47.25%	56.01%	51.76%	59.37%	70.26%	65.90%
Metcalfe, senator, 1910	28.92	23.12	28.59	26.45	30.26	35.93	33.40
Clark, president, 1912	44.02	38.26	42.12	38.98	52.12	49.47	39.97
Shallenberger, senator, 1912	60.61	56.82	57.05	57.91	61.62	70.04	62.17
Shallenberger, governor, 1908	43.11	41.79	38.47	37.89	42.83	61.19	36.18
Metcalfe, governor, 1912	47.03	41.66	48.87	40.40	51.06	52.14	49.14
Wilson, president, 1912	30.03	24.50	31.57	29.07	28.73	34.29	40.55
Dahlman, governor, 1908	24.02	30.11	27.48	27.07	21.27	13.24	23.34
Dahlman, governor, 1910	42.85	52.75	43.99	48.24	40.63	29.74	34.10
Harmon, president, 1912	23.12	34.28	20.85	29.69	16.47	14.24	20.62
Hitchcock, senator, 1910	57.68	60.18	58.84	57.31	57.92	53.37	56.11
Morehead, governor, 1912	52.97	58.34	51.13	59.60	48.94	47.86	50.86

Republican primaries

Norris, senator, 1912	55.53%	50.03%	51.88%	47.69%	57.53%	72.74%	55.78%
La Follette, president, 1912	20.84	18.36	21.19	13.73	22.63	26.67	24.07
Whedon, senator, 1910	25.36	22.98	23.23	21.48	28.56	29.03	25.26
Aldrich, governor, 1910	54.77	51.69	47.44	43.14	58.03	62.42	68.48
Aldrich, governor, 1912	69.03	66.51	64.14	71.54	71.22	70.58	70.36
Roosevelt, president, 1912	62.02	62.78	63.26	62.74	61.45	61.51	62.37
Brown, senator, 1912	44.47	49.97	48.12	52.31	42.47	27.26	44.22
Brown, senator, 1912	44.47	49.97	48.12	52.31	42.47	27.26	44.22
Taft, president, 1912	16.31	19.09	14.20	22.83	15.18	11.08	12.72
Burkett, senator, 1910	52.41	55.65	57.35	55.89	50.43	42.70	52.41
Cady, governor, 1910	35.45	40.50	44.14	46.04	31.54	25.10	22.49
Newton, governor, 1912	30.79	33.49	35.86	28.46	28.77	29.42	29.64

[a] The "more ritualistic" counties were above the median (20 percent) in the percentage of the population born in, or having parents born in, Germany, Austria, or Ireland; the "more pietistic" counties were below the median.

[b] The "more urban" counties were above the median (34 percent) in the percentage of the population living in incorporated cities, towns, or villages in 1910; the "more rural" counties were below the median.

[c] The "lower income" counties were below the median ($2,658) in the mean annual income per farm in 1909; the "higher income" counties were above the median.

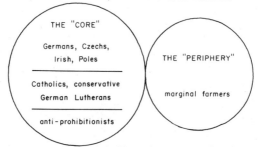

FIGURE 9. The Democratic party in Nebraska—core and periphery.

cratic electorate was composed of perhaps one-fourth to one-third gut Populists, who would bolt the party of Bryan when presented with a Dahlman. The data suggest that these voters made their presence felt in the Democratic primaries in support of candidates like Metcalfe (who was on the staff of Bryan's *Commoner*) and Wilson. Voters who backed Metcalfe or Wilson in the primaries of 1910 and 1912 seem to have been prone to bolt Dahlman in 1910.

The Democratic periphery, as I have described it here, consists of voters whipsawed between the party of morality (the GOP) and the party of Bryan and Populism. Shallenberger sought to guarantee his reelection in 1910 by riding both core and periphery with his daylight saloon bill, which was opposed by the liquor interests but did not deny to any Nebraskan either the right to spend an afternoon in a *Biergarten* or the right to purchase alcoholic beverages for consumption at home in the evening. This delicate balancing act, treading between the ethnocultural values of the core and those of the periphery, failed when Shallenberger lost his foothold on the core in the 1910 primary. Dahlman secured the core, but—with his talk of beer parties on the capitol grounds—alienated the periphery. Few Democrats objected to legislation like the bank guaranty law, the Oregon Pledge Law, or the nonpartisan board of control for state institutions. The horns of the party dilemma were composed, as they had been since the consummation of fusion, of the need to defuse the liquor issue, and thereby to give the lie to Republican charges of being controlled by the liquor interests, without imposing restrictions on the traditional life-styles of ritualistic party members.

Republican voters can also be described in terms of core and periphery, the core consisting of pietistic voters, whether of old-stock American, Swedish, Norwegian, or British descent, without much regard for agricultural prosperity or urban-rural distinctions, most of them sympathetic to temperance or even outright prohibition. Two peripheral groups may be distinguished shading into this core (fig. 10). The left periphery provided a primary base for candidates like La Follette and Whedon; the right periphery served a similar function for candidates like Taft, Cady, and Newton. Aldrich in 1910 and Norris in 1912 rode both the center and the left periphery. Burkett in 1910 and Brown in 1912 sought the center and the right periphery. Theodore Roosevelt seems to have drawn most of the center. The left periphery was centered in rural, low-income, pietistic counties, many with a heritage of Populism; the right periphery was centered in counties largely urban or of high farm income, most of which had little Populism in their pasts. Like the Democratic periphery, these two Republican peripheries appear caught in crosscurrents. La Follette and Whedon voters, the left periphery, seem to have been caught between their commitment to the party of pietistic morality and their economic status, leading them to bolt Republican candidates they deemed not sufficiently attuned to economic problems, like Burkett in 1910 and both Roosevelt and Taft in 1912. Taft, Cady, and Newton voters, the right periphery, seem to have been less than enthusiastic in their commitment to the cold water reform but committed to Republican prosperity and likely to bolt those candidates whose association with the La Follette periphery made them suspect—like Aldrich and Norris in 1912 and Howell in 1914.[10]

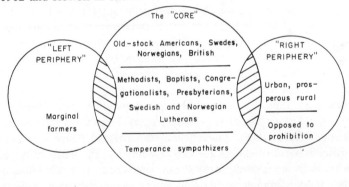

FIGURE 10. The Republican party in Nebraska—core and peripheries.

The 1912 presidential campaign provides an especially good example of these patterns. The vote for Roosevelt correlates more strongly with the ethnicity variable than does the vote for any other Republican in any year of this period save the Aldrich vote of 1910. The Wilson vote has one of the lowest correlations with ethnicity of the vote for any Democratic candidate during this period, but it is nonetheless clear that nearly all of the normal

Democratic vote went to Wilson. He ran somewhat behind the normal party vote in the most ritualistic and most prosperous counties; he held the normal party vote in the lowest-income counties and ran somewhat ahead of it in the most pietistic ones. These losses at the core and gains on the periphery make the coefficient of correlation with ethnicity lower than for most Democratic candidates.[11] It is impossible to determine which of the other candidates benefited most from the Democratic desertions in the core counties, but Taft ran most strongly in the counties where Wilson's losses from the normal party vote were largest. Taft actually ran ahead of Roosevelt in the most ritualistic counties (26 percent to 24 percent, compared with means of 22 percent and 29 percent for all counties), and he ran very close to the Bull Moose candidate in the most prosperous counties (25.7 percent to 27.5 percent). Taft ran most behind Roosevelt where Wilson held the normal Democratic vote—in the most pietistic counties (Taft 18 percent, Roosevelt 32 percent) and the lowest-income counties (Taft 19 percent, Roosevelt 30 percent). Apparently one Democrat out of twelve in the most ritualistic counties bolted Wilson and suppported Taft in preference to the avowed progressivism of both leading candidates. Wilson seems to have held—and even added to—the Democratic periphery, but he lost slightly at the core. Roosevelt held most of the Republican core but lost one periphery entirely to Taft and suffered some losses to Wilson in the other.

Who, then, was the "progressive" voter in Nebraska? In part, the answer to such a question must be an exercise in definitions. If Democrats supported such legislation as the bank guaranty fund or the Oregon Pledge Law, then Democratic voters were, by one definition, "progressive." We want something more, however. The voter most easily labeled "progressive" was the voter caught in cross-pressures, pulled toward both the party of Bryan and the party of La Follette and Norris. We may combine the two earlier diagrams to illustrate the extent to which Democratic progressives like Metcalfe or Wilson and Republican progressives like La Follette or Norris were, in fact, concentrating on the same group of voters (fig. 11). The major criterion for determining the "progressive" voter is economic. Progressive voting behavior in Nebraska was concentrated in the same areas where Populism had raged two decades before, areas of marginal agriculture settled disproportionately by old-stock Protestants. Of all the voters in the state, these were the most cross-pressured between ethnicity and economics, and these were the most willing to cross party lines. The progressive voter in Nebraska was most likely to be old-stock Protestant, a marginal farmer who had been touched by the Populist prairie fire and who looked to leaders like Bryan and La Follette.

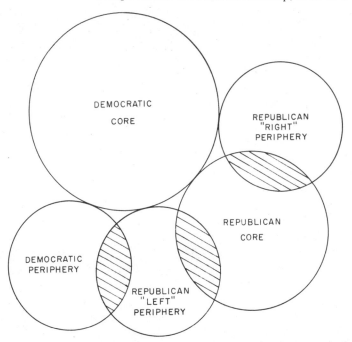

FIGURE 11. Groups within the Republican and Democratic parties.

Political Leadership

Biographical data were located for 398 political leaders who were active from 1906 through 1912; 199 were Republicans, 199 either Democrats or persons affiliated with both the Democratic and Populist parties.[12] Included in the group are most who sought or held statewide office and about 71 percent of those who served in the state legislature. Tabulations were made for all the variables tested for in earlier time periods—ethnicity, occupation, education, and association memberships. Tables 31 and 32 summarize these data.

While the ethnic background of the political leadership continued to show similarities to that of earlier time periods, the leadership groups were less different in this regard that in previous time periods. Data on age, occupation, associational memberships, and education all point to a similar conclusion: leadership groups were less different than formerly. This tendency of

Table 31. Percentage Distribution of Nebraska Political Leaders by Occupation and Place of Birth, 1906–12

Characteristics	Republicans	Democrats
Occupation	N=199	N=199
Agriculture	24.1%	31.2%
The professions		
Law	22.6	20.1
Journalism	6.0	5.0
Total, professions	31.2	29.6
Business		
Merchandising	11.6	9.0
Finance	20.6	19.6
Total, business	39.7	36.2
All other occupations	5.0	3.0
Place of origin[a]	N=199	N=199
Regions of U.S.		
New England	4.5%	1.0%
Middle Atlantic	11.6	4.0
Middle West	51.8	42.2
Border	2.5	4.5
Confederate South	3.0	6.0
Total born in U.S.	73.4	57.8
Outside U.S.		
Germany	7.5	15.1
Ireland	6.5	13.1
Britain exc. Ireland	6.0	2.0
Bohemia	1.0	4.5
Scandinavia	3.5	4.0
Total, outside U.S.	26.1	40.7
Unspecified	0.5	1.5

Note: Columns may not add to 100 owing to rounding.

[a]Based on place of birth, parents' place of birth, surname, and similar evidence.

the leadership of the two parties to become somewhat less distinctive seems to be the result of former Populists moving into positions of leadership in the Democratic party. The Democratic leadership was more Protestant than formerly and had a larger proportion of farmers, included proportionately fewer members of such high-status groups as the Masons and proportionately fewer graduates of distinguished colleges. The direction of all these tendencies is toward the pattern exhibited by Populist leaders in the period 1890–1904. Of the 199 Democratic leaders, nearly one in five had once been either a Populist or a Silver Republican.

TABLE 32. PERCENTAGE DISTRIBUTION OF NEBRASKA POLITICAL LEADERS
BY VARIOUS BIOGRAPHICAL CHARACTERISTICS, 1906–12

Biographical Characteristics	Republicans	Democrats
Date of birth	N=199	N=199
Born before 1841	1.5%	0.5%
Born 1841–50	18.1	15.1
Born 1851–60	29.1	25.1
Born 1861–70	26.1	37.2
Born 1871–80	17.6	14.6
Born after 1880	5.0	3.0
Unspecified	2.5	4.5
Union Army service among		
Leaders born 1836–45	77.8%	42.8%
Spanish American War service		
among leaders born 1871–80	44.7%	39.2%
Attendance at or graduation from		
college or normal school	44.7%	39.2%
Associational memberships	N=113	N=106
Mason	58.4%	38.7%
Other fraternal lodges	72.6	75.5
Professional and commercial		
organizations	19.5	17.0
Agricultural societies	2.7	6.6
Religious affiliations	N=86	N=73
Baptist	4.7%	0.0%
Methodist	33.7	21.9
Quaker	4.7	0.0
Congregational	15.1	8.2
Presbyterian	11.6	19.2
Episcopal	4.7	8.2
Lutheran	8.1	9.6
Roman Catholic	3.5	27.4
Jewish	3.5	0.0
All others	10.5	5.5

Note: Data for date of birth and religious affiliations may not add to 100 owing to rounding.
Percentages for associational memberships and for religious affiliations are based on the
number indicating memberships or affiliations rather than on the total number of subjects.
Percentages for associational memberships will not add to 100 because of multiple memberships.

It is extremely difficult to extract from this group of 398 political leaders a subgroup of unquestioned progressives. Some leaders seemed to move in and out of the progressive camp, like Norris Brown, who in 1906 waged an aggressive antirailroad campaign in his bid for the senate, took the lead in the senate in promoting the income tax amendment, but supported Taft in the 1912 primary and general elections. The legislative reforms of 1907, most directed against the railroads, were passed with the overwhelming support of both parties. The reforms of 1909 and 1911, however, were passed by nearly straight party votes. The best we can do is isolate twenty-nine Republicans who were consistently and unquestionably associated with the progressive wing of their party. These Republican progressives, in their composite portrait, do look somewhat different from others of their party. They were somewhat younger, somewhat more likely to be veterans of the war with Spain, and considerably more likely to have attended college. The group did not include a single Catholic or Lutheran, but other measures of ethnicity are similar to the larger Republican group. Republican progressives were more likely to belong to prestige groups like the Masons, far more likely to be lawyers, and much less likely to be financiers. Among the Republican progressives, 52 percent were professionals, compared with 28 percent of the other Republicans; among the progressives, 17 percent were businessmen compared with 44 percent of the other Republicans.[13]

The political leadership of 1906–12 shows signs of an important shift in attitude regarding tenure in office. Before 1890, officeholding had been seen as a temporary interruption in one's career. The two-term tradition was strong, and only in the state judiciary was long-term continuous service at all common. By 1906 a new attitude had clearly taken hold—serving in public office had become a lifetime occupation. Those best typifying this new attitude were among the most prominent of Nebraska's political leaders. George W. Norris, elected a district judge in 1895, served continuously in elected public office until 1943. Ashton C. Shallenberger was a candidate for some position every year from 1900 to 1934, spending eighteen of those thirty-four years in public office. John H. Morehead ran for elective office in every election from 1910 to 1934 except that of 1916, spending eighteen of those twenty-four years as an officeholder. Moses P. Kinkaid was elected to the House of Representatives in 1902, after an unsuccessful attempt in 1900, and served until his death in 1922. Kinkaid's twenty years in Congress and Norris's forty are in striking contrast to the pattern before 1900, when the longest any Nebraskan had spent in Washington was twelve years.

The New Political System of Progressivism

By 1914 a new political system was in place in Nebraska, characterized by weaker party loyalties and increased ticket-splitting, growing out of voter sensitivity to crosscutting social and economic pressures. This voter sensitivity, in turn, forced candidates to address such issues more closely. Political leadership became more homogeneous, and individual leaders became more closely tied t specific issues and policies, sometimes even when such a commitment placed them at odds with their own party. The replacement of nominating conventions by the direct primary not only encouraged candidates to differentiate themselves from other leaders of their own party but also, in the long run, freed candidates from the bargaining of conventions and encouraged the development of personal organizations that, in turn, permitted them to win nomination after nomination—allowed them, in short, to become professional officeholders. Party organization, ironically, reached its apex at exactly the time it was being undercut by these other forces, an apex symbolized by the Republican state committee's file of some seventy thousand cards that, at the rate of one per voter, represented nearly a third of all the voters in the state. Each card carried information on the voter's ethnicity, religion, occupation, ability to read English, military service, party affiliation, and voting record. While such a massive set of information was essential to the old politics of voter mobilization, it was increasingly anachronistic in the midst of a new politics characterized by weakened party loyalties, candidates with strong personal organizations, and issues that pulled voters one way in one race and the opposite in another on the same ballot.[14]

At a policy level, the new system was characterized by two new approaches—regulation and departisanization. Regulation proved to be a convenient way of removing potentially politically dangerous issues from politics—political leaders could create a commission, make it relatively immune from political pressure, turn a problem over to that commission, and then proudly tell the voters that the problem had been solved. Departisanization—as reflected not only in the direct primary and the independent regulatory commission, but also in the nonpartisan judiciary and the creation of the state board of control for state institutions—was also a means of defusing potentially explosive political situations. By shifting supervision of state institutions from the governor to a nonpartisan, autonomous commission, the governor was relieved of the tedium of the close supervision necessary to prevent politically dangerous charges of mismanagement or corruption and was also relieved of the necessity of selecting among—and inevitably alienating some of—the numerous party faithful who demanded the most routine of jobs.

Perhaps the most important of these structural changes was the replacement of the party convention by the direct primary, a reform that not only relieved party leaders of the necessity of constantly negotiating or reaffirming coalitions among representatives of all party factions, but also lessened the chances of party schism by greatly reducing the stakes. Now party leaders could concentrate on creating a *personal* organization, loyal to an individual leader, stable over time, but not necessarily representative of the major elements within the party. Although such personal factions had long existed, before the direct primary their development had been restrained by the necessity of interacting with—bargaining with—other party factions at the annual state conventions. Between 1906 and 1912, six such personal factions emerged within the Democratic party alone, one led by Shallenberger (strongest in south central Nebraska), another by Morehead (strongest in southeastern Nebraska), others by Dahlman (Omaha), Mullen (statewide), the Bryan brothers plus Edgar Howard and Richard Metcalfe (statewide), and Hitchcock (statewide, but especially Omaha). Among the Republicans, factional leaders included Norris (strongest in south central), Aldrich (east central), Burkett (southeastern), Kinkaid (north central), Victor Rosewater (statewide, but especially Omaha), and Howell (also statewide, but centered in Omaha); with Burkett's defeat in 1910, organizations in the southeast corner of the state began to emerge around Arthur Weaver and Adam McMullen.

Where the state convention system had typically resulted in a state ticket including representatives of several such factions, the direct primary was a winner-takes-all situation, with the losers retiring to lick their wounds and perhaps sit out the general election; some factional leaders, recognizing the regional nature of their organization, settled for a semipermanent seat in the House of Representatives (Shallenberger, Morehead, Kinkaid, and later Howard) or other local office (e.g.,Dahlman's lifetime hold on the Omaha mayoralty.) As local political activists came to focus their loyalties largely upon one person, once elegant party structures—as distinguished from such personal organizations—slowly crumbled.

CHAPTER NINE

Populists, Progressives, and the Transformation of Nebraska Politics

Victorious in death . . . the populist party . . . now passes unbubbling into oblivion. The new progressive party has pre-empted eighteen of its planks. The democrats seized six. The republicans embraced four . . . the work the populist party set out to do has been done, though by other hands, or is about to be done by other hands that once scorned its proposals. . . . The political proposals of the populists, based on the demand for greater popular control of politics and government, have been generally accepted. Their economic plans, free silver, government ownership, popular money, have not been so cordially received. We must wait awhile to see whether the populists now fading into empty air were altogether prophets and not without honor except in their own country.

Nebraska State Journal, 15 August 1912

The Alliancemen who drove their farm wagons in long processions down Main Street to demonstrate their unity in 1890 had thought—hoped—they were initiating a new age in American political life. Their most ambitious proposals, for government ownership of the banking system, transportation, and communication, would never be realized. The mass movement itself never again aroused the degree of popular emotion it had in 1890. By 1893 the state Populist chairman was sending county leaders directions on creating political enthusiasm. The organized party disappeared after the 1916 election; the mass movement had disappeared some two decades before. But those warmed by such political flames carried the embers in their souls. For some, the embers rekindled in the Bull Moose campaign of 1912, or in the Non-Partisan League, or in La Follette's campaign in 1924. For George J. Marshall, son of the 1890 president of the

Franklin County Farmers' Alliance, the embers flared when he wrote the 1930 state Democratic platform "using the language of the old Populist platform so far as it was appropriate to the changed conditions." For a few hardy survivors, the embers burst into flame with Roosevelt's candidacy in 1932.[1]

While the farmers' parades of 1890 did not usher in the millennium, they did mark the beginning of a new stage in Nebraska's political development. From a system dominated by the Republican party and characterized by little continuity of leadership, by a distributive approach to state policy, and by voting behavior determined almost solely by ethnic antagonisms, by 1915 the state had moved to a system of close competition between the two major parties and of professional political leadership with long tenure, a system marked by state policies of regulation and departisanization and by voting behavior highly sensitive to both ethnic and economic issues.

These patterns persisted, for the most part, until at least the late 1930s. The Democrats who came to prominence between 1894 and 1912 continued to dominate their party until the 1930s: Mullen, Hitchcock, Dahlman, Shallenberger, Morehead, Thompson, Charles Bryan, and Edgar Howard all remained active within the party until 1930, when death began to thin their ranks. Among Republicans, Norris, Howell, and McKelvie all continued their party leadership until the mid-1930s. Other prominent Republicans during the 1920s, and 1930s—Adam McMullen, Arthur J. Weaver, Christian "Abe" Sorensen, Hugh Butler, Kenneth Wherry—emerged after 1915, though McMullen and Weaver had played minor parts in state politics before then. The state remained very competitive until 1940. Of twenty-one gubernatorial or senatorial elections between 1914 and 1939, Democrats won ten, Republicans won ten, and Norris, running as an independent recommended by the Democratic state convention, won one; of seventy-five congressional elections between 1914 and 1939, Democrats won thirty-six and Republicans thirty-nine. Despite this degree of competitiveness, officeholders tended to serve for longer and longer periods, a tendency that first clearly emerged during the progressive period. In 1905, only about 30 percent of the state senators had any previous legislative experience, but by 1915 this figure had risen to 65 percent and remained at approximately that level thereafter. Before 1905 very few statehouse officers, congressmen, or senators had served more than two terms, but after 1915 four, six, or even eight terms were not unusual; twenty-nine officeholders served more than fifteen years and five served for thirty years or more. Although the governorship remained bound by the two-term tradition until 1938, former governors remained politically active, often seeking other office.[2]

Detailed analysis of voting behavior after 1914 is beyond the scope of this study, but there is every indication that the ethnic patterns established by the 1880s continued through the 1920s and 1930s. Until 1940, the leading Democratic counties were the very same ones—Catholic and Lutheran, German, Czech, Irish, and Polish—that had been the backbone of the Democratic party since the mid-1880s. After 1940 the German counties—especially the Lutheran ones—left this ethnic coalition, but the others remained. During the 1920s and 1930s marginal agricultural areas continued the pattern of sensitivity to economic issues that had previously been established. The Non-Partisan League candidate for governor in 1920 drew nearly one-quarter of the vote, running most strongly in marginal agricultural areas and in German areas (alienated from the Democrats by the war). La Follette, in 1924, drew about the same proportion from largely the same sources, plus some support from organized labor. Democrats continued to draw some support from marginal farming regions, especially in 1922 and from 1930 to 1938. Roosevelt's strength in 1932 and 1936, and the base for the Democratic statewide sweeps of the 1930s, consisted of the traditionally Democratic ethnics, distressed farmers, and labor. With the exception of the German Lutheran counties—which, since 1940, have been among the most strongly Republican in the state—it was this coalition that was largely responsible for Democratic gubernatorial victories in 1958 and since.[3]

This study of Nebraska politics began with the historiographical dispute over the natures of Populism and progressivism and the relationship between the two. I hoped that a study of Nebraska, where both movements were strong, would produce important insights into the Populist movement, the progressive movement, and linkages between the two. En route to that goal, other conclusions have emerged that seem at least as important as the contributions to the long-standing historiographical argument. This final chapter begins with a look at Populism and progressivism in Nebraska; it concludes with a survey of the transformation of Nebraska politics and of the role of the voter as the moving force in that transformation.

Populism and Progressivism in Nebraska

What, then, was the relationship between the Populist and progressive movements in Nebraska? Were they, as a historian in the progressive tradition put it, "the same ideas traveling in the same direction, with new leaders, new vitality, and new weapons, against the old forces of privilege and corruption''? Or were they, as Hofstadter and others have argued, somewhat similar in their proposals but quite different in their essential natures, with Populism nostalgic, simplistic, even paranoid, and progressivism more complex and sophisticated in its analysis of problems, led by men ''who suffered from the events of their time not through a shrinkage in their means but through the changed pattern in the distribution of deference and power''? Or were the two movements totally different, with Populism (as suggested by Norman Pollack) basically humanitarian and protosocialist and progressivism (as outlined by Kolko) the ''victory of big businessmen in achieving the rationalization of the economy that only the federal government could provide''?[4] We may begin to approach these questions by comparing the two movements in Nebraska along three dimensions: voting behavior, political leadership, and policies.

One way to compare Populist and progressive voting behavior would be to locate strongly Populist voting units that remained roughly stable in their socioeconomic characteristics over the next quarter-century and then determine their voting behavior toward progressivism, as measured in both primary and general elections. But such a survey is largely inconclusive, as a few examples will illustrate.[5]

Upper Driftwood Precinct, Hitchcock County, home of Populist patriarch John Powers, cast 98 percent of its votes for the Populists in 1890, making it the most Populist precinct in the county and one of the most strongly Populist in the state; in 1904 it cast 55 percent of its vote for Watson, indicating a continuing Populist propensity. Six years later, in the 1910 primary for United States senator, Upper Driftwood cast only 25 percent of its vote for Charles O. Whedon, the progressive Republican, and not a single vote for Richard Metcalfe, the progressive Democrat. In the 1912 Republican presidential primary, Upper Driftwood was the precinct most strongly for La Follette in the county (50 percent), and Taft got not a single vote there. In the Democratic presidential primary that year, Clark received 75 percent and Judson Harmon failed to get a single vote. In the 1912 presidential election, Wilson carried Upper Driftwood handily, with 84 percent of the vote, the largest Wilson percentage in the county, and one of the largest in the entire state.

Marshall precinct, Clay County, cast 83 percent of its vote for the Populists in 1890 and 31 percent for Watson in 1904, but in the 1910 senatorial primary both Whedon and Metcalfe did very poorly, well below the countywide average, as did both Wilson and La Follette in 1912. Marshall ranked third of the county's twenty voting units in its support for both Wilson and Roosevelt in the 1912 primaries, but in the general election it was seventh in support for Wilson and tenth for Roosevelt. Wallace Creek Precinct, an old-stock part of largely Irish Greeley County, voted unanimously Populist in 1890 but was well below the county average in support for Whedon (who failed to get a single vote) and Metcalfe in the 1910 senatorial primary and was among the weakest precincts in the county in its support for both Wilson and La Follette in the 1912 presidential primaries. In the 1912 presidential election, Wallace Creek was the second strongest precinct in the county in its support for Taft.

Coefficients of correlation between Populist voting and voting for avowedly progressive candidates are similarly inconclusive. A composite Populist tendency scale, based upon the Populist party vote in 1890, 1892, and 1893, and upon the Populist presidential vote in 1904, correlates at +0.42 with the 1910 primary vote for Metcalfe, at +0.33 with the 1912 primary vote for Wilson, and at +0.22 with the primary vote for Clark. In Republican primaries, the coefficients are no more conclusive: +0.35 for Whedon in 1910, +0.45 for La Follette in 1912, +0.34 for Norris in 1912, and −0.02 for Roosevelt in 1912. All these coefficients are quite low; the strongest relationship, that between Populist voting and support for La Follette, "explains" only 20 percent of the variation in the distribution of the La Follette vote. If eighty-three voting units in five counties, scattered over various parts of the state, are examined to compare support for La Follette with support for the Populists, an interesting pattern emerges. From this data, summarized in table 33, it appears that the areas most strongly for La Follette had, in fact, been strongly Populist but that not *all* areas that had been strongly Populist in the 1890s gave disproportionate support to La Follette.

TABLE 33. COMPARISON OF SUPPORT FOR POPULISM AND LA FOLLETTE

Support for La Follette in 1912 Republican Primary	Number of Precincts	Support for Populism, 1890		
		Mean	Range	
			Low	High
Over 45 percent	6	79%	65%	98%
15 to 45 percent	49	52	9	97
Less than 15 percent	28	45	3	100

One final comparison of voting behavior may be drawn between the social and economic characteristics that were most significantly related, statistically, to voting for the two movements. As I indicated in chapter 4, statistical analysis suggests that Populist voters were motivated, above all else, by their economic distress—that unlike Republican and Democratic voters they were suppressing their ethnic antagonisms in the interest of a unity based on common economic problems. In chapter 8 I suggested that voters most likely to support such progressive candidates as Metcalfe, Shallenberger, and Clarke among the Democrats or Whedon, Norris, and La Follette among the Republicans were those most caught between their ethnic and economic characteristics, most likely to be pulled in one direction by their ethnicity and in the other by their economic situation. In composite, the voter for these candidates was more likely to be pietistic than ritualistic, more likely to be rural than urban, and more likely to be in an area of low farm income than one of higher farm income. It thus appears that the composite characteristics of Populist voters, of Metcalfe, Shallenberger, and Clark voters in Democratic primaries, and of Whedon, Norris, and La Follette voters in Republican primaries, were most similar in their economic and rural-urban dimensions. For other self-avowed progressives, however, patterns of voter support were quite different. Voting for Republicans Brown and Burkett followed exactly the reverse of the pattern described, and primary voting for Theodore Roosevelt showed almost no pattern at all, at least in terms of these variables. While support for Wilson was similar to that for the progressive Democrats already described in the ethnic and urban-rural dimensions, it was the reverse of those patterns in the farm income dimension.

All this suggests (a) that economic distress is the factor that links voting for Populism with voting for Norris–La Follette Republicans or Clark Democrats; (b) that former Populists did not, by any means, form a cohesive voting bloc; and (c) that some candidates widely described as "progressive" had very different sources of voter support, not related to agricultural economics.

The question of continuity between Populist and progressive leadership may be approached in three ways similar to those used to examine voting behavior: examining the response of prominent Populists to progressive issues and candidates; determining the reaction of prominent progressives to the Populist movement; and comparing composite characteristics of the two leadership groups.

Many prominent Populists survived into the progressive period, but only a few continued their active involvement in politics. Among those who remained active, the two most common patterns seem to have been either alignment with the Democrats or participation in the third-party movement spawned by the Non-Partisan League in the early 1920s. Silas Holcomb, suffering from crippling arthritis, moved briefly to Seattle after his term on the state supreme court, but he returned to Nebraska to accept appointment from Democratic governor Morehead as chairman of the state Board of Control. Former senator William V. Allen seldom bolted Democratic candidates, insisted he was a progressive, but opposed a number of typically "progressive" reforms, including county option and the direct primary. Congressman Omer M. Kem left Nebraska after the expiration of his third term in Congress, was elected to the Colorado legislature as a Democrat in 1906, and later was sympathetic to the New Deal. George W. Berge had moved into the Democratic party by 1912 and unsuccessfully sought the Democratic nomination for governor in the 1914 primary. Jacob V. Wolfe ostensibly remained a Populist but supported Democratic progressives. Frank Eager was active in state Democratic politics until as late as the 1930s.[6]

A surprising number of former Populists participated in the new state third party of the early 1920s. A party had been formed in 1920 by delegates from the Non-Partisan League, several Farmers' Union locals, the state Federation of Labor, several central labor councils, and the railway brotherhoods. Out of it, in 1922, grew a state Progressive party that supported La Follette in 1924. The state chairman of the Non-Partisan League in 1918 was James D. Ream, a former Populist state legislator. The state chairman of the Progressive party in 1922 was J. Harlan Edmisten, longtime Populist state chairman and national vice-chairman in 1900, who had taken no active part in politics since then; blindness forced his permanent retirement soon after 1922. State chairman of the La Follette campaign in 1924 was Otto Mutz, a former Populist state senator who, like Edmisten, had not been politically prominent for the preceding twenty years. Michael F. Harrington, prominent at all state Populist conventions through 1904, generally supported Democratic progressives thereafter, but he bolted to Roosevelt in 1912 and to La Follette in 1924, and as early as March of 1932 he announced his support for Franklin D. Roosevelt as the Democratic nominee that year.[7]

Other former Populist leaders occasionally surfaced when some particular issue drew them into politics. John H. Powers, Alliance leader and Populist patriarch, was generally not politically active after the turn of the century, but he did endorse Republican Chester Aldrich for governor in 1910 on the basis of the county option issue. Former governor William A. Poynter supported Republican progressive Sheldon for governor in 1906; he died in 1909 while advocating approval of the eight o'clock closing law before

Governor Shallenberger. Former secretary of state William Porter was not politically conspicuous from 1900 to 1912, but he took part in the formation of the state Progressive party that year. Only a few Populists later took part in Republican politics, none prominently. John O. Yeiser of Omaha generally supported Republican progressives, except when such a course conflicted with the interests of the Douglas County party or with his own ambitions.[8]

Of the 293 Populist leaders active from 1890 to 1905 for whom biographical data were collected, only thirty were politically visible after 1905. Of these thirty, sixteen were Democrats, four were Republicans, six were connected to the Non-Partisan League or the state Progressive party of 1922 and 1924, and the remainder continued to identify themselves as fusion Populists. These data are clearly inadequate for projecting the future political orientation of the Populist leaders of the 1890s. This does indicate, however, that most of the Populist leaders *who remained politically active* retained their affiliation with the Bryanized Democracy, and a significant minority took part in the Progressive party that grew out of the Non-Partisan League activity of the war period.[9]

Few of the Nebraska political leaders of the progressive period had been active Populists. Arthur F. Mullen began his political life as a Populist, under the guidance of Michael F. Harrington, and both Mullen and Harrington were active in state Democratic politics in the early twentieth century. Mullen's political activity continued to his death and included many years as national committeeman and service as Roosevelt's floor manager at the 1932 national convention. William R. Jackson, Populist superintendent of public instruction from 1897 to 1901, was the Democratic candidate for that post in 1910 and was appointed deputy food, drug, and dairy commissioner in 1911 by Governor Aldrich. Addison E. Sheldon, Populist state legislator in 1897, later founded and served as director of the state legislative reference bureau from 1907 to 1919; he was director of the Nebraska State Historical Society until his death. Most prominent Democratic leaders of the early twentieth century had been associated with Bryan in the 1890s and had cooperated with the Populists then. *None* of the most prominent Republican progressives had been participants in the Populist movement, and *none* left a public record of sympathy for it. George W. Norris, Charles O. Whedon, Chester A. Aldrich, Norris Brown, and Elmer Burkett had all opposed Populism in the 1890s, some of them attacking it vigorously. Daniel Nettleton, Speaker of the 1907 House and leader of the progressive Republican forces there, had participated in the 1890 antimonopoly Republican convention and was sometimes referred to as a former Populist, but he had in fact compaigned against McKeighan, the Populist, for Congress in 1890 and continued to take part in county Republican politics through the 1890s. Other leaders of Republican progressivism left no record of their attitudes toward Populism, but none had been involved in active support at a visible level.[10]

A comparison of the collective profiles of the leaders of Populism with those of the progressive movement reveals more differences than similarities. Populist leaders are most different with regard to the various measures of socioeconomic standing and occupation. Only about 5 to 7 percent of the Populist leaders belonged to the high-status Masonic lodge, compared with 20 percent of the progressive Democratic leaders and nearly half of the progressive Republican leaders. Only a third of the Populist leaders had attended college; the same proportion of Republican progressive leaders had attended graduate or professional school. Nearly three-fourths of all Populist leaders were farmers; only a third of the Democrats and a quarter of the progressive Republicans were engaged in agriculture. Only 16 percent of the Populist leaders were professionals, compared with 30 percent of the Democrats and well over half of the most prominent Republican progressives.

These comparisons suggest that the Populist and progressive leadership groups were not drawn from the same, or even from similar, socioeconomic groups. The typical Populist leader was a farmer whose education and associations marked him as lower middle class. He was not, to be sure, typical of most farmers—as indicated by the fact that a third of all Populist leaders had attended college; he was very likely held in esteem by his rural neighbors for his learning or abilities, and he very probably had filled such neighborhood offices as road supervisor, school board member, or justice of the peace. Even among the fifty-four most prominent Populist leaders of the 1890s, 46 percent were farmers. Among progressive political leaders, by contrast, only about 25 percent were farmers, and the most common occupations were professional, especially the law. Progressive leaders tended to have more formal education than Populists and at more distinguished institutions; their membership in socially presitigious fraternal associations like the Masons put them in the upper socioeconomic levels of their communities.

Interestingly, many of the former Populists active in the progressive era were professionals—Mullen, Harrington, Holcomb, Allen, and Berge were all lawyers. Some former Populist officeholders who remained politically visible during or after the progressive period raised their educational level during or after their terms of office in Lincoln—Charles Beal and Frederick Hawxby received law degrees from the University of Nebraska; William R.

Jackson received bachelor's and master's degrees there, as did Addison E. Sheldon, who added a doctorate in history from Columbia University. Most of the Populists who took only a sporadic part in the politics of the progressive period—Powers, Wolfe, Dech—were active or retired farmers. By contrast, all of the three former Populists who served as state chairman of the Non-Partisan League or the Progressive party of the early 1920s were either farmers or retired farmers.

At the level of policy or policy proposals, the two movements were also more different than similar. For the Populists, the origin of most of their grievances could be traced to the emergence of industrialism: giant industrial corporations, allied with corrupt and extravagant officeholders, were making it impossible for farmers and workers to achieve the good life. Farmers suffered most from deflation, moneylenders, railroads, land monopolists, and taxes; workers suffered from exploitation by unfeeling employers, competition with convict labor, the use of Pinkertons, and inability to negotiate with their employers on the basis of equality. The solution to these problems was to be found in the use of government to restrict special privilege and to contain monopoly power. Populist spokesmen extended the labor theory of value to its logical conclusion and advocated the cooperative commonwealth. Nebraska Populist platforms reflected this in arguing that the people, through the government, should own and operate the most essential systems that transferred, but did not create, value—transportation, communication, banking—plus industries that provided public necessities (e.g., coal) and municipal utilities. Labor should be made equal to capital by forcing the arbitration of labor grievances, and laws should alleviate the conditions of the workingman. For this massive redistribution of economic wealth and power to be effective, it was essential that the people improve their control over the medium of redistribution, the government, through direct elections, a secret ballot, and the initiative and referendum. Underlying all Populist proposals was an economic framework based upon the labor theory of value plus a strong faith in the people's inherent virtue and ability to make the correct decisions when given the facts.[11]

Progressives, for the most part, proposed neither reordering of social values nor redistribution of economic power. Few progressives—no Republican progressives—would have been comfortable with the Populist dogma that "wealth belongs to him who creates it." The closest approach the Republican progressives of Nebraska made to such a concept was their suggestion, in 1912, that "all honest labor and toil should be justly compensated." Few progressive proposals—and *no* progressive enactments—posed a serious threat to capital investments. Where Populists had proposed the redistribution of economic power and wealth, progressives proposed regulation. The progressive Republican platform of 1912 echoed Roosevelt in giving first priority to demands for a "permanent non-partisan tariff commission" and "non-partisan industrial commission." Coupled to these demands for regulation, especially among Republican progressives, was a clear admiration for efficiency and businesslike methods in public administration; beginning in 1907, Republican platforms and pronouncements fairly bristled with praise for Republican administrators as demonstrating "business sagacity," "businesslike administration," and "a high standard of efficiency."[12]

Most Republicans—progressive or not—and a minority within the Democratic party sought to extend the principle of regulation to individual behavior as well. Governor Sheldon called for a statewide prohibition law with a local option clause whereby municipalities could suspend it within their limits by a three-fifths vote, and Governor Aldrich made county option his major issue. Republican progressives expressed concern about the growing "divorce evil," blamed it on "the laxness of our marriage laws," and proposed uniform marriage and divorce statutes. Sheldon and Aldrich both expressed concern about the growing number of "defectives" in society, Sheldon proposed the sterilization of "the confirmed criminal and the incurable insane," and Aldrich favoring "absolutely prohibiting the marriage of an habitual drunkard, an epileptic or a mental incompetent." By contrast, of the fourteen state platforms issued by the state Populist party or the state Farmers' Alliance in the 1890s, only two mention liquor at all—the 1891 Alliance platform asking the the cost of criminal prosecutions for violations of liquor laws be paid by the town where the liquor was procured, and the 1894 Alliance platform suggesting that liquor should be sold only by the state, at cost, through salaried officials.[13]

In one area Populists and progressives seem in basic agreement: both favored restructuring the political process with the ostensible objective of increasing the role of the people. Populists, in the 1892s, favored the direct election of all officials, the initiative and referendum, the secret ballot, and the extension of the civil service. Republican progressives, too, favored the initiative and referendum, direct election of United States senators (although they opposed the Oregon Pledge Law), and extension of the civil service principle in state government, and they added the recall, the direct primary, a nationwide presidential primary, the short ballot, a nonpartisan board of control for state institutions, and placing post offices under civil service. Democrats endorsed all of these except the nationwide presidential primary, the short ballot and the placing post offices under civil service and added municipal home rule for Omaha and South Omaha, a nonpartisan judiciary (opposed by Republicans), the nonpartisan election of school superintendents, and equitable legislative apportionment.[14]

Democratic progressivism did not emerge suddenly, as did the Republican variety in 1906; Nebraska Democrats did not falter from the path they chose in 1894, continuing to endorse some Populist proposals and to add to them. To be sure, Democratic progressives did not embrace the cooperative commonwealth, but their policy proposals place them somewhere between Republican progressives and Populists in the area of economics. They endorsed Republican regulation schemes but typically demanded more power for the regulating agency, including, in 1907, the licensing of corporations, and also called for legal distinction "between the natural man and the artificial person, called a corporation." They demanded a national income tax and a national inheritance tax plus careful study of the state tax system to make it as equitable as possible. Perhaps the most publicized Democratic accomplishment was the creation of the state bank deposit guaranty system, which required state-chartered banks (and allowed federally chartered banks) to contribute to an insurance fund to be used to reimburse depositors of a failed bank. The 1913 Democratic legislature also fulfilled a long-standing Democratic promise by passing a workmen's compensation law. Democrats also consistently favored the eight-hour day and some system of conciliation in labor disputes that would allow the state to investigate and publicize but would not include binding arbitration. Other Democratic accomplishments included the Oregon Pledge Law, the initiative and referendum, the state board of control, and nonpartisan election of judicial and educational officials. Some Democratic progressives also continued to promote the cause of public ownership of the railroads.[15]

This survey of policy and policy proposals suggests the Populists and Republican progressives were quite different. Populists advocated a reordering of social values and a redistribution of wealth and economic power. Republican progressives favored no such radical change, proposing regulation but never redistribution. For Populists, regulation was only an interim measure; for Republican progressives it became an end in itself. Democratic progressives fell somewhere between, committed to some redistributive measures—the income and inheritance taxes, designed to reduce "swollen fortunes;" the bank guaranty law, taxing banks in the interests of depositors; workmen's compensation and employer liability; and, at least among some Democratic progressives, government ownership of railroads.[16]

Contemporaries of the two movements in Nebraska tended to ignore the sometimes subtle—but often incredibly obvious—distinctions between Populism and progressivism and to emphasize the extent to which, in

William Allen White's words, the progressives "caught the Populists in swimming and stole all of their clothing except the frayed underdrawers of free silver." Albert Watkins, anti-Populist and antisilver in the 1890s but later a progressive Democrat, titled the section of his 1913 state history dealing with the progressive period "Return of the Republican Prodigal— His Conversion to Populism." The *Nebraska State Journal*, Republican and progressive, suggested in 1912 under the title, "Populism Triumphant," the analysis at the head of this chapter: "the work the populist party set out to do has been done, though by other hands, or is about to be done by other hands that once scorned its proposals." The Populists themselves took a similar view in their 1911 state platform: "The people's independent party of Nebraska . . . rejoices because the principles that it announced twenty years ago . . . have now been accepted in greater or less degree by all parties and all right-thinking men." Although the principles of greater popular participation in politics and government were widely accepted during the progressive years and given wider rhetorical praise than formerly, the heart of the Populist program—government ownership and operation of transportation, communication, banking, and other such services—was never accepted by the progressive movement, nor were Populist proposals for the direct election of the president. For the Populists of 1911 to claim that their "principles" had been universally accepted was a self-congratulatory delusion.[17]

The Transformation of Nebraska Politics

Before the Populist prairie fire raged across the Nebraska plains, politics revolved almost entirely upon a single axis and was largely symbolic. The axis of politics was, of course, ethnic—pitting Catholics and conservative Lutherans, Germans, Czechs, Irish, and Poles, against old-stock Protestants and pietistic immigrants, around a series of issues such as woman suffrage and school attendance laws, but more than anything else around the issue of alcohol. Such single-axis politics, dividing along the lines of ethnoreligious values, were not new to the 1880s; such alignments could be found to the east before Nebraska Territory was even opened to permanent settlement.

Economic issues were either absent or very secondary to the vast majority of voters. Few—if any—of the voters took a burning interest in the tariff rate or railroad subsidies unless, of course, subsidy might mean a transcontinental trunk line in one's own community, bringing growth, new jobs, and prosperity. In the absence of economic *issues*, politics tended to focus upon economic *distribution*—using government to give things in order to bring growth. The things distributed might vary from year to year and from state to federal levels. At the state level, the government could distribute such "things" as normal schools and state hospitals, subsidies for mineral discoveries or for particular crops, or subsidies for railroad construction. At a federal level the "things" included tariff protection and land grants. In the absence of economic issues, distribution of such favors and the distribution of patronage were the major functions of state government. Distribution was politically easy, for coalitions among representatives of communities would typically bargain over the distribution of favors until at least a majority of the representatives felt they had something to take back to the community. If a community's representative failed, it was usually not of great moment, for he did not have a strong stake in being reelected and might even view his service rather grudgingly in the first place.

The ethnic, single-dimension politics of the pre-Populist period was highly conducive to a politics of symbols and to a high degree of party loyalty. Politics in the 1880s seemed to revolve largely around symbols— ritual invocations of party saints and dogmas, ritual exorcisms of the opposing party. Fervor was as high in politics as in church—not surprisingly, given the close connection between the two. The voter's ethnic group identity, religion, and party affiliation were bound together, mutually reinforcing one another. Party loyalty was consequently intense and was vividly displayed during campaigns, when symbols and relics were displayed and invoked and the faithful were exhorted to do battle with the foe. Political leadership was but a part of the larger symbolism. The specific candidate mattered little to Republicans or Democrats; what mattered more was his symbolic nature. In 1888 both parties seemed to achieve the ultimate in this sort of symbolism. The Republican candidate for governor, John Milton Thayer, was born in Massachusetts, graduated from Brown University, came to Nebraska Territory in 1854, became a general in the territorial militia in 1855, practiced law and engaged in territorial politics as an opponent of slavery, volunteered when war broke out in 1861 and left the military as a brigadier general, was elected to the United States Senate in 1867 and sided with the Radical Republicans against Johnson, failed of reelection in 1871, served as governor of Wyoming Territory from 1875 to 1879, returned to Nebraska, was elected state GAR commander in 1886, was elected governor for the first time the same year, and was elected to his second term in 1888. The Democrats nominated John A. McShane, born in Ohio, Catholic and of Irish parentage, educated only through the common schools. He came to Omaha in 1874 and immediately plunged into business ventures and Democratic politics, investing in lumbering, ironworks, and real estate and becoming president of the Union Stock Yards in 1884 and president of the Union Stock Yards Bank in 1887; he was elected to the state legislature in 1880, 1882, and 1884 and to Congress in 1886 when Edward Rosewater bolted the Republican nominee. Both Thayer, the Yankee abolitionist and Civil War veteran, and McShane, the Irish Catholic Omaha businessman and politician, were almost stereotypes of the images their parties projected to the voters. Nominations for office and officeholding itself were largely symbolic exercises; state government actually did very little throughout the period beyond the distributive functions already described. Officeholding was a duty for a few honored party members, and officeholders were amateurs, filling an office for a short period and expecting—sometimes clearly longing—to return to their "normal" life and activities. Symbolic politics with a high degree of party loyalty produced symbolic leadership, amateur leadership, a high degree of turnover in officeholders, and minimal intraparty disputes over issues.[18]

Voter initiative in the early 1890s, in the form of Populism, irrevocably altered this single-dimension, symbolic, amateur political system. Populism sprang from the grass roots; Alliance members led their state leadership into politics, rather than vice versa. Populism was an economic and occupational movement, uniting marginal farmers across ethnic lines of division. Politics became something more than symbolic invocations; politics became a fire, an obsession, a revolution. Politics became mass rallies, excited speeches, singing. Old party lines shattered, new ones formed. The new lines, however, formed not along one dimension, but along two. Economics became as important a determinant of voting as ethnicity. The Populists became the party of marginal farmers, regardless of ethnicity. The Democrats, without the less prosperous of their erstwhile adherents, became a party of more prosperous antiprohibitionists. Republicans, also losing their less prosperous adherents, became concentrated in the towns and in those more prosperous rural areas peopled by old-stock Protestants.

The next crucial step, the coalition of Populists and Democrats, also came as a result of voter initiative. Democratic voters far preceded their party leaders in embracing the new party. Bryan, the most charismatic of a new crop of Democratic leaders, led the party in the same direction Democratic voters had already moved. In the process, the Democratic party made a sharp break with the leadership of the past. Leadership within the Democratic party became tied to economic issues to a far greater extent than formerly. The emergence of Populism not only marked the emergence of a multiple-issue politics with crosscutting lines of cleavage, it also precipitated conversion and schism within the Democratic party, as party leaders fought bitterly over the attitude their party ought take on a range of economic issues. A similar conversion and schism took place within the Republican party, although with less bitterness and with only a small minority aligning themselves with the Populists. Disputes over economic issues, intraparty wrangling and schism, and the weakening of party loyalties all served to focus special attention upon those new party leaders who seemed capable of bringing order from the chaos. Personality became a far more important political force than ever before; Bryan was only the most successful of a field of new faces. Within Bryan's party, the same upheaval produced a host of other leaders—Harrington, Mullen, Dahlman, Shallenberger, Thompson, to name only a few—who would ultimately develop followings of their own rivaling that of the Commoner. The process was much slower within the Republican party, probably because of its greater stability at the grass roots. Republican voters, after the initial losses of 1890, were not moving to the new party; quite the reverse was true, as Republicans recovered the loyalty of some former adherents through the early 1890s.

The end result of this was a new political system. The continuation of multiple, crosscutting determinants of voting behavior made for a system in which party loyalties were permanently weaker, at least among those voters most subject to cross-pressures. The presence of a body of voters receptive to issues and prone to ticket-scratching made for an emphasis on the issues that attracted those votes and for an emphasis on personality as a way of securing votes without issues. The continuation of intense intraparty disputes over nominations (e.g., any of the fusion conventions, the Republican senatorial election of 1900, or the Republican nomination for the United States Senate in 1904) helped move the party leaders to accept a new means of resolving such disputes without creating the schisms characteristic of the 1890s. The new device was the direct primary, which removed the process of nomination from the arena of bargaining (a convention) and placed it instead in the arena of campaigning. Some party leaders sought to capitalize on weakened party loyalties by promoting nonpartisanship; the most prominent example is the creation of the nonpartisan judiciary, which many saw as a way of securing the votes of those with weak loyalties to a party without imposing the barrier of a party label. Certain other divisive issues were dealt with in a similar fashion, through the creation of a nonpartisan regulatory commission, the ultimate solution to the problem of the railroads after the failure in the 1890s of so many efforts to legislate rates. Regulation removed the problem from the arena of political bargaining (in this case, the legislature) and turned it over to nonpartisan commissioners elected directly by the people.

The creation of the new political system was initiated by the voters, in three distinct steps. The emergence of a complex socioeconomic structure, in which the fortunes of Nebraska farmers were tied to decisions by railroad boards of directors and grain exchange brokers, imperiled the self-sufficiency of a simpler past well within the memory of many. The emergence of these economic forces gave rise to demands to control them, and voters initiated the new, multiple-issue politics by creating a new party. Established leaders sought to contain this voter impulse within the old party structure (e.g., the 1890 Republican antimonopoly convention, or the reluctance of Alliance leaders to call an independent political convention), but they failed. The voters' demands were too strong, and the old party structures were shaken or shattered. The new party sought to use the power of government in a way it had never been used before. The new party favored government ownership of the railroads and as an interim measure sought, in both the 1891 and the 1893 legislative sessions, to use the power of government to set railroad rates directly, through law. The second step at which voters took the initiative was in the creation of the Democratic-Populist coalition. Many old party leaders sought to prevent this coalition, even to the point of encouraging party schism. The coalition, preceded by the actions of voters, nonetheless came into existence and dominated state politics for six years. Its aftereffects could be seen within the Democratic party even after the Populist party ended as a significant independent political force. The third step, for which voter initiative was also crucial, was the emergence of a seemingly permanent situation in which multiple-issue politics produced weakened party loyalties and increased emphasis on both issue-oriented politics and the politics of personality. Once again party leaders sought to contain this development through such devices as the direct primary, the initiative and referendum, the nonpartisan judiciary, and the nonpartisan regulatory commission. These efforts were successful in deflecting the major thrust of the voters in marginal agricultural areas, a thrust that, throughout the period from 1890 through at least the 1912 election, was in the direction not of regulation, but of government ownership. Although the thrust was deflected, the tension remained and continued to influence state politics at least until World War II, producing the Non-Partisan League party of 1920, which drew nearly a quarter of the vote, the Progressive party of 1922 and 1924, strong support for George W. Norris throughout the 1920s and 1930s, and a base for "Brother Charley" Bryan's gubernatorial victories of 1922, 1930, and 1932. This tension was finally reduced about the time of World War II, apparently by a combination of assimilation and the final elimination of large numbers of marginal farmers. Both Norris and Bryan lost their last campaigns for office in 1942.[19]

The farmers who drove their wagons in the Alliance parades of 1890 had hoped they were initiating a new political system. And a new political system did emerge in Nebraska. But the new system was not what the farmers of 1890 had sought. The goal of their most optimistic leaders—the cooperative commonwealth—would never be realized. Their enemies—the corporations, the bankers, the railroads—would never come under public ownership, although they would yield to varying degrees of regulation. The status of the farmer improved markedly during the late 1890s and early twentieth century, but the improvement was only temporary. Agricultural depression reappeared after World War I and seemed to become permanent, yielding only when massive numbers of farm families left their land for the cities and those who survived brought a section, two sections, or more together as a single farm unit. Land that had once supported ten families now appeared inadequate to support one. While collecting Nebraska folk songs in the 1930s, Federal Writers' Project researchers found one by Luna E. Kellie, who was secretary of the state Farmers' Alliance through the late 1890s:

> There's a dear old homestead on Nebraska's fertile plain
>   Where I toiled my manhood's strength away;
> All that labor now is lost to me, but it is Shylock's gain,
>   For that dear old home he claims today.
> *Chorus*
> Ah, my dear prairie home! Nevermore in years to come
>   Can I call what I made by toil my own;
> The railroads and banks combined, the lawyers paid to find
>   Out a way to rob me of my home.
>
> It was many years ago that I first saw through this scheme,
>   And I struggled from their meshes to get free;
> But my neighbors all around me then were in a party dream,
>   And they voted to rob my home from me.
> *Chorus*
> Now their homes are gone as well as mine, and they're awake at last,
>   And they now see the great injustice done;
> While some few their homes may save, yet the greater part, alas!
>   Must be homeless for all time to come.
> *Chorus*
> We must now the robbers pay for a chance to till the soil,
>   And when God calls us over the great range,
> All heaven will be owned, I suppose, by men who never toil,
>   So I doubt if we notice the exchange.

Another Writers' Project song, this one anonymous, was more humorous, but no less resigned:

> Of all the years since I began
>   To mix in politics,
> The one that tries my inner man is
>   Eighteen Ninety-six;
> And as this aching void I feel,
>   I cast a wishful glance,
> And count them all from hip to heel,
>   These patches on my pants.[20]

APPENDIX A

Methodology and Data Sources

This appendix addresses certain of the methodological decisions and assumptions involved in the quantitative analysis of voting behavior and the sources of data for both population characteristics and elections.

Methodological Decisions and Assumptions

The key methodological decisions in this study involved the determination of (*a*) appropriate units for analysis, (*b*) appropriate analytical methods, and (*c*) appropriate variables for analysis. Each of these will be taken up in turn.

The determination of the appropriate units for analysis is closely limited by the nature of the historical data. In studying voting behavior, the logical unit of analysis is the voter, and virtually all studies of contemporary voting behavior use the individual voter as the unit of analysis and the public opinion survey as the method. In historical analysis, however, this is not possible, and the research must deal with aggregate data for both election returns and population characteristics. The only major exceptions to the aggregate nature of the data are to be found in the census takers' manuscripts, in which individuals appear with certain of their social and economic characteristics, and in various local histories that include extensive biographical sections. The census manuscripts, however, lack political information and exist only at widely spaced intervals of time (for this study, only 1885 and 1900). Although the biographical sections of the local histories often include political information, the sort of biographical data contained is not necessarily consistent from one entry to the next, does not include all or a reliably random sample of all of the voters in an area, and—like the manuscript census—is specific to a particular time. If the historian is to study voting behavior in the past, the unit of analysis must be something other than the individual voter.

Once the decision is made to utilize aggregate data, the researcher must determine which level of aggregation is most appropriate for the particular study. For Nebraska in the period 1885–1915, some data exist at the level of the precinct, and a good deal more exist at the level of the county. As I indicated in the first chapter of this study, I chose the county as the basic unit of analysis. There are three reasons for this choice: extensive data exist for the county level, far more than for the precinct level; county-level data are more readily available than precinct-level; and the choice of the county as the basic unit of analysis does not preclude the use of selected precinct-level data where such seem to be more appropriate or to be desirable as a check on conclusions drawn from county-level data. The choice of the county as unit of analysis maximizes the types of data available, for county-level social and economic data are readily available in the published census, and county-level voting returns are easily accessible for every election.

By contrast, using precincts as the unit of analysis would present formidable problems in collecting data of both sorts. Social and economic characteristics would have to be tabulated by laboriously counting entries in the 1885 or 1900 census manuscripts and would be limited to those two dates. Where precinct-level election data exist, they are for the most part scattered through the various courthouses of the state, and their preservation has been dependent on the vagaries of dozens of county clerks. In some counties the record books are carefully preserved and readily located; in others the books may be missing or may have suffered damage. Nonetheless, precinct-level data were collected in a number of instances as a check on conclusions drawn from the analysis of county-level data.

As noted in the Preface, analysis was limited to the sixty-one geographically contiguous counties that contained more than five persons to the square mile at the time of the censuses of 1890, 1900, and 1910, thereby limiting analysis to relatively populated and relatively stable counties.

The use of aggregate data, whether at the county or precinct level of aggregation, creates one important danger: that of committing the ecological fallacy. To avoid this danger, I decided to use more than one test for any relationships whenever possible.[1] Two basic forms of analysis were used with the county-level data: (*a*) regression, including scatter diagrams, the derivation of regression coefficients, Pearson product-moment coefficients of correlation, and stepwise multiple regression; and (*b*) cluster analysis.[2] When these methods suggested the possibility of a relationship between variables, I made efforts to confirm such a relationship by reference to actual voting precincts or to the comments of contemporaries. The text of this study incorporates various elements of this process as seems appropriate to any given discussion.

Regression analysis assumes that the relationship between two variables can be expressed in the form of a straight line. The analysis begins, logically, with the construction of a scatter diagram, locating each unit of analysis with reference to the value it has for the independent variable and for the dependent variable. The next step is to determine the location of the straight line that best summarizes the distribution of these separate points. This line, the regression line, is also termed the least-squares line, because the distance from each point to the line, squared (to compensate for negative values), is minimized by the regression line. The line may then be presented in summary form by reference to the regression coefficients, denoted by a and b, where a represents the point at which the regression line intercepts the vertical axis and b represents the slope of the line, that is the number of units of vertical increase for each unit increase on the horizontal axis. So long as b is a positive number, the regression line will run from the lower left of the scatter diagram toward the upper right. Should b have a negative value, the regression line will run from the upper left to the lower right. Once the regression line has been plotted, the next step is to measure the "closeness of fit" between the regression line and the actual points of the scatter diagram. The Pearson product-moment coefficient of correlation does so with a value that varies from 0.00 to $+1.00$ and from -1.00 to 0.00. A coefficient of $+1.00$ indicates that an increase in one unit in the value of the independent variable brings a corresponding increase in the value of the dependent variable for every unit of analysis, that is, each unit of analysis actually lies on the regression line. A value of -1.00 indicates a perfect inverse relationship, that is, that each increase in the value of the independent variable brings a corresponding decrease in the value of the dependent variable and that each unit of analysis is precisely on the regression line. The coefficient of correlation expresses a relationship between the two variables such that the square of the coefficient is understood as the proportionate reduction in error in the prediction of the dependent variable, knowing the independent variable.

Stepwise multiple regression applies the assumption of the Pearson coefficient of correlation to the situation where there is more than one independent variable. Multiple regression also presumes the existence of a linear relationship. The stepwise version of multiple regression starts with a matrix of the coefficients of correlation between each possible pair of variables. The program begins with the independent variable that has the greatest explanatory power for the dependent variable. It then adds a second independent variable to the regression equation, selecting the one that maximizes the explanatory power of the second in conjunction with the first. A third or subsequent variable is then added using the same criterion. The result is a multiple coefficient (R) that is interpreted in the same way as a Pearson coefficient (r), that is, as the square root of the proportionate reduction of error. A stepwise multiple regression summary table provides the multiple coefficient (R), the square of the multiple coefficient representing the proportionate reduction of error (R^2), the change in this multiple coefficient resulting from the introduction of each subsequent variable into the equation, and the simple coefficient (r) between each independent variable and the dependent variable. A large increase in the multiple coefficient indicates significant explanatory value for a second or subsequent independent variable, but a small increase indicates that introducing a second variable is not especially useful in "explaining" variation in the dependent variable. Should two independent variables each have a high coefficient of correlation with the same dependent variable but the second not markedly increase the multiple coefficient when stepped into the regression equation, it might suggest (a) that the two independent variables are closely related and perhaps (b) that both are in fact measures of the same or similar population attributes.

The use of stepwise multiple regression creates some potential problems of interpretation, however. It is possible that any given independent variable may influence the dependent variables in more than one way, that is both directly and indirectly. The latter possibility would include a situation where an independent variable had a direct influence on the dependent variable and also had a direct influence on some other independent variable. It is sometimes suggested that stepwise multiple regression may assign the direct influence of secondary and subsequent independent variables to the first variable put into the equation and thus exaggerate the influence of the first and underestimate the influence of those that follow. An obvious example of such a situation might be the use of the following independent variables: mean annual dollar income per farm, mean value per acre of farmland, number of bushels of corn produced per acre, number of bushels of wheat produced per acre, value of corn produced, value of wheat produced, value of livestock sold, proportion of land area under cultivation, and farm mortgage interest rate. In point of fact, all of these variables measure various aspects of one underlying factor: the viability of agriculture. Whichever of these would have the highest individual correlation with the dependent variable would be stepped into the equation first, and subsequent variables would add little to the explanatory of the first. One way of guarding against this problem is to reduce all independent variables to artificial factors through factor analysis. This option was explored but rejected, since the factors produced, by the nature of the program, had no relation to each other and using them was, in fact, a distortion of reality. As I noted in chapter 2, there was a relationship between the viability of agriculture and the ethnicity of settlers, in that old-stock Americans were more likely than Germans or Czechs to settle in areas of marginal agriculture. The interrelationship between sentiment favoring prohibition (as measured by the 1890 vote) and the prosperity of agriculture (as measured by the 1889 mean annual income per farm) produces a coefficent of correlation of -0.25. Employing factored variables eliminates this interrelationship. I decided instead to use actual variables, selecting one from each of the three major groups of variables revealed by factor analysis and by correlating all independent variables. One group of variables focuses upon the viability of agriculture, and the mean annual farm income was used to represent this group; a second group focuses upon place of residence, and the percentage of the population living in incorporated areas was used to represent this group. The third group focuses upon ethnicity, and three different variables were used here: the vote for prohibition in 1890 for dependent variables from 1886 to 1895; the percentage of the population born in Bohemia, Germany, Ireland, or Poland in 1900 for dependent variables from 1896 through 1904; and the percentage of the population born in or having parents born in Austria, Germany, or Ireland in 1910 for dependent variables from 1906 through 1914. The first method of dealing with this potential problem in the interpretation of the results of stepwise multiple regression was thus the selection of independent variables that did not have a logical causal relationship. The next step was to be alert, nonetheless, to possible statistical relationships between these independent variables and to the possibility that such a statistical inter-relationship might produce a misleading stepwise regression result. When such possibilites arose, other methods of analysis were employed as a check on the conclusions that might have been drawn from the stepwise multiple regression analysis. Examples may be found in chapters 2 and 4. The process described here, however, is not incorporated into those chapters beyond what seems appropriate to illustrate the conclusions drawn.

Cluster analysis, as presented in this study, operates in a quite different fashion in the search for relationships among variables. Whereas correlation and multiple regression presume a linear relationship, seek to identify its direction, and measure the closeness of fit to the regression line, cluster analysis makes no such assumptions and is instead a method of summarizing data by homogeneous clusters of cases. As used in this study cluster analysis consists of specifying parameters for independent variables and averaging the values of the dependent variables for each cluster of units specified by the parameters chosen. In this study, one such analysis consisted of specifying quartiles for independent variables; the program assigns each county to its appropriate quartile, then calculates the mean value of the dependent variable for each quartile. A second variety of this method is to break each of these quartiles for one independent variable down according to the quartile distribution of a second independent variable, then calculate the mean value of the dependent variable for each of the sixteen categories that result. Figures 1 through 4 are based upon such a two-way breakdown. A third variable may also be used in such a cluster analysis; such an operation provided the basis for table 30.

Both cluster analysis and stepwise multiple regression are methods of multivariate analysis, but the two operate in very different fashions. Multiple regression assumes a linear relationship and uses every case to try to find the optimal regression line for "explaining" the relationships among variables. Cluster analysis assigns cases to homogeneous categories and summarizes the value of the dependent variable for these categories; interpretation of the results is left to the analyst. Scatter diagrams, regression coefficients, Pearson coefficients of correlation, stepwise multiple regression, and cluster analysis using two or more independent variables were calculated for every vote for president, governor, and senator between 1886 and 1914, for indexes of party strength for every even-numbered year, for selected elections in odd-numbered years, for all candidates in party primaries, and for a number of popular referenda. Presentation of all of these results would take hundreds of pages, but representative examples are included in the text, and additional examples may be found in Appendix B. These analyses, supplemented by precinct analysis, the observations of contemporaries, and such other operations as are described in the text itself, form the basis for the conclusions drawn about the nature of voting behavior in Nebraska during 1886 through 1914.

Determining the appropriate variables for this analysis sometimes involved selecting from a rich array and at other times involved an attempt to construct an appropriate scale or index from other variables, none of which seemed entirely satisfactory alone. The discussion of these variables may be conveniently broken down into political variables and population variables.

There is a wealth of political data for virtually every year. Even-numbered years from 1886 through 1916 saw elections for at least eight state officers as well as federal officers—governor, lieutenant governor, secretary of state, treasurer, auditor, attorney general, superintendent of public instruction, commissioner of public lands and buildings, and, after 1906, railway commissioner, plus congressmen, United States senator, and presidential electors. Odd-numbered years saw elections for supreme court judge and for two university regents. Despite this wealth of election returns, there are no data that directly indicate the party affiliation of voters, either in the form of voter registration figures (most counties were not required to register voters until much later) or in the form of the number of votes cast on the party line (such ballot lines were in existence for only a few years, and no statewide tabulations were made of them). To develop a measure of the strength of the various parties among the voters, I averaged the seven state executive offices below governor by party, to produce an index of party strength for each county for each even-numbered year. (The same procedure was used with the vote for the two university regents in 1891 and 1893.) The rationale for such a procedure is fairly obvious: these offices seldom drew much attention to the individual candidates, and voting for these offices therefore provides an accurate indication of the voters' party commitments at that time. Averaging the seven eliminates the possibility that some one of them might be partially unrepresentative of party strength—for example, that a candidate might do somewhat better in his home county than the strength of his party would otherwise dictate. Averaging the party vote for all seven offices submerges such individual idiosyncrasies and produces as reliable a measure of party affiliation as is possible. Voting for the heads of the ticket (president, United States senator, governor, and supreme court judge) was analyzed separately from party strength, to determine how the vote for a particular candidate compared with that for the rest of his party and to determine the appeal of particular candidates.

In chapter 8, prior party preference is used as an independent variable in analyzing primary election voting patterns. To determine if a historical pattern of support for Populist candidates was significantly related to patterns of support for candidates in primary elections, it was necessary to derive a measure of Populist voting proclivities. To make such a measure as reliable as possible, I decided that it ought not to be based on any year when fusion was operating and that it ought to include Populist support both in the early 1890s and in the 1904 presidential election. The scale derived, therefore, was the mean of the normalized distribution of the index of Populist party voting strength in 1890, 1892, and 1893 and of Populist presidential voting in 1904. Normalizing these four distributions gives the 1904 presidential vote weight equal to each of the other three, even though in most counties the Populist presidential vote in 1904 was half, a third, or even less of the Populist party vote in the early 1890s.

Some political data were used as independent variables when the data clearly measured an attitude. Thus, for elections from 1886 through 1895, one key independent variable used was the attitude of the county on prohibition, as expressed in voting for or against an amendment to the state constitution in 1890 providing for prohibition. During the progressive period there were a number of such referenda relating to ethnicity—a vote on limiting the suffrage to fully naturalized citizens in 1910 (until then any alien who had filed his declaration of intent could legally vote), a vote on woman suffrage in 1914, and vote on prohibition in 1916.

The first task in determining relationships between voting behavior and population attributes was to select appropriate independent variables. Once again a wealth of data was available in the decennial census publications, covering such attributes as place of birth, parents' place of birth (1910 only), religion, number of people living in incorporated cities, towns, and villages and the number outside such areas, the number of people gainfully employed in various occupations, plus a host of statistics of agriculture—on productivity (in bushels or head or whatever the appropriate unit, as well as in dollars), the number of acres of improved farmland, ownership status (owner-operated, tenant-operated, or manager-operated), value (including land, improvements, implements, and livestock), and mortgage debt information. In reducing the number of independent variables, the first step was to seek relationships among them; Pearson coefficients of correlation were accordingly calculated for all pairs of variables for each census (1890, 1900, and 1910). This made it clear that there were three major groups of independent variables: one revolving around measures of ethnicity (attitude on prohibition, place of birth, religious indicators); a second reflecting an urban-rural dimension (percentage of the population living in incorporated areas, population density, percentage of the gainfully employed population engaged in manufacturing occupations, ratio between the number of farms and the total population, etc.); and a third related to various measures of the prosperity of agriculture (mean value per farm acre, mean dollar income per farm, the percentage of land area in improved farm acreage, corn productivity and wheat productivity, the ratio between wheat acreage and corn acreage, the ratio between corn production and the number of swine, the farm mortgage interest rate, the tenancy rate, etc.). Experimenting with factor analysis confirmed these three as the major dimensions of the population revealed by the data available.

In the final decision, the selection of an independent variable representative of each of the three population attributes, I used three criteria; (*a*) the extent to which a given variable was statistically related to the others in its major group, with an eye to selecting variables having high coefficients of correlation with as many of the others in the group as possible; (*b*) closeness in time to the dependent variables being analyzed so that no independent variable was removed by more than five years time from the dependent variables for which a relationship was tested; and (*c*) an intuitive logic—that is, whether the variable chosen could be easily and quickly seen to be representative of the dimension being tested. Two variables were used throughout the study: the mean annual dollar income per farm (representing the prosperity of agriculture) and the percentage of the population living in incorporated cities, towns, or villages (representing the urban-rural dimension). Three different, but closely related, ethnic variables were used: for analysis of the period 1886–95, the vote for prohibition in 1890; for analysis of the period 1886–1904, the percentage of the population born in Germany, Bohemia (the Czechs), Ireland, or Poland, as of 1900; and for analysis of the period 1906–14, the percentage of the population born in, or having parents born in, Germany (the vast majority German, but with a few German Poles), Austria (the vast majority Czech, but including a few German-speaking Austrians and some Austrian Poles), or Ireland, as of 1910.

Data Sources

The official tallies of the vote, county by county, were kept in a basement storage vault maintained by the secretary of state in the Nebraska state capitol. As a result of my search for these official tallies, and the assistance of State Archivist Duane Reed in that search, the entire collection has now been microfilmed and is available at the Nebraska State Historical Society. Returns are summarized on separate sheets of paper for each year; those for even-numbered years are usually typeset and printed, some of those for odd-numbered years are handwritten. Some of this material may also be found in: *Nebraska Blue Book: 1901 and 1902* (Lincoln: State Journal Co., 1901), pp. 173–369; *Nebraska Blue Book and Historical Register: 1915* (Lincoln: State Journal Co., 1915), pp. 185, 186, 907, 908, 911–36; *Nebraska Blue Book and Historical Register: 1918* (Lincoln: n. p., 1918), pp. 439–94.

Voting returns for the precinct level were obtained in some cases by going to the county courthouse, locating the relevant record book, and copying down the official tallies. This was done for the following counties: Boone County (county seat, Albion); Butler County (county seat, David City); Clay County (county seat, Clay Center); Greeley County (county seat, Greeley); Harlan County (county seat, Alma); Jefferson County (county seat, Fairbury); and Pawnee County (county seat, Pawnee City). Some Hitchcock County records were used at the Nebraska State Histroical Society, as were certain returns for Knox County (only Sparta, Jefferson, and Bohemia precincts were tabulated). Other precinct-level returns were secured from the following newspapers:

Adams County: *Hastings Daily Republican,* 7 November 1895; (Hastings) *Adams County Democrat*, 13 November 1896, 5 November 1897, 18 November 1898, 17 November 1899, 16 November 1900, 21 November 1902, 18 November 1904, 16 November 1906, 13 November 1908, 18 November 1910, 15 November 1912, 20 November 1914, 17 November 1916.

Blaine County: *Brewster News*, 13 November 1896.

Brown County: *Ainsworth Star-Journal*, 6 November 1890, 15 November 1893, 10 November 1894, 13 November 1895, 12 November 1896, 11 November 1897, 17 November 1898.

Butler County: *David City Tribune*, 17 November 1887; (David City) *Butler County Press*, 15 November 1894, 13 November 1896, 5 November 1897, 18 November 1898; (David City) *People's Banner*, 16 November 1899, 17 November 1904.

Cedar County: (Hartington) *Cedar County News*, 15 November 1900, 13 November 1902, 8 November 1906, 16 November 1916; *Hartington Herald*, 13 November 1908, 11 November 1910, 8 November 1912, 13 November 1914; *Beemer Times*, 7 November 1890.

Cherry County: (Valentine) *Republican*, 17 November 1893, 16 November 1894, 15 November 1895, 13 November 1898, 12 November 1897, 17 November 1899, 18 November 1904; (Valentine) *Western News-Democrat*, 17 November 1898.

Cuming County: (West Point) *Progress*, 11 November 1886; *West Point Republican*, 8 November 1895, 5 November 1897, 11 November 1898, 10 November 1899, 9 November 1900, 15 November 1901, 7 November 1902, 11 November 1904, 9 November 1906, 18 September 1908, 6 November 1908, 26 August 1910, 18 November 1910, 8 November 1912, 13 November 1914, 17 November 1916; (West Point) *Cuming County Democrat*, 28 August 1914; (West Point) *Cuming County Advertiser*, 10 November 1891, 15 November 1892, 14 November 1893, 13 November 1894, 10 November 1896; (West Point) *Nebraska Volksblatt*, 8 November 1889.

Dakota County: (Dakota City) *North Nebraska Eagle*, 6 November 1890, 10 November 1892, 8 November 1894, 5 November 1896, 10 November 1898, 6 November 1902, 10 November 1904, 8 November 1906, 11 September 1908, 6 November 1908, 26 August 1910, 11 November 1910, 26 April 1912, 15 November 1912, 13 November 1914, 16 November 1916.

Deuel County: *Chappell Register*, 7 November 1895, 12 November 1896, 17 November 1898, 11 November 1899, 17 November 1904.

Frontier County: (Stockville) *Faber*, 12 November 1896, 17 November 1898, 16 November 1899, 17 November 1904.

Harlan County: (Alma) *News Reporter*, 7 November 1895; *Alma Weekly Register*, 13 November 1896; (Alma) *Harlan County Journal*, 18 November 1904; *Alma Record*, 24 November 1908.

Hayes County: (Hayes Center) *Hayes County Republican*, 8 November 1895, 4 November 1897, 10 November 1898, 10 November 1904.

Hitchcock County: *Trenton Register*, 6 November 1908, 26 August 1910, 18 November 1910, 15 November 1912, 13 November 1914, 17 November 1916.

Holt County: (O'Neill) *Frontier*, 8 November 1888, 14 November 1889, 10 November 1890, 12 November 1891, 17 November 1892, 16 November 1893, 15 November 1894, 21 November 1895, 26 November 1896, 11 November 1897, 17 November 1898, 16 November 1899, 15 November 1900, 13 November 1902, 10 November 1904, 15 November 1906, 12 November 1908, 17 November 1910, 14 November 1912, 12 November 1914, 16 November 1916.

Howard County: *St. Paul Phonograph*, 9 November 1888, 7 November 1890, 10 November 1892, 13 November 1896, 11 November 1898, 9 November 1900, 7 November 1902, 11 November 1904, 23 November 1906, 6 November 1908, 11 Novermber 1910, 7 November 1912.

Kearney County: (Minden) *Kearney County Gazette*, 12 November 1886;

(Minden) *Kearney County Democrat*, 13 November 1888, 11 November 1890; (Minden) *Workman*, 11 November 1892; *Minden Courier*, 15 November 1894, 12 November 1896, 17 November 1898, 15 November 1900, 6 November 1902, 14 November 1912; (Minden) *Kearney County News*, 11 November 1904; *Minden News*, 16 November 1906, 13 November 1908, 26 August 1910, 18 November 1910, 17 November 1916.

Keya Paha County: *Springview Herald*, 12 November 1895, 11 November 1896; (Springview) *Keya Paha Call*, 5 November 1897.

Kimball County: (Kimball) *Western Nebraska Observer*, 17 November 1898, 9 November 1899.

Knox County: *Bloomfield Monitor*, 13 November 1895, 14 November 1900, 13 November 1902, 17 November 1904, 15 November 1906, 12 November 1908, 17 November 1910, 14 November 1912, 12 November 1914, 16 November 1916; *Niobrara Tribune*, 11 November 1896, 10 November 1897, 23 November 1898.

Lincoln County: (North Platte) *Current*, 8 November 1890; (North Platte) *Independent Era*, 13 November 1891; *North Platte Telegraph*, 11 November 1893, 13 November 1897, 19 November 1898.

Pawnee County: (Pawnee City) *Pawnee Republican*, 4 November 1886, 8 November 1888, 13 November 1890, 17 November 1892, 14 November 1894, 12 November 1896.

Platte County: *Columbus Democrat*, 5 November 1886, 16 November 1888; *Columbus Weekly Telegram*, 6 November 1890, 5 November 1891, 10 November 1892, 9 November 1893; *Columbus Telegram*, 8 November 1894, 7 November 1895, 5 November 1896, 11 November 1897, 10 November 1898, 9 November 1899, 8 November 1900, 7 November 1902, 11 November 1904, 9 November 1906, 11 September 1908, 6 November 1908, 19 August 1910, 11 November 1910, 26 April 1912, 15 November 1912, 13 November 1914, 10 November 1916.

Rock County: *Bassett Eagle*, 4 November 1897, 10 November 1898, 9 November 1899.

Saunders County: (Wahoo) *New Era*, 17 November 1892, 16 November 1893, 15 November 1894, 21 November 1895, 5 November 1896; *Wahoo New Era*, 5 November 1897, 11 November 1898, 10 November 1899; (Wahoo) *Saunders County New Era*, 16 November 1900, 7 November 1902, 18 November 1904; *Wahoo Democrat*, 10 September 1908, 13 November 1908, 25 August 1910, 17 November 1910, 2 May 1912, 14 November 1912, 12 November 1914, 16 November 1916.

Sheridan County: *Rushville Standard*, 15 November 1895, 13 November

16 Developed 3 clusters for analytical approach.

19. Ethnicity strongest variable

30-1 The Republican party system was not geared to respond to popular demands in 1896.

49-5 Dem Freexelives League

55-57 - Disagrees with Kleppner on strong relationships between production & population

57 Pops are party based on single issue - economy.

60 ?

66 Bryan not leading but following

70-71 Farmer leaders etc in Pops

71 characteristics of party member & voting

95-7 Persistent pops contrary to my view

90. Cherny's theory of who were realigned in 1896

DJ Very important

42 Was Hicks correct

57 How much continuent?

63 What happened between 1889-1894

1896, 12 November 1897, 18 November 1898, 17 November 1899.
Sioux County: (Harrison) *Sioux County Herald*, 8 November 1890, 12
    November 1891, 10 November 1892, 16 November 1893, 8 November
    1894, 14 November 1894; (Harrison) *Sioux County Journal*, 7
    November 1889, 10 November 1898.
Wheeler County: (Bartlett) *Wheeler County Independent*, 24 November
    1892, 11 November 1897, 17 November 1898.

Variables measuring ethnic attributes at the county level included some
political variables already identified and cited, plus those derived from the
census. County-level tabulations of place of birth and, for 1910 only, of
parents' place of birth may be found in the following locations:

Table 33, Department of the Interior, Census Office, *Report on the Popula-
    tion of the United States at the Eleventh Census: 1890*, part 1
    (Washington D.C.: Government Printing Office, 1895); Table 34,
    Census Office, *Twelfth Census of the United States Taken in the Year
    1900*, vol. 1, *Population* (Washington D.C.: Government Printing
    Office, 1901); Nebraska Table 1, Bureau of the Census, Department of
    Commerce, *Thirteenth Census of the United States Taken in the Year
    1910*, vol. 3 (Washington D.C.: Government Printing Office, 1913).

Religious data were derived based on the number of adherents listed in the
1906 census of religious bodies and expressed as a percentage of the
population. For Protestant bodies this was based on the county population
over twelve years of age (the usual age of confirmation), as reported in the
1910 census. For Roman Catholic church members, the census returns were
85 percent of those reported by the church as having been baptized, and the
percentage Catholic was calculated by restoring the base to 100 percent and
taking the percentage of the entire county population. Population figures
came from Nebraska Table 1 of the 1910 census cited above. Denominational data came from:

Table 4, Department of Commerce and Labor, Bureau of the Census,
    Special Reports: Religious Bodies: 1906, part 1, *Summary and General
    Tables* (Washington D.C.: Government Printing Office, 1910).

Measures of ethnicity at the precinct level were derived by counting
entries in the 1885 and 1900 census schedules, available on microfilm. The
1885 state census microfilm was used at the Nebraska State Historical
Society; that for the 1900 census was used in the National Archives,
Washington, D.C. Determining religious data for rural precincts is difficult,

but one indication is the presence in or near the precinct of a church of an identifiable denomination. County atlases or plat books are useful for locating such churches:

C. H. Scoville, comp., *Plat Book of Butler County Nebraska* (Philadelphia: National Publishing Co., 1889);

Atlas of Cuming County, Nebraska (Mason City, Iowa: Anderson Publishing Co., 1918);

Plat Book of Dixon and Dakota Counties, Nebraska (Philadelphia: National Publishing Co., 1891);

Standard Atlas of Greeley County, Nebraska(Chicago: Geo. A. Ogle, 1904);

Standard Atlas of Holt County, Nebraska (Chicago: Geo. A. Ogle, 1904);

Standard Atlas of Howard County, Nebraska (Chicago: Geo. A. Ogle, 1917);

Untitled plat book of Platte County, dated 1914 (in Nebraska State Historical Society);

Plat Book of Saunders County, Nebraska (Des Moines: Brown-Scoville, 1907).

Agricultural data may be found, by county, as follows:

Unnumbered map showing value per acre and county interest rate. Department of the Interior, Census Office, *Eleventh Census: 1890: Report on Real Estate Mortgages* (Washington D.C.: Government Printing Office, 1895);

Tables 103 and 108, Department of the Interior, Census Office, *Eleventh Census: 1890: Report on Farms and Homes* (Washington D.C.: Government Printing Office, 1896);

Tables 6, 12, and 14, Department of the Interior, Census Office, *Eleventh Census: 1890: Statistics of Agriculture* (Washington D.C.: Government Printing Office, 1894);

Tables 19, 35, and 55, Census Office, *Twelfth Census: 1900*, vol. 5, *Agriculture*, part 1 (Washington D.C.: Government Printing Office, 1901);

Nebraska Tables 1 and 4, Department of Commerce, Bureau of the Census, *Thirteenth Census: 1910*, vol. 3, *Agriculture, 1909 and 1910* (Washington D.C.: Government Printing Office, 1913).

APPENDIX B

Correlation and Regression Coefficients, All General Election Dependent Variables and Major Independent Variables

Dependent Variables	Vote in Favor of Prohibition in 1890			Mean Annual Dollar Income per Farm, 1889			Proportion of Population in Incorporated Areas in 1890		
	r	a	b	r	a	b	r	a	b
Democratic party vote									
1886	−0.78	64.82	−0.57	+0.24	28.85	+0.01	+0.19	33.92	+0.13
1888	−0.85	65.23	−0.55	+0.26	30.58	+0.01	+0.20	35.59	+0.13
1890	−0.79	68.49	−0.90	+0.53	−4.02	+0.05	+0.37	14.66	+0.40
1892	−0.80	56.07	−0.69	+0.51	1.17	+0.03	+0.29	16.50	+0.23
1893	−0.75	58.52	−0.74	+0.42	2.83	+0.03	+0.20	17.97	+0.19
1894 (Fusion)	+0.09	41.94	+0.05	−0.60	59.89	−0.02	−0.53	51.72	−0.27
1894 (Silver)	−0.51	23.04	−0.30	+0.27	0.89	+0.01	+0.14	6.62	+0.08
1894 (Gold)	−0.56	14.06	−0.16	+0.34	1.87	+0.01	+0.16	5.51	+0.04
Democratic vote for governor									
1886	−0.76	64.04	−0.57	+0.25	27.59	+0.01	+0.13	34.48	+0.09
1888	−0.85	67.99	−0.58	+0.31	29.88	+0.02	+0.22	36.45	+0.15
1890	−0.81	72.23	−0.93	+0.56	−3.32	+0.05	+0.41	15.44	+0.45
1892	−0.79	49.20	−0.59	+0.48	4.05	+0.03	+0.27	16.11	+0.19
1894 (Fusion)	−0.08	52.06	−0.04	−0.38	60.10	−0.02	−0.42	56.20	−0.21
1894 (Gold)	−0.42	6.65	−0.07	+0.32	0.99	+0.00	−0.01	3.53	−0.00
Democratic vote for president									
1888	−0.84	64.76	−0.55	+0.29	29.14	+0.01	+0.19	35.21	+0.12
1892	−0.69	27.59	−0.32	+0.42	2.82	+0.01	+0.12	10.93	+0.05
Democratic vote for judge, 1895									
Gold	−0.68	24.37	−0.32	+0.37	0.50	+0.01	+0.20	6.66	+0.09
Silver	−0.56	13.95	−0.18	+0.37	−0.48	+0.01	+0.14	4.19	+0.04

Dependent Variables	Major Independent Variables								
	Vote in Favor of Prohibition in 1890			Mean Annual Dollar Income per Farm, 1889			Proportion of Population in Incorporated Areas in 1890		
	r	a	b	r	a	b	r	a	b
Republican party vote									
1886	+0.57	38.56	+0.35	−0.35	66.22	−0.02	−0.23	58.94	−0.13
1888	+0.74	36.18	+0.36	−0.28	60.09	−0.01	−0.19	55.77	−0.09
1890	+0.23	26.19	+0.14	+0.11	29.60	+0.01	+0.12	30.93	+0.07
1891	−0.41	56.29	−0.27	+0.42	29.33	+0.02	+0.54	33.65	+0.34
1892	+0.23	33.88	+0.12	+0.14	35.99	+0.01	+0.31	35.25	+0.15
1893	+0.29	32.74	+0.15	+0.30	32.00	+0.01	+0.40	34.20	+0.20
1894	+0.20	42.21	+0.09	+0.42	36.97	+0.01	+0.52	40.11	+0.23
Republican vote for governor									
1886	+0.55	39.17	+0.35	−0.36	67.31	−0.02	−0.16	58.51	−0.10
1888	+0.75	33.31	+0.39	−0.33	60.70	−0.01	−0.22	55.18	−0.11
1890	+0.29	23.29	+0.17	+0.04	30.21	+0.00	+0.03	31.00	+0.02
1892	+0.29	31.13	+0.14	+0.09	35.63	+0.00	+0.30	33.90	+0.14
1894	+0.17	40.10	+0.09	+0.30	36.91	+0.01	+0.46	37.99	+0.22
Republican vote for president									
1888	+0.73	36.76	+0.36	−0.30	61.28	−0.01	−0.18	56.06	−0.08
1892	+0.26	35.88	+0.13	+0.14	38.56	+0.00	+0.31	37.75	+0.14
Republican vote for judge, 1895	+0.29	34.51	+0.15	+0.27	34.79	+0.01	+0.35	36.71	+0.17

Dependent Variables	Major Independent Variables								
	Vote in Favor of Prohibition in 1890			Mean Annual Dollar Income per Farm, 1889			Proportion of Population in Incorporated Areas in 1890		
	r	a	b	r	a	b	r	a	b
National party vote for governor,									
1886	+0.23	−0.11	+0.09	+0.04	0.37	+0.00	−0.05	1.83	−0.02
Union Labor party, 1888									
President	+0.31	−1.27	+0.08	−0.15	4.57	−0.00	−0.16	3.72	−0.04
Governor	+0.30	−0.16	+0.07	−0.20	4.90	−0.00	−0.16	3.48	−0.04
Party	+0.31	−1.34	+0.08	−0.15	4.64	−0.00	−0.16	3.78	−0.04
Populist party vote									
1890	+0.55	4.02	+0.74	−0.53	73.89	−0.05	−0.40	53.14	−0.50
1891	+0.31	39.78	+0.23	−0.46	67.16	−0.03	−0.50	60.43	−0.35
1892	+0.58	9.22	+0.53	−0.59	60.31	−0.04	−0.45	45.25	−0.39
1893	+0.55	7.32	+0.55	−0.59	62.16	−0.04	−0.41	44.47	−0.39
1894	+0.38	23.23	+0.30	−0.57	59.18	−0.03	−0.45	46.70	−0.33
1894 (Fusion)	+0.08	41.94	+0.04	−0.60	59.89	−0.02	−0.53	51.72	−0.27
Populist vote for governor									
1890	+0.57	3.49	+0.74	−0.53	72.49	−0.05	−0.40	52.41	−0.49
1892	+0.54	19.18	+0.38	−0.57	57.41	−0.03	−0.49	46.75	−0.33
1894 (Fusion)	−0.08	52.06	−0.04	−0.38	60.10	−0.02	−0.42	56.20	−0.21
Populist vote for president									
1892	+0.27	36.33	+0.15	−0.50	56.88	−0.02	−0.38	48.88	−0.20
Populist vote for judge									
1895	+0.39	26.33	+0.32	−0.56	63.42	−0.03	−0.41	50.14	−0.31

| | Major Independent Variables | | | | | | | | |
| | Proportion of Population Czech, German Irish, or Polish in 1900 | | | Mean Annual Dollar Income per Farm, 1899 | | | Proportion of Population Living in Incorporated Areas in 1900 | | |
Dependent Variables	r	a	b	r	a	b	r	a	b
Fusion party vote									
1896	+0.10	51.09	+0.13	−0.31	60.81	−0.01	−0.56	59.68	−0.24
1898	+0.25	49.10	+0.30	−0.22	57.53	−0.01	−0.48	57.74	−0.19
1900	+0.38	45.26	+0.44	−0.21	54.56	−0.00	−0.36	53.51	−0.14
1902	+0.38	41.33	+0.46	−0.15	49.54	−0.00	−0.37	50.22	−0.15
1904	+0.47	36.16	+0.58	−0.03	42.09	−0.00	−0.43	46.71	−0.17
Fusion vote for governor									
1896	+0.20	52.96	+0.25	−0.22	61.13	−0.01	−0.53	61.95	−0.22
1898	+0.25	49.14	+0.29	−0.23	57.64	−0.01	−0.50	57.82	−0.20
1900	+0.38	46.03	+0.42	−0.18	54.24	−0.00	−0.35	53.81	−0.13
1902	+0.44	42.40	+0.57	−0.05	48.83	−0.00	−0.20	50.11	−0.08
1904	+0.51	40.41	+0.66	+0.10	43.58	+0.00	−0.21	49.23	−0.09
Fusion vote for president									
1896	+0.17	51.43	+0.22	−0.25	60.76	−0.01	−0.55	60.98	−0.25
1900	+0.31	45.02	+0.35	−0.30	55.66	−0.01	−0.31	51.75	−0.12
Vote for president, 1904									
Democratic	+0.67	12.22	+1.25	+0.52	2.35	+0.02	+0.12	21.06	+0.08
Populist	−0.44	17.30	−0.71	−0.65	33.62	−0.02	−0.46	18.54	−0.25

Dependent Variables	Major Independent Variables								
	Proportion of Population Czech, German Irish, or Polish in 1900			Mean Annual Dollar Income per Farm, 1899			Proportion of Population Living in Incorporated Areas in 1900		
	r	*a*	*b*	*r*	*a*	*b*	*r*	*a*	*b*
Republican party vote									
1896	−0.25	46.50	−0.32	+0.17	38.81	+0.00	+0.51	36.87	+0.22
1898	−0.24	49.64	−0.28	+0.24	41.12	+0.01	+0.47	41.42	+0.19
1900	−0.32	51.41	−0.37	+0.29	40.77	+0.01	+0.39	43.49	+0.15
1902	−0.35	54.67	−0.40	+0.17	46.80	+0.00	+0.28	47.67	+0.11
1904	−0.41	58.17	−0.45	+0.06	52.56	+0.00	+0.31	50.58	+0.11
Republican vote for governor									
1896	−0.30	45.13	−0.37	+0.15	37.58	+0.00	+0.51	35.14	+0.22
1898	−0.23	49.64	−0.27	+0.25	40.99	+0.01	+0.49	41.36	+0.19
1900	−0.30	50.50	−0.32	+0.28	41.01	+0.01	+0.38	43.34	+0.14
1902	−0.40	54.24	−0.50	+0.07	47.87	+0.00	+0.14	47.95	+0.06
1904	−0.43	54.61	−0.54	−0.05	51.14	−0.00	+0.13	48.06	+0.05
Republican vote for president									
1896	−0.18	46.48	−0.23	+0.26	37.17	+0.01	+0.55	37.13	+0.24
1900	−0.24	51.93	−0.27	+0.37	40.39	+0.01	+0.33	45.60	+0.13
1904	−0.41	64.66	−0.43	+0.08	58.89	+0.00	+0.27	57.88	+0.09

| | Major Independent Variables | | | | | | | | |
| | Proportion of Population Austrian, German or Irish Stock in 1910 | | | Mean Annual Dollar Income per Farm, 1909 | | | Proportion of Population Living in Incorporated Areas in 1910 | | |
Dependent Variables	r	a	b	r	a	b	r	a	b
Democratic party vote									
1906	+0.60	36.67	+0.36	+0.18	37.95	+0.00	−0.21	47.76	−0.10
1908	+0.52	44.20	+0.24	+0.01	48.78	+0.00	−0.10	50.38	−0.03
1910	+0.80	37.85	+0.50	+0.20	41.13	+0.00	−0.06	49.13	−0.03
1912	+0.45	40.95	+0.21	+0.04	44.22	+0.00	−0.11	46.81	−0.04
1914	+0.67	39.58	+0.36	+0.19	41.17	+0.00	−0.29	51.38	−0.12
Democratic vote for governor									
1906	+0.43	40.00	+0.26	+0.04	44.12	+0.00	−0.25	49.72	−0.12
1908	+0.52	45.27	+0.26	−0.02	50.98	−0.00	−0.07	51.57	−0.03
1910	+0.76	30.16	+0.72	+0.26	31.20	+0.01	+0.24	38.42	+0.17
1912	+0.44	45.23	+0.24	−0.09	53.01	−0.00	+0.08	48.86	+0.03
1914	+0.67	42.22	+0.43	+0.09	47.58	+0.00	−0.07	52.22	−0.03
Democratic vote for senator									
1906	+0.57	39.22	+0.34	+0.22	38.68	+0.00	−0.24	49.96	−0.10
1910	+0.67	44.52	+0.43	+0.20	46.04	+0.00	−0.03	53.82	−0.02
1912	+0.61	39.59	+0.31	+0.13	42.09	+0.00	−0.03	46.34	−0.01
Democratic vote for president									
1908	+0.49	44.97	+0.21	−0.02	49.81	−0.00	−0.02	49.52	−0.01
1912	+0.35	41.13	+0.17	−0.05	45.93	−0.00	+0.02	44.40	+0.01

Note: In every instance but the 1910 gubernatorial election, Democratic candidates also carried the nomination of the People's Independent (Populist) party.

Dependent Variables	Proportion of Population Austrian, German or Irish Stock in 1910			Mean Annual Dollar Income per Farm, 1909			Proportion of Population Living in Incorporated Areas in 1910		
	r	a	b	r	a	b	r	a	b
Republican party vote									
1906	−0.43	55.70	−0.23	−0.10	53.98	−0.00	+0.27	46.85	+0.11
1908	−0.45	53.50	−0.20	+0.03	48.56	+0.00	+0.12	47.86	+0.04
1910	−0.76	57.54	−0.42	−0.10	51.91	−0.00	+0.06	47.95	+0.03
1912	−0.33	53.57	−0.15	+0.16	46.41	+0.00	−0.00	50.54	−0.00
1914	−0.47	48.19	−0.22	+0.04	42.68	+0.00	+0.22	40.89	+0.01
Republican vote for governor									
1906	−0.25	53.57	−0.15	+0.03	49.42	+0.00	+0.29	45.74	+0.13
1908	−0.39	50.71	−0.19	+0.08	44.55	+0.00	+0.09	45.65	+0.03
1910	−0.74	66.32	−0.65	−0.19	62.56	−0.00	−0.27	59.73	−0.18
1912	−0.31	48.60	−0.16	+0.28	37.47	+0.00	−0.17	47.84	−0.07
1914	−0.52	49.59	−0.34	+0.06	40.60	+0.00	−0.03	43.29	−0.01
Republican vote for senator									
1906	−0.56	58.92	−0.32	−0.16	57.49	−0.00	+0.22	48.68	+0.10
1910	−0.58	50.58	−0.35	−0.10	46.82	−0.00	+0.05	42.76	+0.02
1912	−0.56	55.77	−0.27	−0.00	50.33	−0.00	−0.09	51.50	−0.03
Republican vote for president									
1908	−0.33	50.45	−0.14	+0.12	44.56	+0.00	+0.02	47.29	+0.01
1912	+0.51	16.10	+0.29	+0.52	5.08	+0.01	+0.04	21.45	+0.02
Pregressive vote for president									
1912	−0.65	36.45	−0.37	−0.28	38.01	−0.00	−0.14	31.13	−0.06

Note: All Republican candidates in 1912, except for the candidate for president, also carried the nomination of the Progressive party.

Notes

ABBREVIATIONS USED IN NOTES

Bee:	Omaha Bee
Independent:	(Lincoln) Nebraska Independent
LC:	Library of Congress
NH:	Nebraska History
NSHS:	Nebraska State Historical Society
NSJ:	(Lincoln) Nebraska State Journal
Star:	Lincoln Star
W-H:	Omaha World-Herald

PREFACE

1. Leopold Vincent, comp., *Alliance Songster: A Collection of Labor and Comic Songs for the Use of Grange, Alliance, or Debating Clubs* (Winfield Kans.: H. and L. Vincent, 1890), p. 14.

2. These Populist rallies strongly impressed both participants and observers. See descriptions in Addison E. Sheldon, *Nebraska: The Land and the People*, 3 vols. (Chicago and New York: Lewis Publishing Co., 1931), 3:689 (hereafter cited as Sheldon, *Nebraska*); J. Sterling Morton and Albert Watkins, *Illustrated History of Nebraska*, 3 vols. (Lincoln: Jacob North, 1905, 1907; Lincoln: Western Publishing and Engraving Co., 1913), 3:230 (hereafter cited as Watkins, *Nebraska*); Mary Louise Jeffery, "Young Radicals of the Nineties," *NH* 38 (1957): 33–42. See also the descriptions in John D. Hicks, *The Populist Revolt: A History of the Farmers' Alliance and the People's Party* (Minneapolis: University of Minnesota Press, 1931; rpt. Lincoln: University of Nebraska Press, 1961), pp. 167–69, and James C. Olson, *History of Nebraska* (Lincoln: University of Nebraska Press, 1955), pp. 234–35.

3. The historiography of the Populist movement is complex and lengthy. For examples of the approach of the 1920s and 1930s, see Hicks, *Populist Revolt*; Hallie Farmer, "The Economic Background of Frontier Populism," *Mississippi Valley Historical Review (MVHR)* 10 (1924): 406–27; idem, "The Railroads and Frontier Populism," *MVHR* 13 (1926): 387–97; and Chester M. Destler, "Western Radicalism, 1865–1901: Concepts and Origins," *MVHR* 31 (1944): 355–68. The best example of the approach of the 1950s is Richard Hofstadter, *The Age of Reform: From Bryan to F.D.R.* (New York: Random House, 1955). For recent views contrary to Hofstadter, see Norman Pollack, *The Populist Response to Industrial America: Midwestern Populist Thought* (Cambridge: Harvard University Press, 1962), and Lawrence Goodwyn, *Democratic Promise: The Populist Moment in America* (New

York: Oxford University Press, 1976).

4. For examples, see Sheldon Hackney, *Populism to Progressivism in Alabama* (Princeton: Princeton University Press, 1969); O. Gene Clanton, *Kansas Populism: Men and Ideas* (Lawrence: University of Kansas Press, 1969); Stanley B. Parsons, Jr., *The Populist Context: Rural versus Urban Power on a Great Plains Frontier* (Westport, Conn.: Greenwood Press, 1973).

5. For a quick survey of these methods, see Appendix A. The specific programs used throughout this study were those in the Statistical Package for the Social Sciences (SPSS); see Norman Nie et al., *SPSS: Statistical Package for the Social Sciences*, 2d ed. (New York: McGraw-Hill, 1970).

6. The sources for data on social and economic characteristics of the population are described in Appendix A.

CHAPTER ONE

1. George W. Norris, *Fighting Liberal* (New York: Macmillan Co., 1945), p. 5; Sheldon, *Nebraska*, 1:460.

2. The growth percentages for the decade 1880–90 are from Edgar Z. Palmer, "The Correctness of the 1890 Census of Population for Nebraska Cities," *NH* 32 (1951): 259–67. For other data sources, see the full discussion in Appendix A.

3. Watkins, *Nebraska;* Sheldon, *Nebraska*; see also the following M.A. theses at the University of Nebraska: Virginia Bowen Jones, "The Influence of the Railroads on Nebraska State Politics" (1927), Rudolph Alvin Knudsen, "Regulation of Railroad Rates in Nebraska 1867–1906" (1937), Harold Grier, "A History of the Democratic Party in Nebraska, 1854–1890" (1936), and Juliette Herscher, "Early Third Party Movements in Nebraska (1931)."

4. Parsons, *Populist Context* esp. part 2, "The Structure of Power." See also the grass-roots approach in Samuel P. Hays, "Political Parties and the Community-Society Continuum," in *The American Party Systems: Stages of Political Development*, ed. William Nisbet Chambers and Walter Dean Burnham (New York: Oxford University Press, 1967), esp. pp. 153, 157–59, 161; and also Robert H. Wiebe, *The Search for Order: 1877–1920* (New York: Hill and Wang, 1967), esp. pp. 4, 12, 16–17, 27–28, 36–37. See also Jeremy W. Kilar, "Courthouse Politics, Loup City, Sherman County, 1887–1891," *NH* 60 (1979): 36–57.

5. Twenty-eight of Nebraska's present ninety-three counties are composed of sixteen congressional survey townships; sixteen others are very close to this size and configuration. In most of these counties, townships or precincts correspond to congressional survey townships. A number of the counties that deviate from this pattern are in the sparsely populated sandhills cattle country.

6. These generalizations are based on a number of local histories (see the list in the bibliography), on a number of county-seat newspapers (listed in the bibliography), and on such reminiscences and autobiographies as Norris, *Fighting Liberal*; Cass G. Barns, *The Sod House* (Madison, Nebr.: n.p., 1930); Arthur F. Mullen, *Western Democrat* (New York: Wilfred Funk, 1940) James Manahan, *Trials of a Lawyer* (n.p., 1932); or Alfred C. Nielsen, *Life in an American Denmark* (Askov, Minn., American Publishing Co., 1962). See also Kilar, "Courthouse Politics."

7. Parsons, *Populist Context*, part 2, esp. pp. 37–41, 48–57; Lewis Atherton,

Main Street on the Middle Border (Bloomington: Indiana University Press, 1954), pp. 23, 28, 103, 150, 152, 214, 306; Barns, *Sod House*, pp. 132–34, 158 ff.; Nielsen, *American Denmark*, p. 100; Thomas J. Majors Manuscript Collection, *NSHS*; Samuel Maxwell Manuscript Collection, NSHS; Samuel Chapman Manuscript Collection, NSHS.

    8. Population density derivations are discussed in Appendix A. Railroad lines, in map 3 are based on *Poor's Manual of Railroads: 1890* (New York: N. V. and H. W. Poor, 1890), between pp. 760 and 761. Generalizations on the role of the railroads derive from the many local histories, reminiscences, autobiographies, and manuscript collections cited in notes 6 and 7 and in the bibliography; see also Kilar, "Courthouse Politics."

    9. Watkins, *Nebraska*, 3:195, 206, 210–11, 215. The *Bee* and *NSJ* typically carried lengthy accounts of the conventions.

    10. See accounts of the various conventions; *Nebraska Party Platforms: 1858–1940* (Lincoln: Works Projects Administration, 1940), esp. pp. 84, 96–97, 113–14, 125–27, 138–39.

    11. For accounts of campaigns see the sources cited in notes 6 and 7. The diary of John Sanborn, a Franklin County Republican farmer who ran for the state legislature in the early 1890s, probably gives a good picture of prevailing campaign scheduling and practices on the county level; John Sanborn Manuscript Collection, NSHS.

    12. For biographical sketches of the governors, see *Messages and Proclamations of the Governors of Nebraska, 1854–1941*, 4 vols. (Lincoln: Works Projects Administration and NSHS, 1944), 1:477, 505, 565; 2:3–4. The Garber family was the model for the Fletchers of Willa Cather's *A Lost Lady*. See also Earl G. Curtis, "Biography of John Milton Thayer" (M.A. thesis, University of Nebraska, 1933); *Compendium of History, Reminiscence and Biography of Nebraska* (Chicago: Alden Publishing Company, 1912), p. 269.

    13. Watkins, *Nebraska*, 1:744–46, 2:686–88, 3:745–46; Dale J. Hart, "Edward Rosewater and the *Omaha Bee* in Nebraska Politics" (M.A. thesis, University of Nebraska, 1938); Sheldon, *Nebraska*, 1:586–88, 638–39; Wayne A. Alvord, *The Nebraska State Journal*: 1867–1904" (M.A. thesis, University of Nebraska, 1934); 85th Congress, 2d Session, *Biographical Directory of the American Congress: 1774–1961*, House Document no. 442 (Washington, D.C.: Government Printing Office, 1961), pp. 1258–59, 1418–19, 1751; Marie U. Harmer and James L. Sellers, "Charles H. Van Wyck—Soldier and Statesman," *NH* 12 (1929): 322–73; Allen L. Shepherd, "Algernon Sidney Paddock" (M.A. thesis, University of Nebraska, 1967).

    14. Cf. John A. Garraty, *The New Commonwealth: 1877–1890* (New York: Harper and Row, 1968), pp. 229–30; *Messages and Proclamations*, 1:507, 524, 538, 567–72, 587, 592–93, 604, 608; Barns, *Sod House*, pp. 132–34; J. H. Agar, "Nebraska Politics and Nebraska Railroads," *Proceedings and Collections of the Nebraska State Historical Society* 15 (1907): 34–44; George F. Blanchard to Samuel Maxwell, 19 February 1881, box 3, Maxwell MSS, NSHS.

    15. J. W. Savage to Maxwell, 6 October 1881, box 3, Maxwell MSS, NSHS.

    16. F. W. Liedtke, elected state auditor in 1878, was not renominated in 1880 because of alleged improprieties regarding retention of insurance fees; Watkins, *Nebraska*, 3:196. Senator Van Wyck was denied reelection in 1887, Supreme Court Judge Manoah Reese was denied renomination in 1889, and Attorney General

William Leese was denied renomination in 1890, all allegedly because of their antimonopoly sentiments; Watkins, *Nebraska*, 3:221; Sheldon, *Nebraska*, 1:643–45; John D. Barnhart, "The History of the Farmers' Alliance and of the People's Party in Nebraska" (Ph.D. diss., Harvard University, 1930), pp. 177–90; Chapman to Maxwell, 10 January 1889 and 12 October 1889, and other letters in box 4, Maxwell MSS, NSHS.

17. Parsons, *Populist Context*, chap. 4; Barns, *Sod House*, p. 160; Willa Cather, "Two Friends," in *Obscure Destinies* (New York: Alfred Knopf, 1940), p. 208; Annabel L. Beal, "The Populist Party in Custer County, Nebraska: Its Role in Local, State and National Politics, 1889–1906" (Ph.D. diss., University of Nebraska, 1965), p. 20.

18. Watkins, *Nebraska*, 1:594–95, 629–31, 3:717–25; James C. Olson, *J. Sterling Morton* (Lincoln: University of Nebraska Press, 1942); *Messages and Proclamations*, 2:188; *Biographical Directory of the American Congress*, p. 1316; John McShane Manuscript Collection, NSHS; Ralph G. Coad, "Irish Pioneers of Nebraska," *NH 17 (1936):171–77*.

19. *Party Platforms*, pp. 79–81, 85, 88–89, 100–101, 107–8, 115–17, 121, 129–30, 134–35, 141–43; Grier, "History of the Democratic Party in Nebraska," pp. 58–79.

20. Joe A. Fisher, "The Liquor Question in Nebraska, 1880–1920" (M.A. thesis, University of Omaha, 1951); *Party Platforms*, pp. 89, 100–101, 108, 121, 127, 130, 135, 138–39, 142.

21. Olson, *Morton*, pp. 271–72; Frederick C. Luebke, *Immigrants and Politics: The Germans of Nebraska, 1880–1900* (Lincoln: University of Nebraska Press, 1969), chaps. 5 and 7; John R. Kleinschmidt, "The Political Behavior of the Bohemian and Swedish Ethnic Groups in Nebraska, 1884–1900" (M.A. thesis, University of Nebraska, 1968), pp. 95–114.

22. Harmer and Sellers, "Van Wyck"; Hart, "Edward Rosewater"; Watkins, *Nebraska*, 3:206, 216; Sheldon, *Nebraska*, 1:586–88, 608, 639; Barnhard, "History of the Farmers' Alliance," chap. 3, pp. 128–76; W. P. Squire to Thayer, 17 October 1888, and J. W. Bixler to Thayer, 17 November 1888, box 3, Thayer MSS, NSHS; A. E. Sheldon, ed., *Nebraska Blue Book and Historical Register: 1915* (Lincoln: State Journal Co., 1915), pp. 80–88; Ronald M. Gephart, "Politicians, Soldiers, and Strikes: The Reorganization of the Nebraska Militia and the Omaha Strike of 1882," *NH 46* (1965): 89–120; Sheldon, *Nebraska*, 1:598–99.

23. Luebke, *Immigrants*, pp. 71–116, 122–50; Kleinschmidt, "Political Behavior," pp. 95–114; *Party Platforms*, p. 141; Parsons, *Populist Context*, pp. 77–79; Barnhard, "History of the Farmers' Alliance," pp. 128–76.

CHAPTER TWO

1. Olson, *Morton*, pp. 269–70.

2. Robert N. Manley, "A Note on Government and Agriculture: A Nineteenth Century Nebraska View," *NH 45* (1964): 237–52; idem, "Nebraskans and the Federal Government: 1854–1916" (Ph.D. diss., University of Nebraska, 1962), esp. pp. 370–71; *Party Platforms*, pp. 80, 88, 100, 107, 134, 141–42.

3. Paul Kleppner, *The Cross of Culture: A Social Analysis of Midwestern*

Politics, 1850–1900 (New York: Free Press, 1970); Samuel P. Hays, "The Social Analysis of American Political History, 1880–1920," *Political Science Quarterly* 80 (1965): 373–94, esp. p. 387; Luebke, *Immigrants*.

4. Bishop Andrews, ed., *Doctrines and Discipline of the Methodist Episcopal Church: 1896* (New York: Eaton and Mains, 1896; Cincinnati: Curts and Jennings, 1896), pp. 35, 136–37; Hervé Carrier, S. J., *The Sociology of Religious Belonging* (New York: Herder and Herder, 1965); Thomas F. Hoult, *The Sociology of Religion* (New York: Holt, Rinehart and Winston, 1958); Timothy L. Smith, *Revivalism and Social Reform in Mid-Nineteenth-Century America* (New York: Abingdon, 1957), esp. chaps. 3–5, 8–9; Winthrop S. Hudson, *American Protestantism* (Chicago: University of Chicago Press, 1961), esp. part 2; Klepppner, *Cross of Culture*, pp. 69–91.

5. Luebke, *Immigrants*, pp. 48–51; John Tracy Ellis, *American Catholicism*, (Chicago: University of Chicago Press, 1969), esp. chaps. 2–4; Thomas T. McAvoy, C.S.C., *A History of the Catholic Church in the United States* (Notre Dame: University of Notre Dame Press, 1969), esp. chaps. 7–12; Henry Eyster Jacobs, *A History of the Evangelical Lutheran Church in the United States*, 3d ed. (New York: Charles Scribner's Sons, 1900), esp. pp. 406–14, 498–501; Kleppner, *Cross of Culture*, pp. 69–91. See also Sister M. Aquinata Martin, O.P., *The Catholic Church on the Nebraska Frontier (1854–1885)* (Washington: Catholic University of America, 1937).

6. Hays, "Social Analysis," p. 387; Kleppner, *Cross of Culture*, pp. 72–75.

7. For more information on the sources and derivation of data, see Appendix A. The programs used in analyzing these data were all part of SPSS; see Nie et al., *SPSS*.

8. Marcus Lee Hansen, *The Immigrant in American History* (Cambridge: Harvard University Press, 1948), pp. 61–62.

9. Luebke, *Immigrants*, esp. pp. 138, 148–50.

10. Kleinschmidt, "Political Behavior," esp. pp. 161, 188, 194.

11. Edith Swain McDermott, *The Pioneer History of Greeley County, Nebraska* (Greeley: Citizen Publishing Co., 1939), pp. 44–58; Barns, *Sod House*, pp. 162–63; Mullen, *Western Democrat*, p. 45.

12. In 1900 Dannebrog was 78 percent Danish, Dannevirke was 54 percent Danish and 38 percent Polish or Czech. See Appendix A for data sources. See also Nielsen, *American Denmark*.

13. Shell Creek Precinct, Boone County, largely Norwegian, voted 85 percent Republican in 1889; see also Barns, *Sod House*, pp. 162–63.

14. Paul C. Nyholm, *The Americanization of the Danish Lutheran Churches in America* (Minneapolis: Augsburg Publishing House, 1963), pp. 62–63, 76, 79–80, 143, 146; Nielsen, *American Denmark*.

15. Luebke, *Immigrants*, pp. 50, 87–91.

16. At the time of the 1900 census, Kelso Precinct was 37 percent Polish, 22 percent German, 18 percent Danish, and 13 percent Czech. Dannevirke was 20 percent Polish in 1900, 18 percent Czech and 54 percent Danish.

17. Hicks, *Populist Revolt*, pp. 64, 77; Michael Paul Rogin, *The Intellectuals and McCarthy: The Radical Specter* (Cambridge: MIT Press, 1967), p. 109; Stanley B. Parsons, "Who Were the Nebraska Populists?" *NH* 44 (1963): 96–98.

18. The correlations between various economic indicators suggest that wheat farming was more likely to be a prominent activity in the areas of marginal

agriculture—the least productive land, the least improved acreage, the highest interest rates on mortgages. The relationship between wheat farming and radicalism—if there is any relationship—must be understood as primarily economic. Wheat farmers, and other marginal farmers, as will be seen in chapter 4, were receptive to Populism because of their economic situation, regardless of the ratios of wheat acreage to corn acreage.

19. The election of 1891 was the first under the Australian system. For one example of the kind of manipulation possible under the previous system, see Barns, *Sod House*, p. 162.

20. See my dissertation, Cherny, "Populist and Progressive in Nebraska: A Study of Nebraska Politics, 1885–1912" (Columbia University, 1972), pp. 88–89.

21. Olson, *Morton*, pp. 257–331.

22. Olson, *Nebraska*, pp. 208–9; Harmer and Sellers, "Van Wyck"; *Biographical Directory of the American Congress*, pp. 729, 823, 1185, 1200, 1258, 1384, 1418–19, 1743, 1751, 1785–86; Donald D. Snoddy, "The Congressional Career of Archibald Jerrard Weaver, 1882–1887," *NH* 57 (1976): 83–98.

23. The members of this group and sources of information for each are listed in my dissertation, Cherny, "Populist and Progressive in Nebraska," pp. 512–51.

24. All members of the legislature and their sessions of service are listed in *Nebraska Blue Book: 1968* (Lincoln: Joe Christensen, 1968), pp. 152–213.

25. Barnhart, "History of the Farmers' Alliance," pp. 177–202; Hicks, *Populist Revolt*, p. 154.

CHAPTER THREE

1. Olson, *Nebraska*, pp. 229, 235; (Lincoln) *Farmers' Alliance*, 6 September 1890; *NSJ*, 22 August, 5 September 1890; Watkins, *Nebraska*, 3:223, 229–30; Sheldon, *Nebraska*, 1:671, 689; Hicks, *Populist Revolt*, pp. 167–69; Jeffery, "Young Radicals," pp. 33–42.

2. For a more elaborate treatment of voter rationality, see Anthony Downs, *An Economic Theory of Democracy* (New York: Harper and Row, 1957), esp. chaps 2, 3, 11–13.

3. Van Wyck to "My Dr. Friend" (W. V. Allen?), 15 November 1889, and Van Wyck to Allen, 17 December 1889, box 1, Allen MSS, NSHS; M. W. Bruce to Van Wyck, 27 January 1890, Van Wyck MSS, University of Kansas; Dorsey to Maxwell, 25 February 1890, box 4, Samuel Maxwell MSS, NSHS; *NSJ*, 21 May 1890; Hicks, *Populist Revolt*, p. 156; *Party Platforms*, pp. 157–58; Barnhart, "Farmers' Alliance," pp. 177–200; DeLloyd John Guth, "Omer Madison Kem: The People's Congressman" (M.A. thesis, Creighton University, 1962), pp. 45–58; Annabel L Beal, "The Populist Party in Custer County, Nebraska: Its Role in Local, State, and National Politics, 1889–1906" (Ph.D. diss., University of Nebraska, 1965), pp. 35–57.

4. "Confidential Circular" dated 1 May 1890, box 5, Charles Wooster MSS, NSHS; Barnhard, "Farmers' Alliance," p. 200; Hicks, *Populist Revolt*, pp. 151, 157; Olson, *Nebraska*, pp. 226–31; Sheldon, *Nebraska*, 1:674; Watkins, *Nebraska*, 3:223; *Bee*, 5 July, 18 July 1890; David Stephens Trask, "A Natural Partnership: Nebraska's Populists and Democrats and the Development of Fusion," *NH* 56

(1975): 423.

5. Church Howe Scrapbook, NSHS, p. 103; *Party Platform*, pp. 155–57; Sheldon, *Nebraska*, 1:684–85; Watkins, *Nebraska*, 3:228; Olson, *Nebraska*, p. 232.

6. For information on Richards, see C. H. Scoville, comp., *History of the Elkhorn Valley, Nebraska* (Chicago and Omaha: National Publishing Co., 1891), pp. 313–16; *Bee*, 25 July 1890; Reese to Maxwell, 26 July 1890, box 4, Maxwell MSS, NSHS.

7. *NSJ*, 30 July 1890; Mullen, *Western Democrat*, p. 64; *Party Platforms*, pp. 149–50; Trask, "Natural Partnership," p. 423; "Autobiography of John Holbrook Powers" (Trenton, Nebr.: Register Print., n.d.); *Trenton Register*, 17 May 1918; A. E. Sheldon, "Nebraskans I Have Known: II. John Holbrook Powers," *NH* 19 (1938): 331–39; (Lincoln) *Farmers' Alliance*, 9 August, 20 September 1890; *NSJ*, 10 August 1890; *Bee*, 30 July 1890.

8. *Party Platforms*, pp. 148–49; Watkins, *Nebraska*, 1:588–89, 594–95; *Bee*, 15 August 1890; *W-H*, 19 September, 26 September 1890.

9. *Bee*, 30 July, 5 September, 19 September, 20 September, 23 September, 30 October, 1890; *NSJ*, 31 July, 21 August, 22 August, 5 September, 14 September, 11 October, 14 October, 30 October, 2 November 1890.

10. For examples of Populist song and rhetoric, see Vincent, *Alliance Songster;* Jeffrey, "Young Radicals"; Norman Pollack, ed. *The Populist Mind* (Indianapolis and New York: Bobbs-Merrill Co. 1967), esp. pp. 17–18, 37–38, 440–44, 460; Hicks, *Populist Revolt*, pp. 160–70; George Brown Tindall, *A Populist Reader: Selections from the Works of American Populist Leaders* (New York: Harper and Row, 1966); Donald F. Danker, "Populist Cartoons," *Kansas Quarterly* 1 (1969): 11–23; William E. Koch, "Verse and Song from the Populist Era," *Kansas Quarterly* 1 (1969): 123–25.

11. *W-H*, September to November 1890; *Bee*, 14 August 1890; *New York Times*, 28 April 1890; Sheldon, *Nebraska*, 1:686; Watkins, *Nebraska*, 3:229–30; Paolo E. Coletta, *William Jennings Bryan*, 3 vols (Lincoln: University of Nebraska Press, 1964–69), 1:44–45; box 1, Bryan MSS, LC.

12. Sources for election data are discussed in detail in Appendix A. See also Story to Bryan, 5 November 1890, Wagner to Bryan, 6 November 1890, Pool to Bryan, 7 November 1890, box 1, Bryan MSS, LC; Trask, "Partnership," p. 424.

13. *W-H*, 4 January 1891; Watkins, *Nebraska*, 3:230–31, 690–91; Sheldon, *Nebraska*, 1:683, 696–701.

14. Watkins, *Nebraska*, 3:234–27; Sheldon, *Nebraska*, 1:701–8; *WW-H*, 18 June 1891.

15. *State ex rel Thayer v. Boyd*, 31 Nebraska 682; *Boyd v. State of Nebraska ex rel Thayer*, 143 U.S. 135; 36 Law Ed. 103.

16. *Party Platforms*, pp. 165–66; Watkins, *Nebraska*, 3:239; Sheldon, *Nebraska*, 1:709.

17. *Party Platforms*, pp. 161–63; Watkins, *Nebraska*, 3:238; Sheldon, *Nebraska*, 1:710; Paolo E. Coletta, "The Nebraska Democratic State Convention of April 13–14, 1892" *NH* 39 (1958): 320.

18. *Party Platforms*, pp. 168–70; Watkins, *Nebraska*, 3:237; Sheldon, *Nebraska*, 1:710; Maxwell to Majors, 11 September 1891, box 1, Thomas J. Majors MSS, NSHS; Chapman to Maxwell, 7 August 1891, box 4, Maxwell MSS, NSHS.

19. Hicks, *Populist Revolt*, pp. 231–37; for a sense of the influence of the

convention in Nebraska, see Mullen, *Western Democrat*, pp. 58–60.
20. *Party Platforms*, pp. 172–73, 175–76, 179–80.
21. Watkins, *Nebraska*, 3:242–43; Sheldon, *Nebraska*, 1:718–19; Harmer and Sellers, "Van Wyck" pp. 3–36, 81–128, 189–246, 322–73; Van Wyck to "Mark," 1 September 1888, Van Wyck MSS, University of Kansas; Trask, "Partnership," p. 426.
22. Watkins, *Nebraska*, 3:242; Sheldon, *Nebraska*, 1:818; Eleazar Wakely, "Life and Character of Lorenzo Crounse," *Publications of the Nebraska State Historical Society* 18 (1917): 162–78; "Memorial Presented to the Supreme Court, June 8, 1909," box 7, Crounse MSS, NSHS; Crounse to Maxwell, 1 October 1886, box 3, Maxwell MSS, NSHS.
23. Olson, *Morton*, p. 340.
24. *NSJ*, 28 September 1892; Olson, *Morton*, pp. 342–45.
25. *Bee*, 15 August, 18 August, 1 October, 8 October, 20 October, 29 October, 5 November, 1892; *NSJ*, 22 August, 20 September, 21 September, 28 September, 29 September, 10 October, 20 October, 20 October, 23 October, 25 October, 3 November 1892.
26. 15 September, 13 October, 27 October 1892.
27. *NSJ*, 28 September, 30 September, 5 October, 1892; A. L. Bixby, *NSJ*, 12 September 1912.
28. Shumway to Boyd, 8 June 1892, box 1, Boyd MSS, NSHS; unidentified clipping, box 2, J. H. Broady MSS, NSHS; letters from various county clerks to Frank R. Morrisay, box 2, Boyd MSS, NSHS; Paolo E. Coletta, "Williams Jennings Bryan's Second Congressional Campaign," *NH* 40 (1959): 275–92, esp. p. 282; *NSJ*, 28 October, 30 October 1892
29. *Nebraska House Journal*, 23d sess. (1893), pp. 10, 145–47, 167–69, 182–84, 191–*192*, *202*–4, 217–19, 230–32, 255–56, 267–69, 273–74, 296–97, 310–11, 320, 328–29, 346, 362; *Nebraska Senate Journal*, 23d sess. (1893), p. 17; *W–H*, 11–13 January, 20 January, 1 February, 4 February, 26 February, 4 March 1893; Allen to Bryan, 28 January 1893, Allen to Bryan, 4 February 1893, Casper to Bryan, 8 February 1893, Hale to Bryan, 11 January 1893, box 2, Bryan MSS, LC; Olson, *Morton*, pp. 350–51; Watkins, *Nebraska*, 3:247–53; Sheldon, *Nebraska*, 1:725–28; A. E. Sheldon, "Some Unprinted History," *NH* 19 (1938): 204–5; Paolo E. Coletta, "William Jennings Bryan and the Nebraska Senatorial Election of 1893" *NH* 31 (1950): 183–203.
30. *Party Platforms*, pp. 183–84; Leese to Maxwell, 27 July 1893, Barry to Maxwell, 27 August 1893, box 5, Maxwell MSS, NSHS; Sheldon, *Nebraska*, 1:734; Watkins, *Nebraska*, 3:255; N. C. Abbott, "Silas A. Holcomb," *NH* 26 (1945):187–200; 27 (1946):3–17.
31. *Party Platforms*, pp. 181–83; Coletta, *Bryan*, 1:87; Watkins, *Nebraska*, 3:254; Sheldon, *Nebraska*, 1:735–36.
32. *Party Platforms*, pp. 186–87; Johannes M. Klotsche, "The Political Career of Samual Maxwell" (M.A. thesis, University of Nebraska, 1928), pp. 35–37; Crounse to Maxwell, 22 August 1893, Reese to Maxwell, 6 October 1893, box 5, Maxwell MSS, NSHS; Watkins, *Nebraska*, 3:255; Sheldon, *Nebraska*, 1:737.
33. *Party Platforms*, pp. 195–96; *Bee*, 24 August 1894; Martin E. Carlson, "A History of the American Protective Association in Nebraska" (M.A. thesis, Colorado State College of Education at Greeley, 1947), pp. 146, 152; *Biographical*

Directory of the American Congress, p. 1495; Watkins, *Nebraska*, 3:256, 698–99; Sheldon, *Nebraska*, 1:321–22, 745.

34. *Party Platforms*, pp. 192–93; *Bee*, 25 August 1894; (Lincoln) *Wealth-Makers*, 27 September 1894; Abbott, "Holcomb," p. 190; Sheldon, *Nebraska*, 1:748.

35. Unidentified clipping, box 2, Broady MSS, NSHS; Coletta, *Bryan*, 1:99–100; *W-H*, 27 September 1894; *Bee*, 27 September 1894.

36. *Bee*, 21 September 1894; *NSJ*, 24 August, 24 September 1894; (Omaha) *American*, 21 September, 28 September 1894.

37. *Party Platforms*, pp. 189–91; *W-H*, 27 September 1894; *Bee*, 27 September 1894; Trask, "Partnership," p. 430.

38. *W-H*, 27 September 1894; Watkins, *Nebraska*, 3:259; Sheldon, *Nebraska*, 1:750.

39. *NSJ*, 5 August, 13 August, 18 August, 2 September, 25 September 1894; Sheldon to Allen, 26 February 1894, box 1, Allen MSS, NSHS.

40. *NSJ*, 26 August, 9 September, 19 September, 22 September, 23 September, 24 October, 25 October, 29 October 1894; Gillam to Bryan, 20 November 1894, box 3, Bryan MSS, LC; Mullen, *Western Democrat*, p. 97.

41. *Wealth-Makers*, 18 October 1894; *W-H*, 2 October, 21 October 1894; *Bee*, 20 October, 30 October 1894. See the *Bee* daily from 23 August through 3 November 1894 for its attacks on Majors; the weekly *Bee* was distributed without charge throughout the state, in quantities as large as requested by local campaign organizers, for example, to 1,100 residents of Dawes County, four hundred miles from Omaha, based on a list supplied by the local Populist editor; Dawes County cast 1,809 votes for governor, so the *Bee* mailings reached 60 percent of the voters; Sheldon, *Nebraska*, 1:751 n.

42. Sheldon, *Nebraska*, 1:753; Coletta, *Bryan*, 1:103.

43. *Nebraska Senate Journal*, 24th sess. (1895), pp. 179–81; *Messages and Proclamations*, 2:360–68; Sheldon, *Nebraska*, 1:757; Watkins, *Nebraska*, 3:262; Carlson, "American Protective Association," pp. 154–55.

44. Sheldon, "Powers," p. 337; *North Platte Telegraph*, 28 February 1929; Goff to Kellie, 3 March 1896, box 2, Farmers' Alliance MSS, NSHS. Wright was, in fact, a genuine crank, claiming to be able to induce rainfall through magnetism; Wright to Kellie, 20 March 1896, ibid.; Smyth to Bryan, 2 May 1895, box 3, Bryan MSS, LC.

45. *Messages and Proclamations*, 2:237–45, esp. p. 241; Holcomb to Allen, 30 March 1895, box 1, Allen MSS, NSHS; *Wealth-Makers*, 27 September 1894; Goff to Kellie, 8 March, 29 March 1896, box 2, Alliance MSS, NSHS.

46. Edmisten to Maxwell, 18 October, 28 October, 31 October, 1894, box 5, Maxwell MSS, NSHS; Coletta, *Bryan*, 1:108–9; Watkins, *Nebraska*, 3:263; Sheldon, *Nebraska*, 1:758.

47. Cf. John Higham, ed., "A Republican Estimate of Party Problems in 1892," *NH* 33 (1952): 54–57.

48. Allen to Bryan, 4 February 1893, box 2, Bryan MSS, LC; Olson, *Morton*, pp. 265–314, 343; *W-H*, 13 November 1890; Watkins, *Nebraska*, 3:238; *New York Times*, 2 January 1893, p. 2; Shoemaker to Bryan, 12 February 1893, box 2, Bryan MSS, LC; *NSJ*, 6 November 1892; *Bee*, 2 November, 8 November 1892.

49. Cf. the interpretations in Sheldon, *Nebraska*, 1:681–82, 719; and Olson, *Nebraska*, pp. 228–29.

50. Guth, "Omer Madison Kem," pp. 91–135.
51. Albert Shaw, "William V. Allen: Populist," *Review of Reviews* 10 (1894): 30–42.

CHAPTER FOUR

1. William Nisbet Chambers and Walter Dean Burnham, eds., *The American Party Systems: Stages of Political Development* (New York: Oxford University Press, 1967), esp. the articles by Chambers, Burnham, and Hays; Walter Dean Burnham, *Critical Elections and the Mainsprings of American Politics* (New York: W. W. Norton, 1970); Paul Kleppner, *The Third Electoral System, 1853–1892: Parties, Voters, and Political Cultures* (Chapel Hill: University of North Carolina Press, 1979), esp. chap. 9; Michael Paul Rogin and John L. Shover, *Political Change in California: Critical Elections and Social Movements, 1890–1966* (Westport: Greenwood Publishing Corp., 1970); Richard Jensen, *The Winning of the Midwest: Social and Political Conflict, 1888–1896* (Chicago: University of Chicago Press, 1971).
2. Programs used in deriving statistics presented in this chapter were from SPSS; see Nie et al., *SPSS*. For information on sources of election and population data, see Appendix A.
3. (Omaha) *American*, 21 September, 28 September 1894; *NSJ*, 24 September 1894. The list of Bryan-pledged delegates is in *W-H*, 20 September 1894; of those listed, twelve appear in the 1893 Omaha city directory as proprietors of saloons; see pp. 1000–1002.
4. *W-H*, 21 September 1894; *Bee*, 21 September 1894. For background on Omaha, see Howard P. Chudacoff, "Voting and Mobility: An Intra-urban Study of Omaha, Nebraska, 1880–1900" (M.A. thesis, University of Chicago, 1967), and idem, "Men in Motion: Residential Mobility in Omaha, Nebraska, 1880–1920" (Ph.D. diss., University of Chicago, 1969).
5. *W-H*, 21 September 1894; *Bee*, 21 September 1894.
6. These calculations and conclusions regarding party-switching were completed before I read an important article that draws similar conclusions: David Stephens Trask, "A Natural Partnership, Nebraska's Populists and Democrats and the Development of Fusion," *NH* 56 (1975): 419–38. Trask's methodology is quite different from my own, but his conclusions are identical; see esp. pp. 425 and 428. For testimony by contemporaries, see J. R. Farris, "My Recollections of Pioneering in Cherry County," *NH* 19 (1938): 23; Falloon to Bryan, 19 August 1890, box 2, Bryan MSS, LC.
7. These 457 leaders are listed, with sources of information, in my dissertation, Cherny, "Populist and Progressive in Nebraska," pp. 512–51.
8. All of these are from box 1 of the Farmers' Alliance MSS, NSHS: Stewart to Kellie, 17 June 1894; Cummins to Kellie, 2 July 1894; Wright to Kellie, 2 July 1894; Goff to Kellie, 3 March 1896.
9. Watkins, *Nebraska*, 3:197–202, 206–9, 212–14, 216–21, 231–37, 246–53, 262–63; Sheldon, *Nebraska*, 1:589–600, 609–16, 625–32, 639–49, 654–59, 696–708, 723–31, 755–58.
10. *Messages and Proclamations*, 2:135–42, 162–65, 183–86, 215–16.

11. Ibid., 2:237–45, 357–74.
12. See, e.g., the account of the Fillmore County convention, *NSJ*, 5 August 1894.

CHAPTER FIVE

1. *Bee*, 2 July 1902; for sources of political data in this chapter, see Appendix A.
2. For information on the party affiliation of legislators, the journals of the house and senate may be consulted for 1897; for other years, see the many sources of biographical information listed in my dissertation, Cherny, "Populist and Progressive in Nebraska," pp. 512–51. For general coverage of politics in this period, see Watkins, *Nebraska*, 3:263–75; Sheldon, *Nebraska*, 1:759–809; Olson, *Nebraska*, pp. 242–51.
3. Coletta, *Bryan*, 1:213–352; Olson, *Morton*, pp. 388–430; Richard Lowitt, *George W. Norris: The Making of a Progressive* (Syracuse: Syracuse University Press, 1963), pp. 27–93; Mullen, *Western Democrat*, pp. 117–27; James Manahan, *Trials of a Lawyer* (n.p., 1932), pp. 9–39; Luebke, *Immigrants*, esp. pp. 160–78; John W. Bailey, Jr., "The Presidential Election of 1900 in Nebraska; McKinley over Bryan," *NH* 54 (1973); 560–84.
4. See, e.g., Kleppner, *Cross of Culture*, pp. 269–375, esp. pp.345–47, 374–75; or Hays, "Social Analysis," p.387.
5. *W-H*, 13 July 1900; *Bee*, 26 June 1902, 22 June, 4 July, 11 August 1904; *Independent*, 11 August 1904; Sheldon, *Nebraska*, 1:767, 777–78, 805–8; *Party Platforms*, p.266; Trask, "Partnership," pp. 433–36.
6. *W-H*, 4 August 1898; *NSJ*, 4 August 1898; *Lincoln Evening News*, 25 May 1900, in scrapbook 1, box 3, George W. Berge MSS, NSHS; Sheldon, *Nebraska*, 1:765, 770, 781, 796, 809.
7. *W-H*, 3 August, 4 August 1898, 26 June 1902, 12 August 1904; *Bee*, 26 June 1902; *NSJ*, 7 July, 10 July 1900, 14 August 1904; Edmisten to Wooster, 23 June 1900, box 7, Charles Wooster MSS, NSHS.
8. *W-H* was read from 1 July through a week past election day for each even-numbered year during this period; see esp. 26 September, 5 October, 31 October 1896; 17 August, 9 October, 8 November 1898; 11 September, 28 September, 24 October, 2 November 1900; 27 June, 6 October, 30 October 1902; 15 August, 16 August, 20 August, 13 September, 4 October 1904; for the description of Mickey as "ein Feind persönlicher Freiheiten und Rechte," see 3 November 1902. For the issue of imperialism, see Robert W. Cherny, "Anti-Imperialism on the Middle Border, 1898–1900," *Midwest Review*, 2d ser., 1 (1979): 19–34.
9. *Party Platforms*, pp. 206–8, 220–22, 232–34, 244–45, 254–57, 267–68, 273–79, 284–87.
10. *Independent* was read from 1 July through the end of December for each even-numbered year during this period; see esp. 10 September 1896, 14 April, 28 April, 19 May, 26 May, 2 June, 15 September 1898; 23 August, 30 August, 6 September, 13 September, 4 October, 18 October 1900; 19 June 1902, 25 August, 8 September, 3 November 1904; see also Cherny, "Anti-Imperialism."
11. *Party Platforms*, pp. 212–14, 223–25, 234–37, 247–48, 258–59, 268–70, 275, 279–80, 287–88.

12. Coletta, *Bryan*, 1:41–42, 45, 48, 71, 103, 114; "Call to Silver Democrats," box 2, J. H. Broady MSS, NSHS; Manahan, *Trials; Biographical Directory of the American Congress*, pp. 1258, 1585; William Emil Christensen, "Splendid Old Roman: The Political and Journalistic Career of Edgar Howard" (Ph.D. diss., University of Nebraska, 1966), pp. 27–29, 88, 342–43; Sheldon, *Nebraska*, 3:167–68, 504–5.

13. *North Platte Evening Telegraph*, 28 February 1929; Sheldon, *Nebraska*, 3:429–30, 496–98; Watkins, *Nebraska*, 3:535–36; *Compendium of History Reminiscence and Biography of Nebraska* (Chicago: Alden Publishing Co., 1912), p. 102; Andrew G. Wolfenbarger, ed., *Nebraska Legislative Year Book for 1897* (Lincoln: A. G. Wolfenbarger, 1897), p. 101; Sheldon, "Powers," pp. 331–39; Harmer and Sellers, "Van Wyck," pp. 363–70.

14. Sheldon, *Nebraska*, 1:766–67; Watkins, *Nebraska*, 3:264–65, 273; *Joseph S. Bartley v. State of Nebraska*, 53 Nebraska 310; *Eugene Moore v. State of Nebraska*, 53 Nebraska 831; *Messages and Proclamations*, 2:374–78; Bryan to Poynter, 11 December 1899, box 23, Bryan MSS, LC; Paolo E. Coletta, "A Tempest in a Teapot?—Governor Poynter's Appointment of William V. Allen to the United States Senate," *NH* 38 (1957): 155–64; Cherny, "Anti-Imperialism."

15. *Bee* and *NSJ* were read from 1 July through a week past election day for all even-numbered years during this period. For *NSJ*, see esp. 20 September 1896; 17 September, 24 October, 3 November 1898; 1 September, 21 September, 23 September, 6 November 1900; 14 September, 2 October 1902; 10 August, 14 October, 20 October 1904. For *Bee*, see esp. 23 September 1896; 14 October, 5 November 1898; 29 July, 29 August, 25 September, 30 October 1900; 20 June, 11 October 1902; 18 June, 16 September 3 October 1904. See also *Star*, 23 October 1902; 15 September, 1 November 1904. See also Dale J. Hart, "Edward Rosewater and the *Omaha Bee* in Nebraska Politics" (M.A. thesis, University of Nebraska, 1938); Wayne A. Alvord, "*The Nebraska State Journal*: 1867–1904" (M.A. thesis, University of Nebraska, 1934); Cherny, "Anti-Imperialism."

16. *NSJ*, 13 July, 21 August, 22 August, 16 October, 1 November 1896; 2 October 1898; 27 October 1900; 27 October, 2 November 1902; *Bee*, 20 October, 26 October 1896; 2 September 1898. See also the interesting letter from former senator Charles Manderson to Norris, 17 September 1896, box 12, Norris MSS, LC. *Party Platforms*, pp. 216–17, 227, 238–39, 249–51, 262–64, 271–72, 276–77, 280–82, 289–90.

17. *Bee*, 2 July, 18 October 1896; Watkins, *Nebraska*, 1:672, 674–75; *Biographical Directory of the American Congress*, pp. 812, 1031–32; *Memorial and Biographical Record . . . of Butler, Polk, Seward, York, and Fillmore Counties* (Chicago: Geo. A. Ogle, 1899), pp. 482–84; Luebke, *Immigrants*, pp. 172–77; *NSJ*, 30 October 1902.

18. Sheldon, *Nebraska*, 1:774, 784–93, 800–01; Watkins, *Nebraska*, 3:272–73; Olson, *Nebraska*, pp. 247–48; *W-H*, 16 January through 29 March 1901. Olson claims that the deadlock over the senatorial elections resulted because both the Union Pacific and the Burlington wished to place their men in both senatorships. There is no evidence for this in the voting. Rosewater, who held between twelve and thirty-two votes, and the eight legislators who refused to enter the party caucus owing to anti-Thompson sentiment held the key to the election, and neither group was obviously tied to either railroad company. Without their opposition, Meiklejohn,

from Union Pacific territory, would have been elected to the long-term seat and Thompson, the former Burlington superintendent, to the short term. On the Bartley pardon, see Dietrich to Holdrege, 19 March 1904, box 3, Dietrich MSS, NSHS. See also *W-H*, 19 September, 21 September, 5 October, 20 October 1904; and *Independent*, 25 August, 13 October, 27 October, 1904.

19. Olson, *Nebraska*, p. 251; *Independent*, 8 September 1904. The law, allowing candidates to go on the ballot in a preferential vote for senator, was not legally binding on the members of the legislature; *Compiled Statutes of the State of Nebraska: 1881* (11th ed., 1904), chap. 26, para. 3220, sect. 9. The action of the convention was considered by party leaders to be morally binding upon Republicans; see also Claire Mulvey, "The Republican Party in Nebraska: 1900–1916" (M.A. thesis, University of Nebraska, 1934), pp. 43–48.

20. The party was listed as Straight Democrats on the 1894 ballot, as Democrats in 1895 and 1896 (by grace of the Republican secretary of state), and as National Democrats in 1897. See *Bee*, 2 October 1896; *W-H*, 5 August 1896, August 1898; Olson, *Morton*, pp. 388–430.

21. *W-H*, 8 August 1898, 12 July 1900, 31 August 1902, 11 August 1904, 18 September 1906, 28 August 1910, 3 September, 5 September 1912; *NSJ*, 4 August, 20 August 1900, 2 June 1904; *Bee*, 18 July 1900, 6 August 1904; Sheldon, *Nebraska*, 2:312, 3:291, 299; Watkins, *Nebraska*, 3:675–76; Hugh J. Dobbs, *History of Gage County, Nebraska*, (Lincoln: Western Publishing and Engraving Co., 1918), pp. 338–43; Dorsey to McKinley, 12 October 1900, microfilm reel 13, McKinley MSS, LC.

22. For sources of data, see Appendix A.

23 Luebke, *Immigrants*, pp. 158–59.

24. *NSJ*, 20 October 1896; *Party Platforms*, p. 266; *W-H*, 3 August, 7 August 1898; *NSJ*, 4 August 1898.

25. *NSJ*, 26 April 1907; *W-H*, 25 July 1896, 10 October 1900, 26 June 1902, 11 August, 22 February, 27 February 1904; D. W. Reid, comp., *Souvenir of the Nebraska Legislature: 1901–1902* (Lincoln: Jacob North, n.d.), pp. 29, 40; *Biographical Directory of the American Congress*, pp. 1220, 1228, 1278; Nebraska Legislative Reference Bureau, *Nebraska Blue Book: 1930* (Lincoln: n.p., 1930), p. 263; "Arthur J. Weaver," *NH* 26 (1945): 226–27; *Auburn News*, 24 May 1904; box 3, Berge MSS, NSHS; Watkins, *Nebraska*, 3:705–6, 753–54; Sheldon, *Nebraska*, 1:512–13, 661; box 7, Maxwell MSS, NSHS; Wooster MSS, NSHS.

26. *NSJ*, 28 October 1896; Wright to Kellie, 17 September 1896, Kellie to Stebbens, 25 April 1898, box 2, Alliance MSS, NSHS; "The Father of Populism," undated flyer, NSHS; *Bee*, 4 August 1898; *NSJ*, 9 October 1898; clipping from (Schuyler?) *Quill*, box 17, Silas A. Holcomb NSS, NSHS; *Independent*, 11 June 1896.

27. Deaver to Poynter, 23 June 1899, box 1, Poynter MSS, NSHS; Deaver to the president, 13 July 1901, and letters from prominent Republicans endorsing Deaver, Appointment Division File 1129-05 (filed in a mislabeled folder, "Clem, Deaver D.," in the Omaha-O'Neill box), National Archives; *Omaha News*, 23 February 1914; Wharton Barker to McKinley, 11 August 1900, microfilm reel 11, McKinley MSS, LC; *W-H*, 29 September 1908; correspondence between S. R. Smith and George W. Norris, 19 October 1899, 11 January, 13 January 1902, boxes 20 and 22, Norris MSS, LC; *W-H*, 29 July, 27 August, 11 September, 29 September, 17

October, 21 October, 29 October 1900; *Independent*, 14 July, 21 July, 11 August 1904.

CHAPTER SIX

1. Mullen, *Western Democrat*, p. 100; Burnham, *Critical Elections*, esp. chaps. 4 and 5.

2. For the urban-rural interpretation, see William Diamond, "Urban and Rural Voting in 1896," *American Historical Review* 46 (1941): 281–305; Parsons, *Populist Context*, esp. 121–31; Frederick C. Luebke, "Main Street and the Countryside: Patterns of Voting in Nebraska during the Populist Era," *NH* 50 (1969): 257–75. For the economic interpretation, see esp. Hicks, *Populist Revolt*, chaps. 12–14. For the ethnic interpretation, see esp. Kleppner, *Cross of Culture*, pp. 269–375.

3. For sources of all election and population data cited in this chapter, see Appendix A. All operations discussed in this chapter were done with SPSS; see Nie et al, *SPSS*. Pearson coefficients of correlation between the distribution of the party vote in 1898 and in other years confirm that 1898 was typical, ranging from +0.79 to +0.90 for the fusion party vote, 1896–1904, and from +0.80 to +0.92 for the Republican party vote.

4. Of 60 Czech adult males listed in an 1899 history of east-central Nebraska, 72 percent were Democrats and 8 percent were Populists; 17 percent were Republicans; see Kleinschmidt, "Political Behavior of Bohemian and Swedish Ethnic groups," p. 32.

5. We cannot know if the same was true in 1896, because 1900 is the only year for which there exists a complete compilation of election returns by minor civil divisions, as opposed to counties. In 1900 we may be quite certain that Bryan did not carry any incorporated area with more than a thousand people, except for those noted.

6. Of 108 German adult males listed in the 1899 history of east-central Nebraska, 33 percent were Republicans, 29 percent were Democrats, and 8 percent were Populists (for a fusion total of 37 percent). Of the 15 Catholics in the group, none were Republicans, 40 percent were Democrats, 7 percent were Populists, and 40 percent did not state. Of 49 Lutherans, 43 percent were Republicans, 25 percent were Democrats, and 10 percent were Populists. See Luebke, *Immigrants*, pp. 58, 65.

7. Of 53 Swedish adult males listed in the 1899 history, 60 percent were Republicans, 6 percent were Democrats, and 13 percent were Populists; Kleinschmidt, "Political Behavior of Bohemian and Swedish Ethnic Groups," p. 60.

8. In ten urban, ritualistic, high farm income counties, each party drew about 49.5 percent of the vote in 1898; in twelve urban, low farm income counties, fusion drew about 48 percent, the Republican about 51 percent.

9. See, e.g., Burnham, *Critical Elections*, pp. 6–8, 27–30.

10. For coefficents of correlation between the various independent variable and the party vote in other years, see Appendix B.

11. "The political party that had returned to power by the election of 1896, and on the issue of the full dinner pail, was very cautious about giving out information on the

mortgage status of the farmers"; Fred A. Shannon, "The Status of the Midwestern Farmer in 1900," *Mississippi Valley Historical Review* 37 (1950): 505.

12. Many of the letters of congratulation to McKinley in 1902 show similarly strong religious overtones, expressing pleasure at the election of a Christian and at the defeat of vice, sin, corruption, liquor, Populism, and Democracy; box 1, Mickey MSS, NSHS.

13. For a list of these 661 leaders and the sources of information for each, see my dissertation, Cherny, "Populist and Progressive in Nebraska," pp. 512–51.

14. The most prominent example is the book written by 1904 fusion gubernatorial candidate George W. Berge, *The Free Pass Bribery System* (Lincoln: Independent Printing Co., 1905).

CHAPTER SEVEN

1. *NSJ*, 18 September 1912; for overviews of progressivism in Nebraska, see Watkins,*Nebraska*, 3:275–85; Sheldon,*Nebraska*, 1:816–92; Olson,*Nebraska*, pp. 251–57. Sources for election data are discussed in Appendix A.

2. A striking exception to this generalization regarding support for popular democracy measures was the vote on the Oregon Pledge Law; see below, p. 116; legislature activities are summarized in Sheldon, *Nebraska*, 1:824–26, 839–40, 853–56, 882–85; Watkins,*Nebraska*, 3:277–79, 283–85; Olson,*Nebraska*, pp. 252, 254–55.

3. Sheldon, *Nebraska*, 1:842–44, 849; Fitchie to Muir, 21 February 1899, Robert V. Muir MSS, NSHS; Frederick C. Luebke, "The German-American Alliance in Nebraska, 1910–1917,"*NH* 49 (1968): 165–86, esp. pp. 168–69; Robert E. Wenger, "The Anti-Saloon League in Nebraska Politics, 1898–1910," *NH* 52 (1971): 267–92.

4. Sheldon,*Nebraska*, 1: 911, 913, 851, 874, 890; Ann L. Wiegman Wilhite, "Sixty-five Years till Victory: A History of Woman Suffrage in Nebraska," *NH* 49 (1968): 149–64, esp. pp. 158–59.

5. Virginia Speich, "The Political Career of George L. Sheldon, 1907–1909," *NH* 53 (1972): 339–80, esp. pp. 340–44; Sheldon, *Nebraska*, 1:816; Olson, *Nebraska*, p. 251; *NSJ*, 15 August , 23 August 1906; *Party Platforms*, pp. 303–6.

6. *NSJ*, 23 September, 4 November, 5 November 1906; for denials of the pass charges, see *W-H* and also Devoe to McCarl, 28 October, 5 November 1906, box 36, Norris MSS, LC, wherein Devoe terms the*NSJ* pass exposé "a little 'dirty' politics" designed to secure Brown's election. See also Sheldon,*Nebraska*, 1:821–26; Watkins, *Nebraska*, 3:277; Speich, "Sheldon," pp. 345–48.

7. Sheldon, *Nebraska*, 1:833; Olson, *Nebraska*, p. 253; (Lincoln) *Nebraska State Capital*, 25 September 1908;*W-H*, 23 September 1908;*NSJ*, 23 September, 29 October, 1 November, 2 November 1908; *Star*, 25 September, 28 September, 19 October, 30 October 1908;*Bee*, 13 October, 21 October 1908; Speich, "Sheldon," pp. 355–70.

8. McCarl to Norris, 3 July 1910, McCarl to Dravo, 23 July 1910, Aldrich to Norris, 12 July 1910, box 55 Norris MSS, LC; *Bee*, 9 August 1910; Sheldon, *Nebraska*, 1:847, 854; Watkins, *Nebraska*, 1:281; *Party Platforms*, pp. 342–45; *NSJ*, 4 October, 22 October, 5 November 1910; *State Capital*, 29 September, 13

October 1910.

9. Donald F. Danker, "Nebraska and the Presidential Election of 1912," *NH* 37 (1956): 283–310; Corrick to Bassett, 25 January 1912, box 1, Samuel Clay Bassett MSS, NSHS; *Bee*, 28 June, 31 July, 1 August, 27 August, 29 August, 5 September, 14 October 1912. See also Mulvey, "Republican Party in Nebraska," pp. 132–50; C. L. Hartman, "The National Election of 1912 in Nebraska" (M.A. thesis, Univeristy of Omaha, 1940).

10. Justus F. Paul, "The Political Career of Hugh Butler" (Ph.D. diss., Univeristy of Nebraska, 1966).

11. *W-H*, 15 August, 16 August, 17 August, 5 November 1906; *NSJ*, 16 August 1906; *Bee*, 13 August, 17 August 1906; *Independent*, 23 August 1906; Sheldon, *Nebraska*, 1:816–17; Watkins, *Nebraska*, 3:277; Olson, *Nebraska*, p. 252.

12. Mullen, *Western Democrat*, pp. 128–30.

13. *W-H*, 5 October, 27 October, 30 October 1908; *Bee*, 15 September, 18 October 1908; see also Dravo to McCarl, 12 October 1908, and Crane to McCarl, 7 October 1908, box 44, Norris MSS, LC; Sheldon, *Nebraska*, 1:8329–34; Watkins, *Nebraska*, 3:278; Olson, *Nebraska*, p. 253.

14. Mullen, *Western Democrat*, pp. 146–48; Sheldon, *Nebraska*, 1:839–40; Watkins, *Nebraska*, 3:278–79; *Senate Journal*, pp. 726, 1179; *House Journal*, pp. 149, 556.

15. Mullen, *Western Democrat*, pp. 139–42; Mullen, "Omaha and Eight O'Clock" (undated manuscript), Mullen MSS, Creighton University; for another version, see *W-H*, 3 April, 4 April 1909; see also *Senate Journal*, p. 1543, and *House Journal*, p. 933; Sheldon, *Nebraska*, 1:840; Watkins, *Nebraska*, 3:278–79: Olson, *Nebraska*, p. 254.

16. Mullen, *Western Democrat*, pp. 143–44; Charles Bryan to Pettigrew, 28 June 1910, drawer 2, Pettigrew MSS, Pettigrew Museum, Sioux Falls, S.D.; *W-H*, 19 July, 26 July, 28 July 1910; *Bee* 27 July 1910; see also Sheldon, *Nebraska*, 1:845–47; Watkins, *Nebraska*, 3:280–81; Olson, *Nebraska*, p. 254; Coletta, *Bryan*, 2:8–15.

17. *Bee*, 28 July, 30 July, 3 August, 5 August, 10 August, 11 August, 12 August, 16 August 1910; *NSJ*, 12 August, 13 August 1910; Coletta, *Bryan*, 2:14–15.

18. *W-H*, 21 September, 22 September 1910; *Bee*, 6 September, 21 September 1910; *Star*, 5 September 1910; *NSJ*, 18 September, 5 November 1910; Coletta, *Bryan*, 2:15–16.

19 *House Journal*, pp. 663, 708, 721; *Senate Journal*, pp. 463–64.

20. Mullen, *Western Democrat*, pp. 163–66; undated manuscript on the 1912 primary, Mullen MSS, Creighton; *W-H*, 1 August 1912; (Lincoln) *Commoner*, 5 April 1912; Gruenther to Allen, 9 April 1912, box 1, W. V. Allen MSS, NSHS; Sheldon, *Nebraska*, 1:872–78.

21. *W-H*, 10 August, 3 September, 5 September 1912; *Star*, 12 September 1912; *NSJ*, 30 August, 31 October 1912; *Bee*, 11 July 1912.

22. Bryan's last foray into Nebraska politics resulted in his election as a national convention delegate in 1920. He changed his voting residence to Florida in 1921, returning to Nebraska to campaign for his brother in 1922. He went to the 1924 national convention as a Florida delegate. Coletta, *Bryan*, 3:150, 157–58, 165, 176.

23. *W-H*, 16 August, 17 August, 18 August 1906;.

24. *Bee*, 23 July, 26 July, 18 September, 18 October 1908, 19 September, 20

September, 21 September 1910, 14 August 1912; *W-H*, 21 September, 25 October
1910, 30 July, 1 August, 12 October, 18 October, 31 October, 2 November 1912;
NSJ, 21 September 1910, 18 July 1912; *Star*, 20 September 1910.
   25. *NSJ*, 2 October 1906, 30 August 1912; *Bee*, 17 August, 27 September, 29
September 1906, 31 August 1908, 16 July, 27 July, 27 October 1910, 11 July, 1
August 1912; *Greeley Citizen*, 7 September 1906; *W-H*, 4 October, 25 October 1908,
27 July, 13 September, 4 October 1910; *State Capital*, 6 October 1910; *Star*, 12
September 1912. Regarding the final years of the party, see Barnhart, "Farmers'
Alliance," p. 432 and bibliography.
   26. Danker, "Presidential Election of 1912"; Sheldon, *Nebraska*, 1:887,
890–91, 908–13.

<h2 style="text-align:center">CHAPTER EIGHT</h2>

   1. Mullen, *Western Democrat*, pp. 128–30; Hicks, *Populist Revolt*, p. 404;
Theodore Saloutos and John D. Hicks, *Twentieth-Century Populism: Agricultural
Discontent in the Middle West, 1900–1939* (Lincoln: University of Nebraska Press),
p. 33; Destler, "Western Radicalism," p. 367; Russel B. Nye, *Midwestern Progressive Politics: A History of Its Origins and Development, 1870–1958* (New York:
Harper and Row, 1965) p. 182; Hofstadter, *Age of Reform*, pp. 60–93, 130–73, esp.
pp. 71, 133–35.
   2. Hays, "Political Parties and the Community-Society Continuum"; Gabriel
Kolko, *The Triumph of Conservatism: A Reinterpretation of American History,
1900–1915* (New York: Free Press of Glencoe, 1963), esp. pp. 280, 284, 285, 304;
see also Rogin, *Intellectuals and McCarthy*, esp. pp. 117, 146, 179, 184–85.
   3. Sources and derivation of these variables are discussed in Appendix A.
   4. Programs used were those in SPSS; see Nie et al., *SPSS*.
   5. For both 1906 and 1914, the second variable stepped into the regression is the
percentage of the population living in incorporated areas, and for both years for both
parties, this second variable increased the R^2 by only 0.04 to 0.07. In 1912 the farm
income variable was the second stepped into the regression for the Republiccan party
vote, adding 0.08 to R^2. In no other instance did adding a second variable to the
regression increase the R^2 by more than 0.03.
   6. For six counties, Spearman rank-order coefficients of correlation were calculated for the relationship between Populist sympathies (as measured by the 1904
presidential election and the 1910 election for attorney general) and Dahlman's
deficit from the Democratic party vote, separately for each county, using precincts as
the units of analysis; r_s ranged from +0.54 to +0.60 in five of the six counties. The
loss in the Democratic proportion of the party vote between 1908 and 1910 correlates
at +0.67 with the composite scale of Populist tendencies described earlier.
   7. One way to test Mullen's claim is to calculate the difference between the 1906
and 1908 Democratic party votes and assume that all of this difference was due to
Mullen's organizing efforts; this measure of the Mullen organization correlates at
+0.35 with the primary vote for Metcalfe in 1910, at +0.52 with the vote for Clark in
the 1912 presidential primary, and at +0.31 with the difference between the 1908
and 1910 Democratic votes for governor. Mullen remained at the center of the
Democratic organization in the state until his death; see *W-H*, 18 September, 23

October 1940 for accounts of the collapse of the party organization after his death.

8. Undated manuscript on the 1912 election, Mullen MSS, Creighton.

9. The distribution of support for Metcalfe in both 1910 and 1912 correlates with the difference between the 1908 and 1910 Democratic gubernatorial vote at a level of +0.55. The 1910 primary vote for Shallenberger correlates with this measure of party-line crossing at a level of +0.57, and the 1912 primary vote for Wilson correlates at +0.37. The correlation coefficients for the relationship between these primary voting patterns and Aldrich's margin over the 1910 Republican party vote are:

> Primary vote for Metcalfe, 1910 .... +0.50
> Primary vote for Metcalfe, 1912 .... +0.48
> Primary vote for Shallenberger, 1912 .... +0.48
> Primary vote for Wilson, 1912 .... +0.48

Hitchcock's margin over the Democratic party vote and Burkett's deficit from the Republican party vote correlate at +0.29 with the primary vote for Whedon. The difference between Aldrich's vote in 1912 and the Republican party vote that year correlates at a level of +0.5 with the primary vote for Newton. Spearman rank-order coefficients of correlation were calculated for precincts in each of seven counties for the relationship between Morehead's margin over the normal Democratic vote in 1912 and the vote for Taft in the presidential election; in four of the seven counties, the coefficients were at a level of +0.62 to +0.65. Morehead's margin over the 1914 Democratic party vote correlates at +0.39 with the 1912 vote for Taft in the Republican presidential primary. The difference between the combined vote for Roosevelt and Taft and the Republican party vote in 1912 correlates at a level of +0.50 with the primary vote for La Follette. The increase in the Democratic party vote between 1910 and 1912 correlates at +0.64 with the La Follette primary vote.

10. The distribution of the La Follette primary vote correlates at a level of +0.45 with the composite scale of Populist tendencies and the Whedon vote of 1910 correlates at +0.35. The Taft vote of 1912 correlates at −0.56.

11. The coefficients of correlation for the three independent variables and the vote for the three major presidential candidates of 1912 may be found in Appendix B. Second variables do not significantly change the multiple regressions for the Wilson and Roosevelt votes, but adding a second variable (ethnicity) increases the multiple R for the Taft vote from 0.52 (farm income) to 0.64.

From 1906 to 1914, the Democratic party vote averaged 47 percent in all sixty-one counties; Wilson averaged 45 percent. In the counties with the highest proportions of German, Irish, and Austrian stock, the mean Democratic party vote was 51 percent and Wilson got only 47 percent. In the most prosperous quartile of counties, the mean party vote was 47 percent, and Wilson got 43 percent. By contrast, in the quartile lowest in the percentage of German, Irish, and Austrian stock, the party vote was 44 percent and Wilson slightly exceeded this with 44.3 percent. In the quartile with the lowest farm income, the party vote was 46.2 percent and Wilson got 45.6 percent. Wilson actually ran slightly ahead of the 1912 party vote in these lowest income counties, 45.6 percent to 45.5 percent.

12. For a complete list of these leaders and the sources of information for each, see

my dissertation, Cherny "Populist and Progressive in Nebraska," pp. 512–51.

13. Of the Republican progressives, 66 percent had attended college, compared with 41 percent of other Republicans. Of the Republican progressives, 41 percent were lawyers, compared with 22 percent of the other Republicans; 3 percent of the progressives and 24 percent of the other Republicans were financiers (engaged in banking, insurance, real estate, or grain-buying); 10 percent of the progressives and 5 percent of the other Republicans were journalists.

14. For the card file, see *Star*, 23 October 1908.

CHAPTER NINE

1. Beal, "Populist Party in Custer County, Nebraska," pp. 125–26; Sheldon, *Nebraska*, 1:933; *North Platte Evening Telegraph*, 28 February 1929; boxes 25 and 58, C. A. Sorensen MSS, NSHS; Christensen, "Splendid Old Roman," pp. 368, 376; George J. Marshall, letter to the editor, *NH* 23 (1942): 154–55; Mullen, *Western Democrat*, p. 282.

2. Mullen, *Western Democrat*; Christensen, "Splendid Old Roman"; Coletta, *Bryan*, vol. 3, chaps. 5–10; Fred Carey, *Mayor Jim: An Epic of the West* (Omaha: Omaha Printing Co., 1930); *Biographical Directory of the American Congress*, pp. 1059, 1081, 1085, 1355, 1395, 1585; *Star*, 1 April 1954; Richard Lowitt, *George W. Norris: The Persistence of a Progressive, 1913–1933* (Urbana: University of Illinois Press, 1971), chaps. 10–33; Olson, *Nebraska*; James A. Stone, "Agrarian Ideology and the Farm Problem in Nebraska State Politics with Special Reference to Northeast Nebraska, 1920–1933" (Ph.D. diss., University of Nebraska, 1960); Robert W. Cherny, "The 1940 Election in Nebraska, with Special Attention to Isolationist Voting among the Non-urban German Stock Voters of the State" (M.A. thesis, Columbia University, 1967); Paul, "Hugh Butler"; Harl Adams Dalstrom, "Kenneth S. Wherry" (Ph.D. diss., University of Nebraska, 1965); *Messages and Proclamations*, 3:349, 611, 4:3, 515; Sorensen MSS, NSHS; Butler MSS, NSHS; Wherry MSS, University of Nebraska; Norris MSS, LC; Nebraska Legislative Council, *Nebraska Blue Book: 1968*, pp. 152–213.

3. Stone, "Agrarian Ideology"; Cherny, M.A. thesis, "The 1940 Election in Nebraska"; Cherny, "Isolationist Voting in 1940: A Statistical Analysis," *NH* 52 (1971): 293–310, esp. p. 306.

4. Nye, *Midwestern Progressive Politics*, p. 182; Hofstadter, *Age of Reform*, pp. 71, 133–35; Kolko, *Triumph of Conservatism*, pp. 280, 284–85, 304; Pollack, *Populist Response to Industrial America*.

5. Sources for voting data and a discussion of methodolgy may be found in Appendix A.

6. N. C. Abbott, "Silas A. Holcomb (Part Two)," *NH* 27 (1946): 7–14; *W-H*, 19 July 1910; Allen to De France, 29 August 1918, Allen to Weaver, 17 May 1920, box 1, W. V. Allen MSS, NSHS; Guth, "O. M. Kem," esp. pp. 139–67; *Star*, 12 September 1912; Sheldon, *Nebraska*, 3:406–8; *Independent*, 19 July 1906; *NSJ*, 27 October 1910; Frank D. Eager MSS, NSHS.

7. Sheldon, *Nebraska*, 1:933; *North Platte Telegraph*, 28 February 1929; Eunice Mutz Heard, "Twenty-two Years in Keya Paha," *NH* 17 (1936): 91–102; box 58, Sorensen MSS, NSHS; *W-H*, 10 August 1912; Christensen, "Splendid Old

Roman," pp. 367–68.

8. *NSJ*, 1 October 1910; *Bee*, 29 September 1906; Mullen, *Western Democrat*, pp. 139–42; *NSJ*, 1 August 1912; *W-H*, 6 October 1906, 23 July 1912.

9. For the full list of Populist leaders and sources of biographical information for each, see my dissertation, Cherny, "Populist and Progressive in Nebraska," pp. 369–72, 512–51.

10. Mullen, *Western Democrat*; *W-H*, 27 August 1910, 10 August 1912; Christensen, "Splendid Old Roman," pp. 367–68; A. R. Harvey, comp. and ed., *Nebraska Legislative Year Book for the Thirty-second Session, 1911* (Omaha: A. I. Root, 1911), p. 225; *Who's Who in Nebraska, 1940*, p. 739; Norris, *Fighting Liberal*, pp. 103–11; Lowitt, *Norris: Making of a Progressive*, pp. 88–96, 102–52; Sheldon, *Nebraska*, 1:556; *NSJ*, 2 November 1890; *W-H*, 12 September 1898, 22 August 1910; *Clay Center Sun*, 2 November 1890; *NSJ*, 31 July, 14 October, 17 October 1890.

11. This summary of Populist thought is based on party platforms (both state and national), the writings of a range of Populist activists, especially those in the Nebraska Populist press, the few manuscript collections, and the analyses of historians. Probably the historian's treatment that fits best with my own view is Chester M. Destler's "Western Radicalism." For a view that places very heavy emphasis on the cooperative aspect of Populist thought, see Lawrence Goodwyn, *Democratic Promise*. For a critique of Goodwyn's treatment of Nebraska Populism, see my "Lawrence Goodwyn and Nebraska Populism: A Review Essay," to appear in *Great Plains Quarterly* 1 (1981).

12. *Party Platforms*, pp. 303–6, 314–15, 328–30, 342–45, 353–54, 360–65; *NSJ*, 24 October 1908.

13. *W-H*, 27 July 1910; *Bee*, 27 July 1910; *Messages and Proclamations*, 2:647–48, 3:75–77, 93; *Party Platforms*, pp. 164, 191.

14. *Party Platforms*, pp. 298–301, 316–22, 339–42, 355–58.

15. Above, chap. 7, and *Party Platforms*, pp. 298–301, 307–11, 316–22, 332–34, 339–51, 355–58, 368–70.

16. Christensen, "Splendid Old Roman," pp. 208–9.

17. Kenneth W. Hechler, *Insurgency: Personalities and Politics of the Taft Era* (New York: Columbia University Press, 1940), pp. 21–22; *NSJ*, 15 August 1912; *Party Platforms*, pp. 351–52. The 1914 Populist platform acknowledged that "there still remains to be achieved the most important parts" of the Omaha Platform; *Party Platforms*, pp. 370–72.

18 Earl G. Curtis, "John Milton Thayer," *NH* 28 (1947): 225–38, 29 (1948): 55–68, 134–50; *Biographical Directory of the American Cong.*, p. 1316; McShane MSS, NSHS.

19. For the 1920s and 1930s, see notes 2 and 3.

20. Roger Welsch, "Sweet Nebraska Land, "Folkways Album #FH 5337 (New York: Folkways Records and Service Corp., 1965); the liner notes include the text of the songs.

APPENDIX A

1. For a discussion of the ecological fallacy and means for dealing with it, see Charles M. Dollar and Richard J. Jensen, *Historian's Guide to Statistics: Quantitative Analysis and Historical Research* (New York: Holt, Rinehart, and Winston, 1971), pp. 97–104. See also Hubert M. Blalock, Jr., *Causal Inferences in Nonexperimental Research* (Chapel Hill: University of North Carolina Press, 1961), esp. chap. 4; and also Laura Irwin Langbein and Allan J. Lichtman, *Ecological Inference* (Beverly Hills, Calif.: Sage Publications, 1978).

2. All analysis was done using the Statistical Package for the Social Sciences; see Norman H. Nie, et al., *SPSS: Statistical Package for the Social Sciences*, 2d ed., (New York: McGraw-Hill, 1975), esp. chaps. 17 ("Breakdown"), 18 ("Bivariate Correlation Analysis"), and 20 ("Multiple Regression Analysis").

Selected Bibliography

This bibliography is limited to materials useful for the study of Nebraska politics for the period 1885–1915; general works on the period are not included. Sources already discussed in Appendix A are not repeated here.

Primary Sources: Manuscript Collections

Creighton University, Omaha, Nebraska
    Arthur F. Mullen Papers
Library of Congress, Washington, D.C.
    William Jennings Bryan Papers
    Gilbert M. Hitchcock Papers
    William McKinley Papers
    George William Norris Papers
National Archives and Records Service, Washington, D.C.
    Record Group 49. Records of the Office of the Secretary of the Interior. Land Office. Appointment Division File 1120-05, Deaver D. Clem file.
Nebraska State Historical Society, Lincoln
    Chester Hardy Aldrich Papers
    William V. Allen Papers
    George W. Berge Papers
    James E. Boyd Papers
    Jefferson H. Broady Papers
    Norris Brown Papers
    Charles W. Bryan Papers
    William Jennings Bryan Papers
    Samuel Chapman Papers
    Lorenzo Crounse Papers
    James W. Dawes Papers
    Charles Henry Dietrich Papers
    Frank E. Eager Papers
    Farmers' Alliance Papers
    Gere Family Papers
    Francis Gregg Hamer Papers
    William Leese Papers
    John Albert McShane Papers
    John A. Maguire Papers
    Thomas J. Majors Papers

John Hopwood Mickey Papers
John Henry Morehead Papers
Robert V. Muir Papers
George William Norris Papers
People's Independent Party Papers
John A. Piper Papers
Charles W. Pool Papers
William Amos Poynter Papers
Republican Party Papers
John A. Sanborn Papers
Ezra Perin Savage Papers
Andrew J. Sawyer Papers
Ashton Cokayne Shallenberger Papers
George Lawson Sheldon Papers
Christian Abraham Sorensen Papers
John Milton Thayer Papers
Thomas Henry Tibbles Family Papers
Trans-Mississippi and International Exposition Papers
Charles Wooster Papers
University of Kansas, Lawrence. Spencer Research Library
Charles H. Van Wyck Papers, Watkins Collection

Collections of Documents

Messages and Proclamations of the Governors of Nebraska: 1854–1941. Work
    Projects Administration Official Project no. 165–1–81–317. Lincoln: Nebraska
    State Historical Society, 1941.
Nebraska Party Platforms: 1858–1940. Work Projects Administration Official Pro-
    ject no. 665-81-3-19. Lincoln: n.p., 1940.
Pollack, Norman, ed. *The Populist Mind.* Indianapolis and New York: Bobbs-
    Merrill, 1967.

Newspapers

The Nebraska State Historical Society has an excellent collection of Nebraska
    newspapers. The following were consulted:
Albion Argus (1892, 1895–98, 1904–12)
Albion Weekly News (1892–1912)
Alma News Reporter (1896–98)
(Alma) *Schaffer's Alma Record* (1908–12)
Alma Weekly Record (1896, 1902)
Arapahoe Pioneer (1896–1902)
Blair Pilot (1908–12)
(Clay Center) *Clay County Patriot* (1896–1912)
Greeley Citizen (1896–1912)
Greeley Leader (1890). *Greeley Leader-Independent* (1896–1912)

(Lincoln) *Farmers' Alliance, Alliance-Independent, Wealth-Makers, Nebraska Independent* (1890–1906)
(Lincoln) *Nebraska State Capital* (1908–12)
(Lincoln) *Nebraska State Journal* (1890–1914)
Lincoln Star (1902–14)
Madison Mail (1902–3)
(Minden) *Nebraska F.A. & I.U.* (1895–96)
(Omaha) *American* (1894–96)
Omaha Bee (1890–1914)
(Omaha) *True Populist* (1900)
Omaha World-Herald (1890–1914)

In most cases the paper was read from July through a week past election day for even-numbered years. In a few cases, other issues were consulted for specific information.

Autobiographies, Memoirs, and Reminiscences

Barns, Cass G. *The Sod House: Reminiscent Historical and Biographical Sketches Featuring Nebraska Pioneers: 1867–1897.* Madison, Nebr.: n.p., 1930.
Bryan, William Jennings. *The First Battle: A Story of the Campaign of 1896.* Chicago: W. B. Conkey Co., 1896.
Bryan, William Jennings, and Bryan, Mary Baird. *The Memoirs of William Jennings Bryan.* Philadelphia: United Publishers of America, 1925.
Farris, J. R. "My Recollections of Pioneering in Cherry County." *Nebraska History* 19 (1938): 3–27.
Filley, H. Clyde. *Every Day Was New: The Story of the Growth of Nebraska.* New York: Exposition Press, 1950.
Heard, Eunice Mutz. "Twenty-two Years in Keya Paha." *Nebraska History* 17 (1936): 91–102.
Howard, Edgar. "The Cross of Gold Refurbished: A Contemporary Account of the 1896 Convention." Edited by William E. Christensen. *Nebraska History* 46 (1965): 225–34.
Jeffrey, Mary Louise. "Young Radicals of the Nineties." *Nebraska History* 38 (1957): 25–43.
Johnson, Alvin. *Pioneer's Progress: An Autobiography.* New York: Viking Press, 1952.
Kellie, Luna E. "Luna E. Kellie and the Farmers' Alliance." Edited by Douglas Bakken. *Nebraska History* 50 (1969): 185–206.
Manahan, James. *Trials of a Lawyer.* N.p.: Kathryn Manahan, 1932.
Marshall, George J. Letter to the Editor. *Nebraska History* 23 (1942): 154–55.
Mercer, Samuel D. "A Republican Estimate of Party Problems in 1892." Edited by John Higham. *Nebraska History* 23 (1952): 54–57.
Morearty, Ed. F. *Omaha Memories: Recollections of Events, Men and Affairs in Omaha, Nebraska, from 1897 to 1917.* Omaha: Schwartz Printing Co., 1917.
Mullen, Arthur F. *Western Democrat.* New York: Wilfred Funk, 1940.
Nielsen, Alfred C. *Life in an American Denmark.* Askov, Minn.: American Publishing Co., 1962.

214 / *Bibliography*

Norris, George W. *Fighting Liberal*. New York: Macmillan Co., 1945.
————. "Nebraska: A Reflective View by George W. Norris." Edited by Richard Lowitt. *Nebraska History* 49 (1968): 139–48.
Powers, John Holbrook. *Autobiography*. Trenton, Nebr.: Register, n.d.
Sheldon, Addison E. "Populist Recollections." *Nebraska History* 19 (1938): 45.

Blue Books, Legislative Yearbooks, Etc.

Carr, Daniel M., ed. *Portrait and Biographical Album of the State Officers and Members of the Nebraska Legislature Twenty-eighth Session: 1903–1904*. Fremont: Progress Publishing Co., 1903.
Hall, Charles L. *Biographical Manual of the Members and Officers of the Sixteenth Legislature of Nebraska*. Lincoln: State Journal Co., 1881.
————. *Biographical Manual of the Members and Officers of the Twentieth Legislature of Nebraska*. Lincoln: State Journal Co., 1887.
Harvey, A. R., comp. and ed. *Nebraska Legislative Year Book for the Thirty-second Session, 1911*. Omaha: A. I. Root, 1911.
Howard, William A., comp. *Biographical Sketches of the Nebraska Legislature and National and State Officers of Nebraska*. Lincoln: Jacob North, 1895.
Nebraska Blue Book: 1899 and 1900. Lincoln: State Journal Co., 1899.
Nebraska Blue Book: 1901 and 1902. Lincoln: State Journal Co., 1901.
Reid, D. W., comp. *Souvenir of the Nebraska Legislature: 1901–02*. Lincoln: Jacob North, n.d.
Sheldon, Addison E., ed. *Nebraska Blue Book and Historical Register: 1915*. Lincoln: State Journal Co., 1915.
Wolfe, J. M., comp. *Souvenir of the Nebraska Legislature: 1895–96*. Omaha: Omaha Publishing Co., 1895.
Wolfenbarger, Andrew G., ed. *Nebraska Legislative Year Book for 1897*. Lincoln: A. G. Wolfenbarger, 1897.

Local Histories.

Bassett, Samuel Clay. *Buffalo County, Nebraska, and Its People*. Chicago: S. J. Clarke Publishing Co., 1916.
Biographical and Historical Memoirs of Adams, Clay, Hall and Hamilton Counties, Nebraska. Chicago: Goodspeed Publishing Co., 1890.
Biographical Souvenir of the Counties of Buffalo, Kearney and Phelps, Nebraska. Chicago: F. A. Battey, 1890.
Compendium of History Reminiscence and Biography of Nebraska. Chicago: Alden Publishing Co., 1912.
Compendium of History Reminiscence and Biography of Western Nebraska. Chicago: Alden Publishing Co., 1909.
Dobbs, Hugh J. *History of Gage County, Nebraska*. Lincoln: Western Publishing and Engraving Co., 1918.
Halderson, H. *Tri-county Pioneers*. Newman Grove, Nebr.: H. Halderson, n.d.

Memorial and Biographical Record and Illustrated Compendium of Biography . . . of Butler, Polk, York and Fillmore Counties, Nebraska. Chicago: Geo. A. Ogle, 1899.

Savage, James; Bell, John T.; and Butterfield, Consul W. *History of the City of Omaha Nebraska and South Omaha.* New York and Chicago: Munsell, 1894.

Scoville, C. H., comp. *History of the Elkhorn Valley, Nebraska.* Chicago and Omaha: National Publishing Co., 1892.

Sorensen, Alfred. *The Story of Omaha from the Pioneer Days to the Present Time.* Omaha: National Publishing Co., 1923.

Books

Bogue, Allen G. *Money at Interest: The Farm Mortgage on the Middle Border.* Ithaca: Cornell University Press, 1955.

Brunner, Edmund de S. *Immigrant Farmers and Their Children.* Garden City: Doubleday, Doran, 1929.

Carey, Fred. *Mayor Jim: An Epic of the West.* Omaha: Omaha Printing Co., 1930.

Chudacoff, Howard P. *Mobile Americans: Residential and Social Mobility in Omaha, 1880–1920.* New York: Oxford University Press, 1972.

Coletta, Paolo E. *William Jennings Bryan.* 3 vols. Lincoln: University of Nebraska Press, 1964–69.

Creigh, Dorothy Weyers. *Nebraska: A Bicentennial History.* New York: W. W. Norton, 1977.

Dick, Everett. *The Sod-House Frontier: 1854–1890.* New York: D. Appleton-Century Co., 1937.

Diller, Robert. *Farm Ownership, Tenancy, and Land Use in a Nebraska Community.* Chicago: University of Chicago Press, 1941.

Glad, Paul W. *The Trumpet Soundeth: William Jennings Bryan and His Democracy, 1896–1912.* Lincoln: University of Nebraska Press, 1960.

Hicks, John D. *The Populist Revolt: A History of the Farmers' Alliance and the People's Party.* Minneapolis: University of Minnesota Press, 1931; rpt. Lincoln: University of Nebraska Press, 1961.

Hinman, Eleanor H. *History of Farm Land Prices in Eleven Nebraska Counties, 1873–1933.* University of Nebraska Agricultural Experiment Station Research Bulletin no. 72. Lincoln: University of Nebraska [?], 1934.

Hinman, Eleanor H., and Rankin, J. O. *Farm Mortgage History of Eleven Southeastern Nebraska Townships, 1870–1932.* University of Nebraska Agricultural Experiment Station Research Bulletin no. 67. Lincoln: University of Nebraska [?], 1933.

Koenig, Louis W. *Bryan: A Political Biography of William Jennings Bryan.* New York: G. P. Putnam's Sons, 1971.

Kutak, Robert I. *The Story of a Bohemian-American Village: A Study of Social Persistence and Change.* Louisville: Standard Printing Co., 1933.

Levine, Lawrence W. *Defender of the Faith: William Jennings Bryan: The Last Decade, 1915–1925.* New York: Oxford University Press, 1968.

Lief, Alfred. *Democracy's Norris: The Biography of a Lonely Crusade.* New York: Stackpole Sons, 1939.

Lowitt, Richard. *George W. Norris*. 2 vols. Syracuse: Syracuse University Press, 1963; Urbana: University of Illinois Press, 1971.

Luebke, Frederick C. *Immigrants and Politics: The Germans of Nebraska, 1880–1900*. Lincoln: University of Nebraska Press, 1969.

Morton, J. Sterling, succeeded by Watkins, Albert, editor-in-chief, and Miller, Geo., assoc. ed. *Illustrated History of Nebraska: A History of Nebraska from the Earliest Explorations of the Trans-Mississippi Region*. 3 vols. Lincoln: Jacob North, 1905, 1907; Lincoln: Western Publishing and Engraving Co., 1913.

Nyholm, Paul C. *The Americanization of the Danish Lutheran Churches in America*. Minneapolis: Augsburg Publishing House, 1963.

Okada, Yasuo. *Public Lands and Pioneer Farmers: Gage County, Nebraska, 1850–1900*. Tokyo: Kokusai Printing Co., 1971.

Olson, James C. *History of Nebraska*. Lincoln: University of Nebraska Press, 1955.

———. *J. Sterling Morton*. Lincoln: University of Nebraska Press, 1942.

Parsons, Stanley B., Jr. *The Populist Context: Rural versus Urban Power on a Great Plains Frontier*. Westport, Conn.: Greenwood Press, 1973.

Pederson, James F., and Wald, Kenneth D. *Shall the People Rule? A History of the Democratic Party in Nebraska Politics*. Lincoln: Jacob North, 1972.

Rosicky, Rose. *A History of Czechs (Bohemians) in Nebraska*. Omaha: National Printing Co., 1929.

Sheldon, Addison Erwin. *Land Systems and Land Policies in Nebraska*. Publications of the Nebraska State Historical Society no. 22. Lincoln: Nebraska State Historical Society, 1936.

———. *Nebraska: The Land and the People*. 3 vols. Chicago and New York: Lewis Publishing Co., 1931.

Zucker, Norman L. *George W. Norris: Gentle Knight of American Democracy*. Urbana: University of Illinois Press, 1966.

Articles

Abbott, N. C. "Silas A. Holcomb." *Nebraska History* 26 (1945): 187–200; 27 (1946): 3–17.

Ager, J. H. "Nebraska Politics and Nebraska Railroads." *Proceedings and Collections of the Nebraska State Historical Society* 15 (1907): 34–44.

Bailey, John W., Jr., "The Presidential Election of 1900 in Nebraska: McKinley over Bryan." *Nebraska History* 54 (1973): 560–84.

Barnhart, John D. "Rainfall and the Populist Party in Nebraska." *American Political Science Review* 19 (1925): 527–40.

Bentley, Arthur F. "The Condition of the Western Farmer as Illustrated by the Economic History of a Nebraska Township." *Johns Hopkins University Studies in Historical and Political Science* 11 (1893): 285–370.

Berry, Myrtle, comp. "Local Nebraska History—A Bibliography." *Nebraska History* 26 (1945): 104–15.

Breckinridge, Adam C. "Nebraska as a Pioneer in the Initiative and Referendum." *Nebraska History* 34 (1953): 215–24.

Cherny, Robert W. "Anti-Imperialism on the Middle Border, 1898–1900." *Midwest Review*, 2d ser., 1 (1979): 19–34.

Chudacoff, Howard P. "A New Look at Ethnic Neighborhoods: Residential Dispersion and the Concept of Visibility in a Medium-sized City." *Journal of American History* 60 (1973): 76–93.

———. "Where Rolls the Dark Missouri Down." *Nebraska History* 52 (1971): 1–30.

Coad, Ralph. "Irish Pioneers of Nebraska." *Nebraska History* 17 (1936): 171–77.

Coletta, Paolo E. "Bryan, Cleveland and the Disrupted Democracy." *Nebraska History* 41 (1960): 1–28.

———. "The Morning Star of the Reformation: William Jennings Bryan's First Congressional Campaign." *Nebraska History* 37 (1956): 103–20.

———. "The Nebraska Democratic State Convention of April 13–14, 1892." *Nebraska History* 39 (1958): 317–34.

———. "The Patronage Battle between Bryan and Hitchcock." *Nebraska History* 49 (1968): 121–37.

———. "A Tempest in a Teapot?—Governor Poynter's Appointment of William V. Allen to the United States Senate." *Nebraska History* 38 (1957): 155–64.

———. "William Jennings Bryan and the Nebraska Senatorial Election of 1893." *Nebraska History* 31 (1950): 183–203.

———. "William Jennings Bryan's First Nebraska Years." *Nebraska History* 33 (1952): 71–94.

———. "William Jennings Bryan's Second Congressional Campaign." *Nebraska History* 40 (1959): 275–92.

———. "The Youth of William Jennings Bryan—Beginnings of a Christian Statesman." *Nebraska History* 31 (1950): 1–24.

Curtis, Earl G. "John Milton Thayer." *Nebraska History* 28 (1947): 225–38; 29 (1948): 55–68, 134–50.

Danker, Donald F. "Nebraska and the Presidential Election of 1912." *Nebraska History* 37 (1956): 283–310.

———. "Populist Cartoons." *Kansas Quarterly* 1 (1969): 11–23.

Davis, John Kyle. "The Gray Wolf: Tom Dennison of Omaha." *Nebraska History* 58 (1977): 25–52.

Destler, Chester McArthur. "Western Radicalism, 1865–1901: Concepts and Origins." *Mississippi Valley Historical Review* 31 (1944): 335–68.

Dietrich, Margretta S. "Senator Charles H. Dietrich." *Publications of the Nebraska State Historical Society* 31 (1930): 135–74.

Furnas, Robert W. "Brief Biography of and Tribute to the Memory of the Late Charles H. Gere." *Proceedings and Collections of the Nebraska State Historical Society* 15 (1907): 158–61.

Gephart, Ronald M. "Politicians, Soldiers, and Strikes: The Reorganization of the Nebraska Militia and the Omaha Strike of 1881." *Nebraska History* 46 (1965): 89–120

Harmer, Marie U., and Sellers, James. L "Charles H. Van Wyck—Soldier and Statesman." *Nebraska History* 12 (1929): 81–128, 190–246, 322–73.

Hicks, John D. "My Nine Years at the University of Nebraska." *Nebraska History* 46 (1965): 1–28.

———. "Writing *The Populist Revolt*." *Kansas Quarterly* 1 (1969): 7–10.

House, Boyce, "Bryan at Baltimore, the Democratic National Convention of 1912." *Nebraska History* 41 (1960): 29–52.

218 / *Bibliography*

Johnson, Hildegard Binder. "The Location of German Immigrants in the Middle West." *Annals of the Association of American Geographers* 41 (1951): 1–11.
Johnson, J. R. "Imperialism in Nebraska, 1898–1904." *Nebraska History* 44 (1963): 141–66.
———. "William Jennings Bryan, the Soldier." *Nebraska History* 31 (1950): 95–106.
Kilar, Jeremy W. "Courthouse Politics, Loup City, Sherman County, 1887–1891." *Nebraska History* 60 (1979): 36–57.
Koch, William E. "Verse and Song from the Populist Era." *Kansas Quarterly* 1 (1969): 123–25.
Loudon, Betty, comp. "Nebraska History in Graduate Theses." *Nebraska History* 56 (1975): 289–92.
Lowitt, Richard. "Blackledge on Norris: Reflections on Nebraska Justice in the 1890's." *Nebraska History* 26 (1965): 67–76.
———. "George W. Norris: A Country Boy in an Urbanizing Nation." *Nebraska History* 52 (1971): 233–38.
———. "George W. Norris and the Kinkaid Act of 1904: A Footnote." *Nebraska History* 57 (1976): 399–404.
———. "George W. Norris, James J. Hill, and the Railroad Rate Bill." *Nebraska History* 40 (1959): 137–46.
———. "Norris and Nebraska, 1885–1890." *Nebraska History* 39 (1958): 23–40.
———. "Populism and Politics: The Start of George W. Norris's Political Career." *Nebraska History* 42 (1961): 75–94.
Luebke, Frederick C. "The German-American Alliance in Nebraska, 1910–1917." *Nebraska History* 49 (1969): 165–85.
———. "Main Street and the Countryside: Patterns of Voting in Nebraska during the Populist Era." *Nebraska History* 50 (1969): 257–76.
Manley, Robert N. "A Note on Government and Agriculture: A Nineteenth Century Nebraska View." *Nebraska History* 45 (1964): 237–52.
Miller, D. Paul. "Peter Jansen: A Nebraska Pioneer." *Nebraska History* 35 (1954): 223–30.
Monkkonen, Eric. "Can Nebraska or Any State Regulate Railroads? *Smyth* v. *Ames*, 1898." *Nebraska History* 54 (1973): 365–82.
Osnes, Larry G. "Charles W. Bryan: 'His Brother's Keeper.' " *Nebraska History* 48 (1967): 45–68.
Palmer, Edgar Z. "The Correctness of the 1890 Census of Population for Nebraska Cities." *Nebraska History* 32 (1951): 259–67.
Parsons, Stanley B. "Who Were the Nebraska Populists?" *Nebraska History* 44 (1963): 83–99.
Perkey, Elton A. "The First Farmers' Alliance in Nebraska." *Nebraska History* 57 (1976): 242–47.
Peterson, Paul V. "William Jennings Bryan, *World-Herald* Editor. *Nebraska History* 49 (1868): 349–72.
Pixton, John E. "Charles G. Dawes and the Nebraska Freight Rate Fight." *Nebraska History* 32 (1951):155–85.
Saloutos, Theodore. "The Professors and the Populists." *Agricultural History* 40 (1966): 234–54.
Shaw, Albert. "William V. Allen: Populist: A Character Sketch and Interview."

Review of Reviews 10 (1894): 30–42.

Shedd, George C. "Hibbard Houston Shedd." *Proceedings and Collections of the Nebraska State Historical Society* 15 (1907): 168–74.

Sheldon, Addison E. "The Deficiency Judgment: A Story of the Nebraska Nineties, the Farmers' Alliance, and the Supreme Court." *Nebraska History* 13 (1932): 289–94.

————. "The Editor's Table." *Nebraska History* 21 (1940): 19–20.

————. "Nebraskans I Have Known: I. William Vincent Allen." *Nebraska History* 19 (1938): 191–207.

————. "Nebraskans I Have Known: II. John Holbrook Powers." *Nebraska History* 19 (1938): 331–39.

————. "Nebraskans I Have Known: III. Samuel Clay Bassett." *Nebraska History* 20 (1939): 159–60.

————. "Some Unprinted History." *Nebraska History* 19 (1938): 204–5.

Shepherd, Allen L. "Gentile in Zion: Algernon Sidney Paddock and the Utah Commission, 1882–1886." *Nebraska History* 57 (1976): 359–78.

Sherman, Richard G. "Charles G. Dawes, a Nebraska Businessman, 1887–1894: The Making of an Entrepreneur." *Nebraska History* 46 (1965): 193–208.

Snoddy, Donald D. "The Congressional Career of Archibald Jerrard Weaver. 1882–1887." *Nebraska History* 57 (1976): 83–98.

Sorensen, Alfred. "Biographical Sketch of Edward Creighton." *Nebraska History* 17 (1936): 163–69.

Sparlin, Estal E. "Bryan and the 1912 Democratic Convention." *Mississippi Valley Historical Review* 22 (1936): 537–46.

Speich, Virginia. "The Political Career of George L. Sheldon, 1907–1909." *Nebraska History* 53 (1972): 339–80.

Thompson, J. M. "The Farmers' Alliance in Nebraska: Something of Its Origin, Growth, and Influence." *Proceedings and Collections of the Nebraska State Historical Society* 10 (1902): 199–206.

Trask, David F. "A Note on the Politics of Populism." *Nebraska History* 46 (1965): 157–62.

Trask, David Stephens. "Formation and Failure: The Populist Party in Seward County, 1890–1892." *Nebraska History* 51 (1970): 281–302.

————. "A Natural Partnership: Nebraska's Populists and Democrats and the Development of Fusion." *Nebraska History* 56 (1975): 419–38.

Turner, Tim, comp. "Nebraska History in Graduate Theses." *Nebraska History* 54 (1973): 120–22.

Wakeley, Eleazer. "Life and Character of Lorenzo Crounse." *Publications of the Nebraska State Historical Society* 18 (1917): 162–78.

Walker, Samuel. "George Howard Gibson, Christian Socialist among the Populists." *Nebraska History* 55 (1974): 553–72.

Watkins, Albert. "Jefferson H. Broady—An Appreciation." *Publications of the Nebraska State Historical Society* 18 (1917): 68–74.

Welsch, Roger L. "Populism and Folklore." *Kansas Quarterly* 1 (1969): 114–22.

Wenger, Robert W. "The Anti-Saloon League in Nebraska Politics, 1898–1910." *Nebraska History* 52 (1971): 267–92.

Wilson, Raymond, comp. "Nebraska History in Graduate Theses at the University of Nebraska–Omaha." *Nebraska History* 56 (1975): 279–88.

Zucker, Norman L. "George W. Norris, Nebraska Moralist." *Nebraska History* 42 (1961): 95–124.

———. "George W. Norris: Progressive from the Plains." *Nebraska History* 45 (1964):147–66.

Unpublished Material

Alvord, Wayne A. "*The Nebraska State Journal*: 1867–1904." M.A. thesis, University of Nebraska, 1934.

Barnhart, John D. "The History of the Farmers' Alliance and of the People's Party in Nebraska." Ph.D. diss., Harvard University, 1931.

Beal, Annabel L. "The Populist Party in Custer County, Nebraska: Its Role in Local, State, and National Politics, 1889–1906." Ph.D. diss., University of Nebraska, 1965.

Bowman, Clifford Ernest. "The Populist Press of Nebraska, 1888–1896." M.A. thesis, University of Nebraska, 1936.

Carlson, Martin E. "A History of the American Protective Association in Nebraska." M.A. thesis, Colorado State College of Education at Greeley, 1947.

Cherny, Robert W. "Populist and Progressive in Nebraska: A Study of Nebraska Politics, 1885–1912." Ph.D. diss., Columbia University, 1972.

Christensen, William Emil. "The Legislative Career of Edgar Howard." M.A. thesis, University of Nebraska, 1955.

———. "Splendid Old Roman: The Political and Journalistic Career of Edgar Howard." Ph.D. diss., University of Nebraska, 1966.

Coulter, Thomas Chalmer. "A History of Woman Suffrage in Nebraska, 1856–1920." Ph.D. diss., Ohio State University, 1967.

Curtis, Earl G. "Biography of John Milton Thayer." M.A. thesis, University of Nebraska, 1933.

Davis, Thomas Milburn. "George Ward Holdrege and the Burlington Lines West." Ph.D. diss., University of Nebraska, 1941.

Fisher, Joe A. "The Liquor Question in Nebraska, 1880–1920." M.A. thesis, University of Omaha, 1951.

Folsom, Burton W., III. "Ethnoreligious Response to Progressivism and War: German-Americans and Nebraska Politics, 1908–1924." M.A. thesis, University of Nebraska–Lincoln, 1973.

Fosbury, Eva May. "Biography of John Mellen Thurston." M.A. thesis, University of Nebraska, 1920.

Grier, Harold. "A History of the Democratic Party in Nebraska, 1854–1890." M.A. thesis, University of Nebraska, 1936.

Guth, DeLloyd John. "Omer Madison Kem: The People's Congressman." M.A. thesis, Creighton University, 1962.

Hart, Dale J. "Edward Rosewater and the *Omaha Bee* in Nebraska Politics." M.A. thesis, University of Nebraska, 1938.

Hartman, C. L. "The National Election of 1912 in Nebraska." M.A. thesis, University of Omaha, 1940.

Herscher, Juliette. "Early Third Party Movements in Nebraska." M.A. thesis, University of Nebraska, 1931.

Hodwalker, Theodore. "Public Career of David Butler, First Governor of Nebraska." M.A. thesis, University of Nebraska, 1936.
Jacob, Roger J. "A Study of the Editorial Attitude of the Omaha *World-Herald* toward the Cuban Crisis, 1895–1898." M.A. thesis, University of Omaha, 1967.
Jones, Virginia Bowen. "The Influence of the Railroads on Nebraska State Politics." M.A. thesis, University of Nebraska, 1927.
Kleinschmidt, John Raubold. "The Political Behavior of the Bohemian and Swedish Ethnic Groups in Nebraska, 1884–1900." M.A. thesis, University of Nebraska, 1968.
Klotsche, Johannes M. "The Political Career of Samuel Maxwell." M.A. thesis, University of Nebraska, 1928.
Knibbs, Joseph Charles. "The Political Map of Nebraska: 1900–1934." M.A. thesis, University of Nebraska, 1935.
Knollenberg, Helen. "The Political Career of Church Howe in Nebraska." M.A. thesis, University of Nebraska, 1933.
Knudsen, Rudolph Alvin. "Regulation of Railroad Rates in Nebraska, 1867–1906." M.A. thesis, University of Nebraska, 1937.
Kubicek, Clarence John. "The Czechs of Butler County, Nebraska." M.A. thesis, University of Nebraska, 1927.
Luebke, Frederick C. "The Political Behavior of an Immigrant Group: The Germans of Nebraska, 1880–1900." Ph.D. diss., University of Nebraska, 1966.
McGinnis, Mabel Margaret. "Doctor George L. Miller (a Biography)." M.A. thesis, University of Nebraska, 1934.
McIntyre, Kenneth E. "The Morton-Bryan Controversy." M.A. thesis, University of Nebraska, 1943.
Manley, Robert N. "Nebraska and the Federal Government: 1854–1916." Ph.D. diss., University of Nebraska, 1962.
Mellberg, Russell J. "The Public Career of Moses P. Kinkaid." M.A. thesis, University of Nebraska, 1933.
Mulvey, Claire. "The Republican Party in Nebraska: 1900–1916." M.A. thesis, University of Nebraska, 1934.
Parsons, Stanley B., Jr. "The Populist Context: Nebraska Farmers and Their Antagonists." Ph.D. diss., University of Iowa, 1964.
Raymond, Bruce Munson. "A Study of Political and Economic Conditions in Nebraska in the Early Nineties." M.A. thesis, University of Nebraska, 1923.
Rosewater, Victor. "The Life and Times of Edward Rosewater." Nebraska State Historical Society.
Rowley, Richard Dean. "Samuel Maxwell, Dean of Nebraska Jurisprudence." M.A. thesis, University of Nebraska, 1928.
Scheele, Paul E. "State Convention and State Primary: A Presentation and Comparison of Methods of Selecting and Influencing Delegates from Nebraska to the Democratic National Convention, 1900 to 1960." M.A. thesis, University of Nebraska, 1962.
Schmidt, William F. "Municipal Reform in Omaha from 1906 to 1914 as Seen through the Eyes of the Omaha Press." M.A. thesis, University of Omaha, 1963.
Shepherd, Allen La Vern. "Algernon Sidney Paddock: A Biography." M.A. thesis, University of Nebraska, 1967.
Smith, Carl A. "Party Alignments in Nebraska, 1908–1916." M.A. thesis, Univer-

sity of Nebraska, 1950.

Sorensen, Barbara. "A King and a Prince among Pioneers: Edward and John A. Creighton." M.A. thesis, Creighton University, 1961.

Stone, David Michael. "Politics and Elites in Nebraska, 1890–1895." M.A. thesis, University of Nebraska, 1968.

Storms, Helen Elizabeth. "A Study of the Nebraska State Election of 1890." M.A. thesis, University of Nebraska, 1931.

Trask, David Stephens. "Anti-Populism in Nebraska." M.A. thesis, University of Nebraska, 1968.

———. "The Nebraska Populist Party: A Social and Political Analysis." Ph.D. diss., University of Nebraska–Lincoln, 1971.

Walker, Samuel Emlen. "Populism and Industrialism: The Ideology of the Official Organ of the Nebraska Populist Movement." M.A. thesis, University of Nebraska–Omaha, 1970.

Zimmerman, William F. "Legislative History of Nebraska Populism, 1890–1895." M.A. thesis, University of Nebraska, 1926.

Index

Aldrich, Chester A., 156, 159; and elections of 1910 and 1912, 112, 113, 118, 121, 126, 133, 155; voter support for, 130, 135–41 passim
Allen, Thomas S., 118
Allen, William V., 43, 80–81, 87, 157; opposed to county option, 117, 121, 155
American Protective Association (APA), 38–39, 43–45, 48, 52, 63–66, 85, 87
Antelope County, 129
Anti-Imperialist League, 84
Anti-Monopoly Party, 11, 24

Babcock, Heman A., 7
Baptists, 15
Bartley, Joseph, 80–81, 83
Beal, Charles, 157
Berge, George W., 80, 121, 132, 155, 157; and election of 1904, 78, 103, 108, 119, 120; and election of 1906, 114, 115
Bibb, Robert S., 85
Boone County, 60, 66, 95
Boyd, James E., 26, 35, 85, 108; and election of 1890, 34–36, 50; as governor, 37–38, 51, 72, 97; and Omaha Democrats, 9, 45, 64
Broady, Jefferson H., 38
Brown, Norris, 107, 111, 113, 146, 156; voter support for, 135, 136, 154
Bryan, Charles, 86, 121
Bryan, William Jennings, 81, 84; and election of 1890, 36; and election of 1891, 38; and election of 1892, 39, 42; and election of 1893, 43; and election of 1894, 44–45, 47, 63–64; and election of 1895, 48; and elections of 1896 and 1900, 74; breaks with party, 1910, 114; and Bryan Volunteers, 115, 131; cooperates with Populists, 50–51, 65–66, 120; voter support for, 63–65, 94, 120, 142, 148
Bryan Democrats, 114, 121

Bryan Volunteers, 115, 131. See also Mullen, Arthur F.
Buffalo County Alliance, 87
Burkett, Elmer, 84, 112–13, 130, 133; 156; voter support for, 135, 136, 148, 154
Burrows Township, Platte County, 23
Burt County, 129
Butler County, 129

Cady, A. E., 112, 135, 136, 140, 141
Calvinists, German, 15
Castor, Tobias, 45, 84
Cather, Willa, 9
Catholics. See Roman Catholic church
Cherry County, 66
Civil War, the, and electorate, 28, 29, 107
Clay County, 23, 60, 66, 152–53
Cobb, Amasa, 38
Colfax County, 129
Columbus, Platte County, 94
Commoner, the, 84, 118, 140
Congregationalists, 15
Conservative, the, 84
Cook, Daniel, 85
Cosmo Precinct, Kearney County, 22
County option, 112, 116, 117, 121, 126, 155. See also Prohibition
County Option League, 121
Creighton, John A., 9
Crounse, Lorenzo, 39–40, 41, 44, 72
Cub Creek Precinct, Jefferson County, 23
Cuming County, 129
Custer County, 130
Czechs, 10, 21, 124, 129, 140; and support of Bryan, 63–64, 94, 95

Dahlman, James C.: and election of 1908, 132; and election of 1910, 112, 120, 126, 129–30; and Free Coinage League, 79; and fusion, 78; voter support for, 133–40 passim, 148; as a "wet," 117–18, 126, 129–30

223

Dakota County, 22
Dale, W. F. 121
Danes, 21–22, 57, 95
Dannebrog Precinct, Howard County, 22
Dannevirke Precinct, Howard County, 22, 23, 57
Dawes, James W., 7
Deaver, D. Clem, 87
Dech, William H., 119, 120, 158
Democratic party. *See also* Elections; Fusion; Prohibition; Voting behavior
—and American Protective Association, 38, 39, 44, 45, 63, 64, 66
—and ethnocultural conflict: 1880s, 9–11, 14–24; 1890–95, 49, 55–60; 1896–1904, 78, 87–88, 94, 102; 1905–15, 110–12, 116–18, 129–30
—and factionalism: 1890–95, 50–51; 1893, 43–45; 1894, 62–65, 67; 1906–12, 114–19, 132–33, 148
—and fusion: 1882, 1884, 11; 1890–95, 71, 73; 1892, 41–43; 1894, 45–47, 61–67; 1896–1904, 74–81; 1906–14, 114–21
—image of: 1880s, 9–12, 13, 26; 1890–95, 49, 52; 1896–1904, 76–79, 87–88; 1906–14, 114–21
—leadership of, collective biographical data of: 1880s, 26–30; 1890–95, 67–71; 1896–1904, 104–6; 1906–14, 143–46
—in Omaha, 9, 45, 62–64
—and packing-house faction, 9
—progressives in, 107, 109–11, 114–19, 121, 132–33, 160
—and prohibition: 1880s, 9, 10, 16–20, 24; 1890–95, 36, 37, 39; 1898, 77–78; 1902–1904, 78; 1908–10, 116–19, 129–30
—support for: 1880s, 16, 21–22, 23, 25; 1890–95, 57–90; 1896–1904, 89–102; 1906–14, 124–36, 137–40
Destler, Chester McA., 123
Dietrich, Charles, 82, 83, 84, 94
Direct primary, 132
Disciples of Christ, 15
Douglas County, 45, 112, 113. *See also* Omaha, Douglas County

Eager, De Witt, 121
Eager, Frank, 155
Edgerton, Joseph, 38
Edmisten, J. Harlan, 47, 80, 87, 155
Eight o'clock law, 116–17. *See also* County option; Prohibition

Elder, Samuel M., 37, 87
Elections: 1890, 33–37; 1891, 37–38; 1892, 38–42; 1893, 43–44; 1894, 44–47; 1895, 45; 1896 and 1897, 74; 1898, 74, 77, 79, 90–94; 1899, 74; 1900, 74, 77, 78, 79, 94–96; 1902, 74, 78, 79; 1904, 74, 77, 78, 79, 96–99, 103; 1906, 111; 1908, 111–12; 1910, 112; 1912, 112–113; 1914, 113
Episcopalians, 15, 67
Eureka Precinct, Jefferson County, 57

Farmers Alliance, 11, 31, 33, 34, 36
Furnas County, 130
Fusion: 1882 and 1884, 11; 1890–95, 50–51; 1890, 36; 1891, 38; 1892, 40–43; 1894, 45–47, 61–67; 1895, 47–48; 1896–1904, 74–81, 90–96, 101–102; 1898, 90–94; 1906–14, 114–15, 124–36

Gaffin, James N., 80, 87
Garber, Silas, 7
Gere, Charles, 7, 107. *See also Nebraska State Journal*
German-American Alliance, 110
Germans, 10–11, 103, 124, 129, 140; support Bryan, 63–64, 94, 95
Gilbert, Edward A., 86
Gold Democrats, 59, 64–66, 84–86, 99. *See also* Democratic party, and factionalism
Greeley County, 22, 57, 153
Greene, William L., 43, 82
Gruenther, Christian, 114, 115, 118

Hall, Philip L., 79
Harmon, Judson, 133, 135, 136
Harrington, Michael F.: as Populist, 78, 80, 87; as Democrat splits with Bryan, 117, 120–21; as Democratic progressive, 119, 155, 156, 157
Harrison, T. O. C., 44
Hawxby, Frederick, 157
Hayes, Samuel P., 14, 15, 124
Hayward, Monroe, 81, 82, 83
Hicks, John D., 123
Hitchcock, Gilbert M.: asserts progressive stance, 132; aspires to U.S. Senate, 81; Democratic factionalism and, 118, 119, 131, 133; and election of 1910, 117; proposes Democratic-Independent fusion, 38; as son-in-law of Lorenzo Crounse, 40; supports Democratic platforms, 1896–1904, 78–79; support for, 136, 137,

148. See also *Omaha World-Herald*
Hitchcock County, 57, 60, 66, 130, 152
Hofstadter, Richard, 123, 152
Holcomb, Silas A., 66, 80, 155; and election of 1893, 43; and election of 1894, 44, 45, 46; and elections of 1896 and 1899, 74; as governor, 47–48, 72–73, 81, 87
Howard, Edgar, 78, 79, 148
Howard County, 22, 57, 129
Howe, Church, 7, 107
Howe, Mart, 87
Howell, R. Beecher, 113, 114, 141, 148

Independent Party, 34, 36, 37, 39. *See also* Farmers Alliance; Fusion; Populist party
Irish, 10–11, 21–22, 57, 124, 129, 140, 153; support Bryan, 63, 94
Irvine, Frank, 43, 85
Italians, 63

Jackson, William R., 156, 158
Jefferson County, 23, 57, 60
Jones, W. A., 48

Kearney County, 22
Kelso Precinct, Howard County, 23
Kem, Omer M., 36, 42, 46, 155
Kinkaid, Moses P., 146, 148
Kleinschmidt, John R., 21
Kleppner, Paul, 14, 15–16, 55–56
Kolko, Gabriel, 124, 152

La Follette League, 112, 113
Lancaster County, 95
Laws, Gilbert L., 86
Lease, William, 33
(Lincoln) *Alliance Independent,* 41
(Lincoln) *Nebraska Independent,* 79
Lobeck, Charles O., 86
Luebke, Frederick C., 14, 21
Lutherans, 68; Danish, 15; German, 15, 63; Missouri Synod, 21, 95; Norwegian, 15, 63; Swedish, 15, 63
Lyman, John N., 86

McCarthy, J. J., 113
MacColl, John H. "Jack," 82
McKeighan, William, 36, 42, 156
McMullen, Adam, 148
McShane, John A., 9, 11, 26, 162–63; and election of 1894, 45, 64; reenters politics in 1912, 85, 119
Madison County, 95

Mahoney, T. J., 48, 64, 85, 119
Majors, Thomas J., 44–46, 47, 64, 107
Manahan, James, 79
Manderson, Charles, 7, 107
Manley, Robert, 13
Manuel, Cassius B., 121
Marshall Precinct, Clay County, 152–53
Martin, Euclid, 45, 63, 64, 85
Mattes, John, Jr., 85
Maxwell, Samuel, 8, 44, 48, 86
Meiklejohn, George, 83
Mennonites, 23
Metcalfe, Richard, 117, 118, 119, 132, 133; voter support for, 136–140 passim, 148, 154
Methodist Episcopal Church, 14, 15, 67, 102–3
Methodists, British, 15
Mickey, John H., 82–83, 107; and elections of 1902 and 1904, 78, 79, 84, 102–3
Middle-of-the-Road Populists, 84, 87
Miller, George, Dr., 9, 26, 68, 107; and election of 1891, 38; and election of 1894, 45, 64; and fusion, 50; supports McKinley, 84, 85
Morehead, John H., 146; and election of 1912, 118, 119, 133; as governor, 155; opposes Bryan, 131; voter support for, 129, 135–139, 148
Morton, J. Sterling, 9, 26, 40, 50, 51, 68, 107; and elections of 1882 and 1884, 10–11; and election of 1892, 40, 50; and election of 1894, 64; and elections of 1896 and 1900, 84–85
Mullen, Arthur F., 119, 148, 156, 157; and Bryan Volunteers, 115, 130–131; discusses Populists and Democratic voting, 130–32; and eight o'clock law, 116; and election of 1912, 118–19, 133
Mutz, Otto, 121, 155

Nance, Albinus, 7
Nance County, 129
National Democrats. *See* Gold Democrats
Nebraska Anti-Saloon League, 78, 102, 110
Nebraska Bi-metallic Union, 79–80
Nebraska Democratic Free Coinage League, 44, 45, 79
Nebraska State Journal, 7, 35, 46, 82, 112, 161. *See also* Charles Gere
Nettleton, Daniel, 156
Newberry Bill, 37
Non-Partisan League, 86

Norris, George W., 1, 114, 121, 146, 156; and election of 1902, 80, 87; and election of 1912, 119, 133; voter support for, 133, 135, 136, 141, 142, 148, 154
Norval, T. L., 48
Norwegians, 21, 95, 140
Nye, Russel, 123

O'Connor Precinct, Greeley County, 22
Oldham, Willis D., 117
Omaha, Douglas County, 1, 11, 82, 94; Democratic party in, 9, 26, 44–45, 62–64; home rule for, 159–60
Omaha Bee, 82, 112; and election of 1893, 44; and election of 1894, 45, 46; and election of 1896, 81; and election of 1902, 75. *See also* Rosewater, Edward
Omaha Herald, 9
Omaha World Herald: promotes fusion, 1891, 36, 38; and election of 1892, 40; and election of 1894, 45; editorial positions of, 1896–1904, 78–79; praises legislature of 1907, 111. *See also* Hitchcock, Gilbert M.
O'Neill, Holt County, 22, 94

Paddock, Algernon S., 7, 43, 107
Parrington, Vernon, 123
Pawnee County, 57, 60, 129
People's Independent Party of Nebraska. *See* Populist party
Personal Liberty League, 110
Phelps, C. J., 48
Pietists, 14–16, 22–23, 90–96, 102–3, 136–42, 144–45. *See also* Voting behavior
Platte County, 23, 94, 114
Poles, 10, 21, 23, 57, 94, 95, 129, 146
Polk County, 24
Pollack, Norman, 152
Populist party
—and American Protective Association, 43, 85
—decline of, 104, 119–21, 123, 124
—and factionalism, 50
—and fusion: 1890–95,71, 73; 1893, 43; 1894, 45–47, 61–67; 1896–1904, 74–81; 1906–14, 114–21
—image of: 1892, 34, 40–41; 1890–95, 49–52, 73; 1896–1904, 79–81, 87–88
—leadership of, collective biographical data of: 1890–95, 34, 68–71; 1896–1904, 104–6, 114, 115, 117, 156

—support for, compared to progressives, 152–54
—voter support for: 1890–95, 54–57; 1896–1904, 96–104; 1906–14, 131–32
Populism compared with progressivism, 123, 151–61
Porter, William F., 121, 156
Post, Alfred M., 38
Powers, John H., 34, 44, 57, 80, 158; and election of 1890, 34, 36; and election of 1894, 44; appointed labor commissioner, 47; favors County option, 121, 155
Poynter, William A., 80, 120, 155; and election of 1898, 77; and fusion, 77–78, 87; as governor, 81; voter support for, 94
Presbyterians, 15, 67; Ulster, 15
Progressive party, 113, 121
Progressives, Democratic. *See* Democratic Party, progressives in
Progressives, Republican. *See* Republican Party
Progressivism in Nebraska, 109–22, 147–48; leaders of, 123, 124, 157; voter support for, 137–42, 152–54; support for, compared with support for populism, 123, 157–61
Prohibition, 6, 10, 16, 20, 21, 23–24, 26; 1890–95, 39, 52, 57, 59; 1896–1904, 82; 1905–15, 110–11, 112, 116–18, 121, 126, 129–30
Prohibition party, 24, 110
Protestants, 64, 140. *See also* Pietists; individual sects

Quakers, 15

Railroads: regulation of, 37, 111, 146; opposition to, 83–84, 107–8, 146
Reese, Manoah B., 31, 33, 38, 44
Republican party
—ethnocultural conflict and: 1880s, 14–20; 1896–1904, 82–83; 1908–10, 112
—image of: 1880s, 3–8, 10, 13–16, 25–26; 1890–95, 49–51; 1896–1904, 77, 81–84, 88; 1906–14, 111–14
—leadership of, collective biographical data of: 1880s, 21–30; 1890–95, 67–71; 1896–1904, 104–6; 1906–14, 143–46
—and railroads, 6, 31, 33; 1890–95, 49; 1894, 73; 1903, 83–84
—support for: 1880s, 16–20, 25–26; 1890–95, 60–61; 1896–1904, 89–93; 97–104; 1906–14, 124–36, 138–42
Richards, Lucius D., 33, 36, 37

Here is thesis & explaination

re arguments that follow

Step-wise multiple regression used

35

Richardson County, 66, 118
Ritualists, 14–16, 29, 90–96, 136–42, 144–45. *See also* Roman Catholic church; Voting behavior
Roman Catholic church, 21, 45, 57, 68–69; and voting behavior, 63–64, 66, 94, 95. *See also* Ritualists; Voting behavior
Rosewater, Edward, 7, 11, 107, 112; aspires to United States Senate, 83, 111; counters third party agitation, 1890, 33; encourages ticket-splitting, 97; and election of 1892, 39; and election of 1893, 44; and election of 1894, 45, 46, 62; and election of 1902, 75; opposes prohibition, 82. See also *Omaha Bee*
Rosewater, Victor, 112, 113, 148
Russian-Germans, 21, 22, 23

Sabbatarianism, 21, 23–24
Savage, Ezra, 83
School Creek Township, Clay County, 23
Shallenberger, Ashton C., 79–80, 107, 146; and decline of Populists, 120; and election of 1908, 112, 115; and election of 1910, 117, 132, 133; and election of 1912, 118–19; as governor, 115–16
Sheldon, Addison E., 1, 156, 158
Sheldon, George L., 107, 111, 112, 120, 155, 159
Silver Democrats, 45, 46, 48, 59
Silver Republicans, 77, 78, 84, 86–87
Smythe, Constantine J., 45, 48, 63, 78, 79, 80
South Pass Precinct, Lancaster County, 95
Spalding Precinct, Greeley County, 57
Stebbins, Lucien, 87
Straight Democrats. *See* Gold Democrats
Stuefer, William, 83
Sturdevant, Phelps D., 11, 45, 46, 85
Summit Precinct, Dakota County, 22
Sutton Township, Clay County, 23
Swedes, 21, 95, 140

Temperance. *See* Prohibition
Terry, Menzo, 131, 132
Thayer, John Milton, 7, 162
Thomas, Elmer E., 121
Thompson, D. E., 83
Thompson, William H., 81, 133; and election of 1898, 78; and election of 1906,

114; and election of 1912, 118–19, 133; and fusion, 78–79
Thurston, John M., 43, 47, 83
Tibbles, Thomas, 79, 87. See also (Lincoln) *Nebraska Independent*
Ticket-splitting, 97–104, 129–30
True Populist, The, 87. *See also* Deaver, D. Clem
Turkey Creek Precinct, Pawnee County, 57

Union Labor Party, 11, 24–25, 31
Upper Driftwood Precinct, Hitchcock County, 57, 152

Vandervoort, Paul, 87
Van Wyck, Charles H., 7, 11, 39, 80; and election of 1890, 36; and election of 1892, 39, 41, 50
Voting behavior
—and ethnicity-religion: 1880s, 14–16, 20–24, 25–26; 1890–95, 54–61; 1896–1904, 89–104; 1906–14, 124–36; 1910, 126
—and farm income: 1880s, 14, 16–20; 1890–95, 54–61; 1896–1904, 89–104; 1906–14, 124–36
—general patterns of: 1880s, 25–26; 1885–1915, 161–65
—and prohibition: 1880s, 16–19, 32; 1890–95, 54–61; 1896–1904, 89–104; 1906–14, 124–36
—and rural-urban dimension: 1880s, 20, 24; 1890–95, 54–61; 1896–1904, 89–104; 1906–14, 124–36

Wallace Creek Precinct, Greeley County, 153
Watkins, Albert, 1, 161
Weaver, Archibald, 86
Weaver, Arthur J., 86, 146, 148
Weaver, James, 120
Whedon, Charles O., 113, 133, 156; voter support for, 135–41 passim, 154
Wilber, Saline County, 94
Wolfe, Jacob V., 121, 155, 158
Woman suffrage, 21, 23–24
Wooster, Charles, 86
Wright, Walter F., 47

Yeiser, John O., 156